The Shyness & Social Anxiety Workbook

Proven, Step-by-Step Techniques for Overcoming your Fear

By
Martin M. Antony, Ph.D.
Richard P. Swinson, MD

EasyRead Large

Copyright Page from the Original Book

Publisher's Note

Distributed in Canada by Raincoast Books

Copyright © 2008 by Martin M. Antony and Richard P. Swinson
New Harbinger Publications, Inc.
5674 Shattuck Avenue
Oakland, CA 94609
www.newharbinger.com

Cover design by Amy Shoup
Text design by Michele Waters
Acquired by Catharine Sutker
Edited by Carole Honeychurch

Library of Congress Cataloging-in-Publication Data

Antony, Martin M.
  The shyness and social anxiety workbook : proven, step-by-step techniques for overcoming your fear / Martin M. Antony and Richard P. Swinson. -- 2nd ed.
    p. cm.
  Rev. ed. of: The shyness & social anxiety workbook.
  Includes bibliographical references (p.   ).
  ISBN-13: 978-1-57224-553-2 (pbk. : alk. paper)
  ISBN-10: 1-57224-553-0 (pbk. : alk. paper) 1. Bashfulness--Problems, exercises, etc. 2. Social phobia--Problems, exercises, etc. I. Swinson, Richard P. II. Antony, Martin M. Shyness & social anxiety workbook. III. Title.
  BF575.B3A58 2008
  158.2--dc22

                        2008016264

10   09   08

10   9   8   7   6   5   4   3   2   1

First printing

TABLE OF CONTENTS

"Social anxiety and shyness can become so intense that they prevent people from enjoying life. This book is ideal for anyone who wants to learn to be more comfortable around other people. Drs. Antony and Swinson have taken proven treatments for social anxiety and adapted them for a non-professional audience. The step-by-step strategies described in this book have been shown to be effective, are easy to understand, and are sure to help the reader cope better in social situations. Anyone who experiences significant anxiety when performing or when interacting with other people should read this book!"

—Aaron T. Beck, MD, university professor of psychiatry at the University of Pennsylvaniao

"If you have trouble with social anxiety, you will find the book by Drs. Antony and Swinson to be an excellent resource. This highly experienced duo has provided an excellent road map to guide you through your efforts to overcome your anxiety and improve the quality of your life. Based on the tried and true methods of cognitive-behavioral therapy and on the results of many scientific studies, the techniques described in this book will help you feel better when you are with other people or the center of attention. The only thing you have to do is work hard and apply them. Best wishes for your journey along that road."

Richard Heimberg, Ph.D., director of the Adult Anxiety Clinic of Temple University, Philadelphia

"Drs. Antony and Swinson provide practical advice in a highly readable format. This book will be invaluable to people whose social anxiety prevents them from leading full and happy lives."

—Murray B. Stein, MD, professor of psychiatry and director of anxiety and traumatic stress disorders program at the University of California, San Diego

"This is an excellent resource written by world-renowned and skilled clinicians and researchers in the area of anxiety disorders. Drs. Antony and Swinson present the most up-to-date information about social anxiety and its treatment in a way that is clear and, most importantly, that provides step-by-step tools for overcoming this disorder. This is a must-read for persons suffering with social anxiety."

—Michelle G. Craske, Ph.D., professor of psychology at the University of California, Los Angeles

"This workbook by Antony and Swinson gives the millions of people whose lives are limited by social fears the hope to control their future. The book is clear, practical, easy to follow, and, above all, based on solid, scientific ground. The sections on trou-bleshooting are especially valuable to really help fine-tune the techniques. I would strongly recommend this book to anyone who is serious about overcoming their social fears."

—Ronald M. Rapee, Ph.D., professor of psychology at Macquarie University, Sydney, Australia, author of *Overcoming Shyness and Social Phobia*

"This volume, written by a team composed of a psychologist and a psychiatrist, is an outstanding workbook for any individual suffering from social anxiety or shyness and wishing to undertake a structured self-help program to overcome it. The book can be used alone or in conjunction with therapy. The authors are experts in their field and they offer strategies that are solidly grounded in the latest research literature. The workbook format provides readers with the exercises and worksheets they need to do the difficult work required to overcome their shyness and social anxiety."

—Jacqueline B. Persons, Ph.D., director of the San Francisco Bay Area Center for Cognitive Therapy and clinical professor in the department of psychology at the University of California, Berkeley

For our students.

—MMA and RPS

Acknowledgments

There are many people without whom this workbook would not have been possible. First, we wish to acknowledge those who were instrumental in developing and investigating the treatments described in this book. Dr. Aaron T. Beck pioneered many of the cognitive strategies that are used throughout the world to treat anxiety, depression, and many other conditions. We are also indebted to Drs. Isaac Marks, S. Rachman, Joseph Wolpe, David Barlow, and others who helped to develop and study the exposure-based strategies that are now commonplace for the treatment of anxiety. We also acknowledge the important contributions of Drs. Richard Heimberg, Samuel Turner, Deborah Beidel, David M. Clark, and others who adapted these cognitive and behavioral methods for the treatment of social anxiety.

A special thank-you goes out to our colleagues, clients, and patients who provided many helpful suggestions over the years that informed this second edition of *The Shyness and Social Anxiety Workbook.* Finally, we wish to express our gratitude to the staff at New Harbinger Publications (including Carole Honeychurch, Matthew McKay, Catharine Sutker, Amy Shoup, Dorothy Smyk, and many others), who worked closely with us through all stages of developing, editing, and marketing this book.

vi

—Martin M. Antony, Ph.D.
Richard P. Swinson, M.D.
Toronto, Canada

Introduction

Shyness and social anxiety are universal. From time to time, almost everyone has felt nervous speaking in front of a group or anxious when interacting with another person. We wonder if a presentation has gone well or whether we have made a good impression on a first date or a job interview. In fact, even some celebrities, who make their living in the public eye, have been described as excessively shy from time to time, including Harrison Ford (actor), Mary Chapin Carpenter (singer), Michelle Pfeiffer (actor), David Bowie (rock star), David Letterman (talk-show host), Nicole Kidman (actor), and Carrie Underwood (*American Idol* winner). There have also been reports in the media about musical performers like Barbra Streisand, Carly Simon, and Donny Osmond suffering from performance anxiety. Even radio "shock jock" Howard Stern has described himself as being painfully shy when he is outside the safe confines of his on-air studio. (FYI, details on other shy celebrities can be found at www.shakeyourshyness.com/shypeople.htm .)

Shyness and social anxiety can range in intensity from being fairly mild to completely incapacitating. In extreme cases, social anxiety may prevent an individual from developing friendships, working, or even standing in a public place. Regardless of whether your fears are minor or completely overwhelming, the strategies described in this book will help you to deal more effectively with social anxiety.

We recommend that you read this workbook in the order in which the chapters appear. The initial chapters are designed to educate you about the nature of social anxiety and to teach you how to evaluate the main features of your own social anxiety. Then we discuss the costs and benefits of different treatment approaches and help you to select among available treatment options. Subsequent chapters provide detailed information about particular treatment strategies including medications, cognitive therapy for changing your anxious thoughts, using exposure to confront the situations you fear, and fine-tuning your communication and performance skills. The final chapter of the book discusses strategies for maintaining your improvements.

This book is different from other self-help books in a number of ways. Of the many books on social anxiety and shyness that you will find in your local bookstore, this was the first to be written in a workbook format. It is filled with exercises and practices designed to teach you basic strategies for overcoming shyness and social anxiety. We encourage you to fill in the blank worksheets and forms located throughout the text. In addition, we encourage you to make copies of the forms for your personal use so you can continue to use them over the coming months.

This book also differs from many others because the strategies we recommend have all been investigated extensively in well-designed clinical studies. In addition to specializing in helping people deal more effectively with their anxiety, we also are actively involved in research on the nature and treatment of anxiety. It is a well-established fact that when the techniques described in this book are used in a therapeutic setting, people generally experience a significant decrease in their social and performance anxiety (Rodebaugh, Holaway, and Heimberg 2004). Essentially, we have taken strategies that have proven to be useful in therapy and adapted them into a self-help format. Recently, investigators have also shown that our self-help approach (using the first edition of this book) can also be effective for reducing social anxiety (Moore, Braddock, and Abramowitz 2007). This workbook is designed so that it can be used alone or coupled with regular visits to a professional therapist. In fact, a motive for writing this book was to have a good reference our own clients and patients can use as they progress through therapy.

This second edition has been thoroughly updated with the latest scientific knowledge and references concerning the nature and treatment of social anxiety (for example, the section on the genetic underpinnings of social anxiety now includes a discussion of the Human Genome Project, which hadn't been completed when the first edition was published). The chapter on medications has also been revised to include the latest information on medications that have only recently been studied for treatment of social anxiety. Sections that were previously unclear or out of date have been completely rewritten. We have added many new examples and several forms and diaries have been updated and simplified. New sections have been added as well, including a discussion of strategies for improving motivation for treatment and sections for family members and friends of people who suffer from social anxiety. Finally, the lists of recommended readings and Internet resources have been thoroughly updated.

The journey to overcoming your shyness and social anxiety may not be an easy one. Some aspects of your fear will be easier and quicker to overcome than others. Also, for every two or three steps forward, you may experience what feels like a step back. Nevertheless, the techniques described in this book have been shown to reduce social and performance fears in most people who use them consistently. With hard work and perseverance, these strategies will provide you with the opportunity to make big, positive changes in your life.

PART 1

Understanding Your Social Anxiety

CHAPTER 1

Shyness and Social Anxiety

Rachel was a twenty-six-year-old woman who worked as an assistant manager of a small bookstore. She was referred to our Anxiety Treatment and Research Centre to get help for intense anxiety about her upcoming wedding. Rachel wasn't afraid of being married; in fact, she looked forward to spending years together with her husband. She was terrified of the wedding itself. The idea of being on display in front of such a large audience was almost unthinkable. In fact, she had postponed her wedding twice before because of her fear of being the center of attention.

Rachel's anxiety involved more than just a fear of her wedding. She reported that she'd always been shy, even when she was very young. When she was in high school, her anxiety around people had become so intense that it was affecting her school life. She was convinced that her classmates would find her dull or boring, or that they would notice her anxiety and assume that she was incompetent. Typically, Rachel avoided doing oral reports at school and didn't take any classes where she felt her performance might be observed or judged by her classmates (such as physical education). On a few occasions, she even asked for special permission to hand in a written essay instead of doing a presentation in front of the class. Despite being an excellent student, she generally tended to be very quiet in class and rarely asked questions or participated in class discussions.

Throughout college, Rachel found it difficult to make new friends. Although people enjoyed her company and often invited her to parties and other social events, she rarely accepted the invitations. She had a long list of excuses to get out of socializing with other people. She was comfortable only with her family and a few longtime friends, but aside from those, she usually avoided contact with other people.

After college, Rachel began working at a bookstore, and after a short time, she was promoted to assistant manager. She was always comfortable dealing with customers at her store, and she gradually became more comfortable talking to her coworkers. However, she avoided eating lunch with other staff members, and she never attended any social events, including the company's annual holiday party.

Rachel lived with her social anxiety for years, despite how it interfered with her education, work, and social life. It was not until the anxiety prevented her from having the kind of wedding she and her fiance wanted that she decided to seek help.

Rachel's story is not that different from those of other people who experience intense feelings of shyness, social anxiety, and performance-related fears. The types of anxious beliefs and behaviors that she reported are similar to those that many socially anxious people describe. After her evaluation at our center, Rachel began a twelve-session course of cognitive behavioral therapy (CBT) and gradually learned to cope with her anxiety more effectively. By the end of treatment, her avoidance of social situations had decreased significantly, and Rachel was much more comfortable in situations that previously made her very anxious.

CBT involves (1) identifying the thought patterns and behaviors that contribute to people's negative feelings, such as anxiety, and (2) teaching people new ways of thinking and behaving to better manage their anxiety. This book will teach you the strategies commonly used in CBT for social anxiety. Before exploring those strategies, however, we will begin this chapter in the same way we usually begin treatment with the individuals we see in our program—with an overview of the nature of fear and anxiety in general, and of social anxiety in particular.

ANXIETY, WORRY, FEAR, AND PANIC

Everyone knows what it feels like to be afraid. Fear is a basic human emotion. In humans, fear is controlled, in part, by an area of the brain called the limbic system. The *limbic system* includes some of the deepest, most primitive structures of the brain—structures shared by many less "evolved" animals. In fact, there is reason to believe that the emotion of fear is present across most, if not all, animal species. Most organisms display specific patterns of behavior when confronted with danger and often these "fearful" behaviors include forms of aggression or escape. Therefore, the intense feelings we experience when we are exposed to an immediate danger often are called the "fight-or-flight" response.

Although most people use the terms "anxiety" and "fear" interchangeably, behavioral scientists who study emotions assign somewhat different meanings to these and other related terms (Barlow 2002; Suárez et al., in press). *Anxiety* is a future-oriented feeling of dread or apprehension associated with the sense that events are both uncontrollable and unpredictable. In other words, anxiety is a nagging feeling that occurs when a person believes a negative event may occur in the future and that nothing can be done to prevent it.

People who feel anxious tend to dwell upon and ruminate about the possibility of danger. This tendency to dwell on future negative events is called worry. Anxiety is also associated with uncomfortable physical feelings such as arousal (for example, sweatiness, increased pulse), tension (for instance, tight muscles), and pain (like headaches).

There is no question that when anxiety is too intense it can interfere with performance; however, mild to moderate amounts of anxiety are actually helpful. If you never became even slightly anxious under any circumstances, you probably wouldn't bother doing the things that must be done. Why would you bother preparing an assignment on time, dressing nicely for a date, or eating healthy food if you weren't concerned about the consequences of not doing these things? In part, it is anxiety that motivates us to work hard, prepare for challenges, and protect ourselves from possible threats.

In contrast to anxiety, *fear* is a basic emotion that occurs when an individual is confronted with an immediate real or imagined danger. Fear leads to a sudden, intense physiological alarm reaction that essentially has one purpose—to get the person away from the danger as quickly as possible. When people feel fearful, their bodies go into overdrive to ensure that escape is fast and successful. Heart rate and blood pressure increase to transfer blood to the large muscles. Breathing quickens to improve the flow of oxygen throughout the body. People sweat to cool off the body and perform more efficiently. In fact, all of these symptoms of arousal and fear are designed to make escape easier, allowing for survival in the face of danger.

Panic attack is the clinical term used to describe the experience of intense fear that takes place even though no realistic danger is actually present. Panic attacks can be triggered by specific situations that people fear (for example, giving an oral presentation, being in a high place, seeing a snake) or they sometimes occur out of the blue, without any obvious trigger. Panic attacks are discussed in more detail later in this chapter.

To summarize, fear is an emotional reaction to an immediate danger, whereas anxiety is a state of apprehension about some future threat. For example, worrying about giving a presentation that is a week away is a reflection of anxiety, whereas experiencing an adrenaline rush while in the midst of giving a presentation is usually an example of fear.

Here are a few points to remember:

1. Anxiety and fear are normal emotions every-one experiences from time to time.

2. Anxiety and fear are time-limited. Even though they feel as though they may continue forever, they always decrease over time.

3. Anxiety and fear have a helpful function in that they prepare you for future threats and protect you from danger. So, your goal should not be to rid yourself of *all* fear and anxiety. Rather, your goal should be to reduce your anxiety to a level that no longer interferes significantly with your life.

WHAT IS A SOCIAL SITUATION?

A social situation is any situation in which you and other people are present. Social situations can include those that involve interacting with others (these are often referred to as *interpersonal situations*) or situations in which you are the focus of attention or might be noticed by others (these are often called *performance situations*). Examples of interpersonal situations and performance situations that may be feared by people with high levels of social anxiety include:

Interpersonal Situations

- Asking someone out on a date

- Talking to someone in <u>authority</u>

- Initiating or <u>maintaining</u> a conversation ✳
- Going to a party
- Having friends over for dinner
- Meeting new people ✳
- Talking on the telephone ✳
- Expressing a personal opinion ✳ *Around certain people.*
- Having a job interview ✳
- Being assertive (for example, saying no when you don't want to do something)
- Returning an item to a store *(when younger)*
- Sending back food in a restaurant
- Making eye contact

Performance Situations

- Public speaking ✳
- Speaking in meetings ✳
- Playing sports or participating in aerobics

- Performing a piano recital in front of others

- Having others watch you work ✱ *certain situations*

- Leaving a recorded message on somebody's voice mail

- Getting married

- Acting on a stage

- Reading out loud in front of others ✱

- Eating or drinking in front of others

- Using public bathrooms with others in the room

- Writing with others watching (for example, completing a form in public)

- Making a mistake in public (for example, falling down, dropping your keys, and so on)

- Walking or jogging on a busy street or some other public place

- Introducing yourself to a group of people ✱

- Shopping in a busy store

WHAT IS SOCIAL ANXIETY?

Social anxiety refers to nervousness or discomfort in social situations, usually because of fear about doing something embarrassing or foolish, making a bad impression, or being judged critically by others. For many people, social anxiety is limited to certain types of social situations. For example, some people are very uncomfortable in formal work-related situations, like presentations and meetings, but are quite comfortable in more casual situations, like parties and socializing with friends. Others may show the exact opposite pattern, with formal work situations being easier than unstructured social gatherings. In fact, it's not unusual to hear of a celebrity who is quite comfortable performing in front of large audiences but who otherwise feels shy and nervous when interacting with people one-on-one or in small groups.

The intensity of social anxiety and the range of feared social situations vary from person to person. For example, some people experience fear that is fairly manageable, whereas others are completely overwhelmed by the intensity of their fear. For some people, the fear is limited to a single social situation (for example, using public restrooms, public speaking), whereas for others, the social anxiety occurs in almost all social situations.

The experience of social anxiety is related to a number of common personality styles and traits including *shyness, introversion,* and *perfectionism.* People who are shy often feel uncomfortable in certain social situations, particularly when they involve interacting with others or meeting new people. People who are introverted tend to be quieter and more withdrawn in social situations and may prefer being alone, compared with people who are extroverted or outgoing. However, introverted people are not necessarily anxious or fearful when socializing. Finally, the trait of perfectionism is associated with a tendency to hold overly high standards for oneself that are difficult or impossible to meet. Perfectionism can lead people to feel anxious in public for fear that other people will notice their "flaws" and judge them negatively. Perfectionism is discussed again later in this chapter.

HOW COMMON IS SOCIAL ANXIETY?

It is difficult to obtain accurate estimates of the prevalence of social anxiety because different studies have tended to define social anxiety differently and used different questions when interviewing people about their anxiety. Nevertheless, researchers have consistently found that shyness and social anxiety are common experiences. For example, in a survey of more than 1,000 people from across the United States and elsewhere, psychologist Phillip Zimbardo and his colleagues (Carducci and Zimbardo 1995; Henderson and Zimbardo 1999; Zimbardo, Pilkonis, and Norwood 1975) found that 40 percent of those who were asked currently considered themselves to be chronically shy, to the point of it being a problem. Another 40 percent reported that they had previously considered themselves to be shy. Fifteen percent more considered themselves to be shy in some situations and only 5 percent reported that they were never shy. More recent surveys suggest that the prevalence of shyness may be even higher (for a review of studies on the prevalence of shyness, see Henderson and Zimbardo 1999).

Researchers have also studied the prevalence of social anxiety disorder (a condition associated with extreme social anxiety that will be described later in this chapter). In a recently published survey of more than 9,000 Americans (Kessler et al. 2005), about 12 percent of people reported having the necessary symptoms to receive a diagnosis of social anxiety disorder at some point in their lives. In fact, social anxiety disorder was found to be the fourth most prevalent psychological problem in this study, after depression, alcohol abuse, and specific phobias (for example, phobias of animals, blood, needles, heights, flying, and so on). Other researchers have found the prevalence of social anxiety disorder to be lower than 12 percent, but almost all studies have confirmed that social anxiety disorder is a common problem (Kessler et al., in press).

Differences Between Men and Women

Shyness and social anxiety are common across both sexes, although most studies have found that social anxiety disorder is slightly more prevalent in women than in men (Somers et al. 2006). There are a number of possible explanations for why women are more likely than men to report fearing social situations. First, it's possible that men are actually more anxious in social situations than they are willing to admit. For example, there is evidence from studies of other phobias that men underestimate their levels of fear (Pierce and Kirkpatrick 1992). Also, in Western societies, women are often expected to be more socially active than men. Therefore, men may be able to avoid certain types of social situations more easily than women, without being harassed about their absence and without experiencing as much social pressure from others in their day-to-day lives.

There also may be differences in the types of social situations that men and women fear. One study found that men with social anxiety disorder were more fearful than women of urinating in public bathrooms and returning items to stores, whereas women with social anxiety disorder were more fearful than men of situations such as talking to people in authority, public speaking, being the center of attention, expressing disagreement, and throwing a party (Turk et al. 1998).

Cultural Differences

It is challenging to measure social anxiety across cultures because signs of social anxiety in one culture may have a very different meaning in another culture. For example, whereas some cultures may view poor eye contact as a sign of shyness or social anxiety, other cultures often avert their eyes from contact with another as an appropriate sign of respect. Cultures also differ with respect to their use of pauses and silence during conversation, the preferred physical distance from others, and the appropriate tone of voice (Sue 1990).

Despite the difficulties in measuring social anxiety across cultures, studies generally suggest that social anxiety and shyness are common across different ethnic groups. However, it should be noted that in the United States and Canada, the majority of people who seek treatment for social anxiety disorder tend to be white and have a European background. Although people from nonwhite, non-European backgrounds are just as likely to experience problems with social anxiety, they are less likely to seek help from a mental health professional.

HOW DOES SOCIAL ANXIETY AFFECT PEOPLE's LIVES?

In this section, we will discuss how a person's social anxiety can affect relationships, work and school, and other day-to-day activities. After reading each section, take a few moments to consider how your social anxiety affects each of these areas of your life, and then describe this in the space provided.

Relationships

Social anxiety can make it difficult for people to establish and maintain healthy relationships. It can affect all levels of relationships, from those with strangers and casual acquaintances to those with family and significant others. For many people, even the most basic forms of social interaction (such as making small talk, asking other people for directions, saying hello to a neighbor) are very difficult. For such a person, dating may be completely out of the question. Social anxiety may be more manageable around more familiar people, such as close friends and family—but not always. For some people, anxiety may actually increase as a relationship becomes more intimate. Also, social anxiety can interfere with existing relationships, particularly if a socially anxious person's partner wants to socialize with others on a more regular basis. The following case examples illustrate how social anxiety can have a negative impact on a person's relationships.

- William has never been in a romantic relationship. Although others have expressed interest in dating him, he always makes excuses not to go out and usually doesn't return their phone calls. William desperately wants to be in a relationship, but he just can't find the courage to take the initial steps.

- Cindy is generally comfortable with her male colleagues at work, and she has several male friends with whom she socializes occasionally. However, as her relationships with men become closer, she is increasingly fearful that the other person will discover the "real" Cindy and reject her. She has ended several relationships with men just as they were becoming close.

- Jerry frequently argues with his girlfriend about his unwillingness to spend time with her friends. Although he was quite shy and anxious when they first started dating, recently his social anxiety has put more of a strain on their relationship. Because of his anxiety, they have been spending a lot of time alone while she has wanted to socialize as a couple with other people.

- Norm has gradually lost many of his friends over the years. For a while after finishing high school, he kept in touch with his closest friends. However, because of his anxiety, he often dreaded returning their calls and almost never accepted their invitations to get together. Eventually, his friends stopped calling him.

- Alison's roommate consistently plays loud music after midnight, making it impossible for her to sleep. Despite feeling very frustrated and angry, Alison avoids asking her roommate to turn down her music for fear that her words won't come out right or that her roommate will think she is an idiot.

- When talking to people whom she doesn't know well, Julia tends to speak very quietly, keep her distance, and avoid eye contact. As a result, people at work have started to leave her alone and they rarely invite her to lunch anymore.

In the space below, record the ways in which social anxiety has affected your friendships and relationships.

[space left intentionally blank in the original book]

Education and Career

Significant social anxiety can have an impact on a person's education and career. It can affect the types of courses you take in school and the types of jobs you might accept. It can also affect job performance as well as your enjoyment of school or work. Consider the following case examples:

- Naveen turned down a promotion at work that involved significant supervisory responsibilities, including chairing a weekly staff meeting and training groups of staff. Although the promotion would have provided him with a significant increase in salary, Naveen was terrified of speaking in front of groups, and he couldn't even imagine being able to lead the weekly meetings.

- Ruth dropped out of college partway through her third year. As a fresh-man and sophomore, Ruth had been able to be anonymous in her large classes. However, when her classes became smaller in her junior year, she felt increased pressure to participate in class. She began avoiding her lectures and eventually left school.

- Len dreads going into work each day. He is terrified to speak to his cowork-ers and avoids speaking to his boss at all costs. Although he never misses work, Len keeps the time he must talk to others at a minimum. He rarely takes a break for fear that others will ask him to have lunch or to spend their breaks with him.

- Cheryl has been out of work for two years. Although she often hears of jobs that might be interesting, the thought of having to go through a formal interview is completely overwhelming. On several occasions she has arranged for job interviews and then failed to show up because of her social anxiety.

- People at work think that Jason is a snob. He tends to be very serious, and he speaks very little to others. Even when someone asks him a question, he tends to answer with only one or two words. In reality, he isn't a snob; he is just very shy and anxious around people at work.

In the space below, record the ways in which social anxiety has affected your work or education.

[space left intentionally blank in the original book]

Other Day-to-Day Activities

Just about any activity that involves contact with other people can be affected by social anxiety. The following examples illustrate the range of situations and activities that are often difficult for people who are socially anxious.

- Sita avoids going shopping on Saturdays because the stores are so crowded and she is fearful of having other people watch her. In fact, just walking down a busy street is sometimes difficult for her.

- Michael screens all of his phone calls. He is very anxious when speaking to people on the phone because he finds it is more difficult to know how they are reacting to what he says as compared to speaking in person.

- Kalinda has stopped going to the gym. She was finding that exercising in front of other people was causing her too much anxiety. Instead she exercises at home, where no one can see her.

- Reid noticed a small hole in a sweater that he had just purchased. Although he had not worn the sweater and it still had all the original tags, he was unable to return the sweater for fear of looking foolish in front of the salesperson.

In the space below, record the ways in which social anxiety has affected your day-to-day functioning.

[space left intentionally blank in the original book]

SOCIAL ANXIETY DISORDER (SOCIAL PHOBIA)

When social anxiety becomes particularly severe, it may develop into a condition known as social anxiety disorder. *Social anxiety disorder* (also called *social phobia*) is one of several anxiety disorders listed in the *Diagnostic and Statistical Manual of Mental Disorders, Fourth Edition, Text Revision* (DSM-IV-TR; American Psychiatric Association 2000). The DSM-IV-TR is the guide used by mental health practitioners to identify and diagnose various types of psychological problems. DSM-IV-TR diagnoses don't tell us much about the *causes* of the disorder. Instead, the disorders listed in the DSM-IV-TR are simply descriptions of behaviors and experiences that cause interference or distress in a person's life. In short, they are a way of classifying emotional and psychological problems.

Although there is strong evidence that some of the DSM-IV-TR disorders (for example, schizophrenia, Alzheimer's disease) are associated with a biological dysfunction, the evidence is much less clear for other disorders. The problems listed in the DSM-IV-TR range from severe mental illnesses to disorders that most people would consider "bad habits." In fact, the DSM-IV-TR even includes such problems as nicotine dependence and impaired sleep resulting from jet lag or shift work.

If your anxiety symptoms meet the diagnostic criteria for social anxiety disorder, that does not mean that you are sick, have a disease, or are mentally ill. What it does mean is that you are experiencing social anxiety at a level that bothers you or interferes with aspects of your functioning. Remember that almost everyone experiences social anxiety, shyness, or performance anxiety from time to time. The social anxiety experienced by people with social anxiety disorder is associated with the same types of anxious thoughts and behaviors that most people experience. The difference is that people with social anxiety disorder experience social anxiety at a more intense level, more frequently, and often in a wider range of situations than people without social anxiety disorder. Fortunately, social anxiety disorder responds extremely well to the types of treatment discussed throughout this book.

Diagnostic Criteria for Social Anxiety Disorder

A diagnosis of social anxiety disorder requires that a person have an intense and persistent fear of one or more social or performance situations. Typically, the fear is related to anxiety over being scrutinized by others or doing something embarrassing or humiliating. In addition, the fear must bother the individual or cause significant interference in his or her life. In other words, a person would not receive a diagnosis of social anxiety disorder if he or she had a strong fear of public speaking but didn't need to speak in front of groups and didn't care about having the fear. On the other hand, a person who fears public speaking and needs to speak in front of groups (for example, a schoolteacher) might be considered to have social anxiety disorder if the criteria are all met.

Social anxiety is often a feature of other problems. For example, people with eating disorders may be nervous about having other people notice their unusual eating habits. People who wash their hands excessively due to obsessive-compulsive disorder (OCD) may avoid people either for fear of being contaminated by others or for fear of having other people notice their OCD symptoms (such as frequent washing, red hands from washing, and so on). In these examples, the social anxiety would be viewed as part of the other problem, rather than as social anxiety disorder per se. For social anxiety disorder to be diagnosed as a separate problem, there must also be extreme social anxiety that is unrelated to any other problems that are present. For example, the person might have a general fear of looking stupid, appearing boring to others, or making mistakes in front of other peo-ple—over and above the anxiety about having others notice his or her compulsive washing or unusual eating habits.

Diagnosing social anxiety disorder is a complicated task. The information outlined in this section gives you an idea of how mental health professionals distinguish different types of problems from social anxiety disorder. However, this overview will probably not be enough for the purpose of self-diagnosis. If you want to be sure about whether your symptoms meet the diagnostic criteria for social anxiety disorder, we recommend that you see a psychiatrist or psychologist who has experience and expertise in the assessment of anxiety disorders.

Unfortunately, even professionals sometimes have difficulty agreeing about whether the diagnostic criteria for a particular disorder are met. For many people, the criteria outlined in the DSM-IV-TR don't fit as neatly as we might like, which makes diagnosis especially challenging. Fortunately, the exact diagnosis isn't always necessary for selecting an effective treatment. The strategies described in this book will be useful for overcoming shyness and performance anxiety regardless of whether the full criteria for social anxiety disorder are met.

One final note about the diagnosis of social anxiety disorder: if all of the criteria for social anxiety disorder are met and the person is fearful of *almost all* social situations, the person is said to have generalized social anxiety disorder.

THREE COMPONENTS OF SOCIAL ANXIETY

In an effort to define shyness, Cheek and Watson (1989) surveyed 180 shy individuals about the types of experiences that are associated with shyness and social anxiety. Eighty-four percent of the participants' responses to the survey fell into one of three categories: the physical aspects of social anxiety (uncomfortable feelings and sensations), the cognitive aspects of social anxiety (anxious thoughts, expectations, predictions), and the behavioral aspects of social anxiety (for example, avoidance of social situations).

Cognitive behavioral treatments for social anxiety encourage people to think of their social anxiety in terms of these three components. In other words, when you feel anxious, you should pay attention to what you feel, think, and do. Breaking down your social anxiety into these components will help to make the problem feel less overwhelming and will set the stage for using the strategies outlined in this book.

Social Anxiety and Physical Feelings

Anxiety in social situations is often associated with a long list of physical arousal symptoms, and some of these feelings may themselves be sources of fear and anxiety. For example, people with elevated social anxiety are often especially fearful of symptoms that may be noticeable to other people, such as shaky hands, sweating, blushing, and a trembling voice. Examples of feelings that you may experience in social situations include:

- Racing or pounding heart

- Breathlessness or smothering feelings

- Dizziness or lightheadedness

- Difficulty swallowing, choking feelings, or a "lump" in the throat

- Quivering or shakiness (for example, in the hands, knees, lips, or whole body)

- Blushing

- Nausea, diarrhea, or "butterflies" in the stomach

- Excessive sweating

- Shaky voice

- Tearfulness, crying

- Poor concentration or forgetting what you were trying to say

- Blurred vision

- Numbness and tingling sensations

- Feelings of unreality or being detached

- Tightness or weakness in the muscles (for example, wobbly legs, sore neck)

- Chest pain or tightness in chest muscles

- Dry mouth

- Hot flushes or chills

People who are socially anxious differ from one another with respect to the ways in which they experience these feelings when they are anxious. Some people report many different physical symptoms. Others report only a few of these feelings. In fact, some people are not aware of any physical sensations when they are anxious.

There is also evidence that people are often unable to accurately report the intensity of these sensations. People who are socially anxious often report that their physical symptoms are very intense, particularly those symptoms that might be visible to other people. This is, however, often not the case. For the majority of people who are socially anxious, their symptoms are much less noticeable than they think. For example, a study by Mulkens, de Jong, Dobbelaar, and Bögels (1999) found that when socially anxious individuals are exposed to a stressful social situation, they are more likely than nonanxious individuals to believe that they are blushing. However, the study also found that there were no differences between socially anxious and nonanxious people with respect to the actual intensity of blushing.

Although in most cases people's anxiety symptoms are less noticeable than they think, there is no question that a small number of individuals have a tendency to blush, shake, or sweat that is clearly excessive and may actually be quite noticeable to other people. In other words, some people blush easily and others don't. Some people have shakier hands than others, and some people perspire more than others. However, not everyone who blushes, sweats, and shakes excessively also experiences intense fear when around other people. In fact, many people are not terribly concerned about experiencing these symptoms in front of other people.

In other words, experiencing these symptoms is not the problem. Rather, it is your beliefs about the meaning and possible consequences of these symptoms that contributes to your social anxiety. If you didn't care whether other people noticed your physical anxiety symptoms you would probably be much less anxious in social and performance situations. Furthermore, you would probably experience fewer of these uncomfortable symptoms.

Not surprisingly, the physical sensations that you experience when you are anxious or fearful are similar to those that you experience during any intense emotion, including excitement and anger. The differences between fear, excitement, and anger manifest not so much in the way they feel physically, but rather in the types of thoughts and behaviors associated with each of these emotions. It is to these aspects of social anxiety that we now turn our attention.

Social Anxiety and Thinking

Strictly speaking, people don't react emotionally to the situations and events in their lives. Rather, they react to their beliefs and interpretations concerning these events and situations. In other words, given an identical situation, different people might have completely different emotional responses, depending on their beliefs about the situation.

Consider the following example. Imagine that you have interviewed for a job and are waiting to hear about the outcome of the interview. You were told that you would hear within a week. Two weeks have passed, and you still haven't heard from anyone about whether you were selected for the position. How would you feel? What emotions would you be experiencing? Well, you might be nervous if you thought the lack of a call was a sign that you didn't get the job. On the other hand, if you thought no call was a sign that decisions had not yet been made, you might feel more optimistic. You might be angry if you believed that the interviewer was treating you disrespectfully by not calling.

Often our beliefs are accurate; however, sometimes our beliefs are exaggerated or incorrect. For example, some people who are socially anxious are quick to assume that another person doesn't like them just because he or she seems uninterested during a conversation. In reality, there are many reasons why a person might look uninterested when talking to you. Some of these include:

- The other person is not interested in the topic of the conversation but still likes you as an individual.

- The other person is hungry.

- The other person is in a hurry (for example, he or she is late for an appointment).

- The other person is tired.

- The other person is feeling sick or unwell.

- The other person is shy or socially anxious.

- The other person is thinking about something stressful that happened earlier in the day.

- The other person is worrying about something that is coming up.

- The other person is someone who generally doesn't enjoy conversations.

- The other person is someone who always looks somewhat uninterested, even when he or she is having a good time.

- You are incorrectly assuming that the other person is uninterested even though he or she is showing all the usual signs of interest.

If you are anxious in social situations, the chances are that you are either interpreting the situations as threatening in some way or are predicting that something negative is likely to occur. The more often you experience social or performance anxiety, the more often you probably engage in this style of anxious thinking. We will provide a more detailed discussion of the role of thoughts in social anxiety in chapter 6. For now, here are common beliefs held by people who are socially anxious:

- It's essential that everyone likes me.

- If someone doesn't like me, it means I am unlikable.

- If someone rejects me, I deserve it.

- People should always be interested in what I am saying.

- People should never have a disapproving or bored look on their face when I am talking.

- People should never talk about me behind my back.

- If I make a mistake at work, I'll get fired.

- People will be angry with me if I make a mistake.

- I'll make a fool of myself if I give a presentation.

- People can tell when I'm nervous.

- People find me unattractive, boring, stupid, lazy, incompetent, weird, weak, and so on.

- People are untrustworthy, judgmental, and nasty.

- I should be able to hide my anxiety symptoms.

- It's awful to blush, shake, or sweat in front of others.

- If my hands shake at work, it will be a disaster.

- Anxiety is a sign of weakness.

- I should not appear anxious in front of others.

- I won't be able to speak if I'm too anxious.

Social Anxiety and Behavior

The most common behavioral response to feeling anxious or frightened is to either avoid the anxiety-provoking situation completely or to do something else to reduce the anxiety as quickly as possible. The reason people engage in these behaviors is because they are very effective at reducing discomfort—*in the short term.* However, in the long term, these behaviors have the effect of maintaining fear and anxiety in social situations because they prevent people from learning that their anxiety-provoking predictions are unlikely to come true. Following are some examples of behaviors that people often use to reduce their anxiety in social situations. Notice that some of these are examples involving complete escape or avoidance. However, other examples involve partial avoidance, efforts to reduce anxiety, or attempts to protect oneself in the situation. These behaviors are often called *safety behaviors,* because they are carried out in an effort to feel safer in the feared situation:

- Turning down an invitation to a party

- Making an excuse not to have dinner with a friend

- Never answering questions in class

- Always arriving late for meetings and leaving early in order to avoid making small talk

- Offering to help with the dishes at a party in order to avoid talking to the guests

- Making an excuse to get off the telephone with a friend or coworker

- Distracting yourself from your anxious thoughts

- Having the room dark during your presentation in order to keep the audience focused on the slides rather than on you

- Filling out a check before arriving at a store in order to avoid having to write in front of others

- Avoiding eye contact and talking very quietly during conversations with others

- Wearing makeup and a turtleneck sweater to hide your blushing

- Always attending the office holiday party with a close friend, spouse, or other safe person, even though other guests usually attend alone

- Always arriving for meetings early to ensure that it will not be necessary to enter the room after everyone else is already seated

- Having a couple of glasses of wine before meeting another person for a date

Interactions Among the Three Components

The cycle of fear and anxiety can begin with any of the three components we've just discussed. For example, you may be talking to a colleague at work when you notice yourself perspiring slightly (physical component). That may lead to anxious thoughts about whether your colleague is noticing your sweaty brow and wondering if there is something wrong with you (cognitive component). As your anxiety increases, the intensity of your physical sensations increases and you continue to think anxious thoughts. Eventually, you may make an excuse to leave the situation (behavioral component).

Alternatively, the cycle may begin with the cognitive component. For example, before giving a presentation, you may tell yourself that you are going to lose your train of thought and that others will notice how uncomfortable you are. You imagine that the others will interpret your discomfort as a sign of weakness (cognitive component). As you continue to dwell on these anxious thoughts, you notice your face beginning to feel flushed and your heart rate increasing (physical component). Finally, you make a decision to read your presentation word for word to be sure that your anxiety doesn't cause you to lose your place during the presentation (behavioral component).

Finally, the cycle may start with the behavioral component, namely avoidance and safety behaviors. By putting off getting together with friends for a long time (behavioral component), you are more likely to experience anxious thoughts (cognitive component) about what might happen when you do see them, as well as uncomfortable physical feelings when you are actually in the situation (physical component). Although avoiding anxiety-provoking situations can be comforting in the short term, it also can have the effect of making the situation even more uncomfortable when you finally confront it. The longer you put off an unpleasant task, the harder it is to start the task when you finally decide to do it.

Exercise: Components of Social Anxiety

Over the next week or so, photocopy and use the Three Components of Social Anxiety Monitoring Form (found at the end of this chapter) to record your anxiety in terms of the three components of fear. Try to complete the form each time you encounter a feared social situation (if possible, at least three times in the next week). In the first column, record the situation (including time and place). In the second column, record the intensity of your fear using a scale from 0 (no fear) to 100 (maximum fear). In the third column, record the physical sensations that you experienced in the situation. In the fourth column, record any anxiety-provoking thoughts or predictions that you are aware of regarding the situation. Finally, in the fifth column, record any avoidance behaviors or any other anxious behaviors used to reduce your anxiety. In addition to the blank form, a sample completed form is included.

OTHER PROBLEMS AND FEATURES

Social anxiety is often associated with other problems. These may include panic attacks in social situations, excessively high standards and perfectionism, depressed mood, a negative body image, substance abuse, or difficulty trusting others. We will now discuss each of these associated difficulties.

Panic Attacks

If you experience intense social anxiety, the chances are good that you have had panic attacks in social and performance situations. As discussed at the beginning of this chapter, a panic attack is a rush of fear that occurs in the absence of any realistic danger. According to the definition of a panic attack, the fear must peak within ten minutes, although it usually peaks immediately or within a few seconds. Also, to meet the full criteria for a panic attack, there must be at least four symptoms from a list of thirteen, including racing heart, chest discomfort, dizziness, breathlessness, shaking, stomach discomfort, sweating, choking feelings, hot flashes or chills, feelings of unreality or detachment, numbness or tingling, and fears of dying, going crazy, or losing control.

For those who suffer from social anxiety, panic attacks tend to be triggered by exposure to feared social situations or even just thinking about being in a feared situation. In addition, people who are socially anxious are often fearful of experiencing panic symptoms. Because panic-attack symptoms are often incorrectly viewed as a sign that one is about to lose control, it's no wonder that people who are socially anxious would want to avoid having panic attacks in front of others. Even though people who experience panic attacks often are afraid of losing control, going crazy, fainting, having a heart attack, or experiencing some other physical or social catastrophe, such consequences are extremely unlikely. In other words, panic attacks are uncomfortable, but they aren't dangerous. In fact, the symptoms often are not even noticeable to other people.

Perfectionism

Research from our organization (Antony et al. 1998) and elsewhere has found that social anxiety is associated with elevated levels of perfectionism. Perfectionists hold standards that are unrealistically high and overly rigid. They may have exaggerated concerns about making mistakes and often go out of their way to ensure that mistakes are avoided.

In social anxiety, people tend to place too much importance on making a perfect impression on others. If they are not guaranteed to be approved of by others, they may feel very anxious in social situations or avoid socializing altogether. Perfectionism is different from simply having high standards. High standards are often useful because they motivate us to work hard and succeed. In the case of perfectionism, however, the standards are so high and so inflexible that they actually interfere with performance by causing a person to overprepare for tasks (for instance, spending hours rehearsing a presentation), procrastinate (such as putting off preparing for a presentation), or be overly critical of his or her own performance.

Depression

Given the impact of social anxiety on a person's functioning, it is no wonder that a substantial number of people with social anxiety disorder also experience depression. Severe social anxiety can lead to isolation, loneliness, and deep sadness. Social anxiety disorder can prevent a person from living up to his or her potential, which, in turn, can lead to feelings of hopelessness and depression. Depression can also increase the severity of social anxiety.

People who are depressed are often embarrassed about feeling down, may assume that others don't want to be around them, and may avoid being around other people. Social anxiety and depression are associated with similar thought patterns as well—specifically, negative thoughts about oneself and about one's relationships. Finally, there is reason to think that social anxiety disorder and depression may be related to similar biological processes in the brain. In fact, the treatments discussed in this book (including both psychological treatments and medications) have been shown to be useful for both anxiety and depression.

Body Image Problems

People who are unhappy with their physical appearance may feel anxious when socializing or being watched by others. For example, people with eating disorders such as anorexia nervosa and bulimia nervosa may avoid activities that involve eating in front of others or showing their bodies (such as wearing shorts, swimming, or exercising in public). People who are overweight may also be concerned about having their physical appearance judged negatively by others. In fact, dissatisfaction with any aspect of one's physical appearance (for example, losing your hair, not liking your nose, and so on) can lead some people to experience social anxiety.

Substance Abuse

Some people who experience excessive levels of social anxiety use alcohol or other drugs to help cope with social situations. In most cases, this may involve only having an extra glass of wine at a party or having a beer when eating out with friends. However, for some people, using alcohol or drugs to manage anxiety can become a problem if the drug or alcohol use becomes excessive. If you frequently use excessive amounts of alcohol or other drugs to feel more comfortable in social situations, it may be important to address this issue at the same time that you are working on your social anxiety.

Anger and Mistrust of Others

In addition to fearing negative judgment from others, some people with high levels of social anxiety may also have difficulty trusting others. They may avoid confiding in others, not only for fear of being judged, but also because they're afraid that other people will not be able to keep a secret. Social anxiety is also sometimes associated with elevated levels of anger and irritability. For example, some people with social anxiety disorder may become very angry or hostile when being looked at by others. They may also become angry at perceived rejections by other people.

OVERCOMING SOCIAL ANXIETY

Two general approaches have been shown to be useful for overcoming social anxiety: psychological strategies and medications. We'll discuss each of these briefly.

Psychological Strategies

Although there are many different types of psychotherapy practiced by mental health professionals, there are only a small number of strategies that have been shown to be effective for reducing social anxiety in a relatively brief amount of time. The chapters in this book discuss three general approaches that repeatedly have been shown to be effective for treating social anxiety disorder:

1. Exposure-based strategies will teach you to approach feared situations gradually, over and over again, until they no longer provoke fear.

2. Cognitive strategies will be used to help you to identify your anxiety-provoking thoughts and to replace them with more realistic ways of thinking.

3. Instruction in basic communication skills will teach you to communicate more assertively, meet people more easily, give effective pre-sentations, and use nonverbal communication appropriately.

Medications

There are a number of medications that have been shown to be effective for decreasing social anxiety. These include a range of antidepressants as well as certain tranquilizers. As long as the person continues to take the medication, these treatments are about as effective as the psychological strategies discussed in this book. For some people, the combination of medication and psychological treatment is the most effective approach. In chapter 5 we will discuss the benefits and costs of using particular medications for treating your social anxiety. (Table 1.1 and 1.2)

47

Three Components of Social Anxiety Monitoring Form

Place/Situation/Time	Fear (0–00)	Physical Feelings	Anxiety-Provoking Thoughts	Anxious Behaviors

Table 1.1

Three Components of Social Anxiety Monitoring Form—Completed Sample

Place/Situation/Time	Fear (0–100)	Physical Feelings	Anxiety-Provoking Thoughts	Anxious Behaviors
At a party on Tuesday night, I said to Mike, "It's been ages since I saw you last," and he responded by reminding me that I just saw him last week!	90	Heart racing, sweating, shaking, short of breath	I can't believe I said that! Mike must think I'm an idiot for forgetting that I just saw him. Maybe he thinks I don't care enough to remember him. He must notice that I am a nervous wreck!	Apologized to Mike about 5 times, and then went to the bathroom to get away from him. After about 10 minutes, I made an excuse and left the party.
Wednesday evening. Preparing for a brief presentation on Friday.	70	Heart racing, muscle tightness	I will lose my train of thought. People will think I am incompetent. I will lose my job if I blow this presentation.	Had two glasses of wine to calm down. Rehearsed my presentation about 20 times. Asked a coworker to present with me.
Saturday afternoon. Walking through the mall.	50	Feeling flushed, palms are sweaty, heart is racing	People are staring at me. They can tell I'm anxious. They are probably thinking I look funny or that I walk funny.	I avoided eye contact with other people. After about 5 minutes, left the mall, even though I hadn't finished my shopping!

Table 1.2

CHAPTER 2

Why Do You Have These Fears?

BIOLOGICAL FACTORS

As with any emotion or personality trait, our biology affects the tendency to experience anxiety in social situations (Mathew and Ho 2006). Biological processes such as natural selection or evolution, genetics, brain activity, and alterations in the levels of certain neurotransmitters in the brain may all contribute to social anxiety. We'll discuss each of these in this section.

Natural Selection: The Evolutionary Function of Social Anxiety

Natural selection is the process by which members of a species who are best able to adapt to their environments are the most likely to reproduce successfully, thereby causing the species to evolve gradually and to survive over a long period of time. It makes sense that through natural selection, those among us who are most fit and healthy might be more likely to survive and to reproduce than those who are less so. However, several authors have argued that many of the *illnesses* from which humans suffer may also have developed according to the same laws of natural selection that are thought to have guided the more "positive" aspects of human evolution (Moalem and Prince 2007; Nesse and Williams 1994).

For example, in their book, *Why We Get Sick: The New Science of Darwinian Medicine,* Drs. Randolph Nesse and George Williams discuss how a number of uncomfortable conditions such as sneezing from allergies, suffering from colds or fevers, and experiencing pain from injuries all serve to protect us from potential dangers. The same processes that lead to allergies, colds, and fever also help the body to rid itself of potentially dangerous toxins and parasitic viruses. Likewise, pain following an injury is a warning sign that prevents us from moving our bodies in ways that could worsen the injury.

Might anxiety also improve our chances of survival? As we mentioned in chapter 1, the fight-or-flight response associated with fear and panic protects us from potential danger. When we are afraid, our bodies quickly become mobilized either to meet the danger head on or to escape from the danger as quickly as possible. All of the sensations that we experience when we are frightened (for instance, increased pulse, faster breathing, sweating, hyperventilation, and so on) are designed to help us meet the physical demands of confronting the threat (fighting) or escaping to safety (flight).

From an evolutionary perspective, it makes sense that we humans would develop a propensity for experiencing social anxiety. We are social beings, and as such, we are very much dependent on those around us. None of us could survive without the help of others. As infants and children, we are completely dependent on our parents for food, shelter, comfort, and education. As we grow up, we continue to depend on other people. We depend on our employers to provide us with money for food and shelter. We depend on other people to build our homes, grow our food, heal our injuries, entertain us, and to help us meet most of our day-to-day needs. Because of our dependence on one another, we learn at a very young age that it is important to get along well with people. Essentially, we want other people to like us. After all, consistently making a bad impression on other people might lead to isolation, unemployment, and many other negative consequences.

Feeling anxious in social situations serves to remind each of us to pay attention to the effects our behavior has on those around us. If we didn't think about the impact of our behavior on others, we would probably get into trouble more often than not. We wouldn't bother dressing nicely or being polite. We might always say exactly what's on our mind without considering whether it might be hurtful. Feeling anxious in social situations protects us from offending other people and from doing things that might lead others to judge us in negative ways. So, not only is it normal to feel shy or socially anxious from time to time, it is also helpful.

Of course, social anxiety and shyness are not always helpful. Extreme social anxiety may lead to impaired concentration, which, in turn, can cause a person to make more errors at work or school. In addition, socially anxious people often avoid taking social risks and may therefore find it difficult to make friends or to find work. Whereas mild to moderate levels of social anxiety are completely normal and potentially helpful, extreme social anxiety can interfere with a person's functioning.

So, from an evolutionary perspective, people with social anxiety disorder do not have an *illness,* per se. Rather, they have *too much of a good thing.* Social anxiety is helpful in small doses, but when it is too intense, it can make life more difficult.

Genetics and Social Anxiety

Social anxiety disorder appears to run in families. For example, a study by Stein, Chartier, Hazen, Kozak, et al. (1998) found that having a close relative (for example, a parent, sibling, or child) with *generalized* social anxiety disorder (extreme anxiety in most social situations) made an individual ten times as likely to have social anxiety disorder, compared with individuals who didn't have a socially anxious relative. In contrast, more narrowly focused social fears (for example, a fear of public speaking only) were less likely to run in families.

Of course, the existence of social anxiety disorder in multiple family members does not necessarily mean that the social anxiety is transmitted by genes. Environmental factors (for example, learning from one's parents and siblings) can also contribute to the family members sharing certain behaviors and tendencies. To tease out the effects of genetic influences from the effects of environment and learning, scientists have relied on three main types of studies:

1. **Twin studies.** Twin studies examine the frequency of a problem across pairs of *identical twins* (twins who are 100 percent genetically identical) vs. pairs of *fraternal twins* (twins who share, on average, 50 percent of their genetic material). Because twin pairs tend to be raised in similar environments regardless of whether they are identical twins or fraternal twins, a higher social anxiety concordance rate in identical twins than in fraternal twins is thought to be evidence that genetics may have played a larger role in the

development of the social anxiety (the term *concordance rate* refers to the probability of one person having a particular problem if his or her twin also has the problem).

2. **Adoption studies.** In adoption studies, scientists interview both the biological parents and the adoptive parents of people who were adopted as children and who also have the particular problem being studied. If the researcher finds that social anxiety disorder occurs much more frequently in the biological parents of the socially anxious adoptees than in the adoptive parents, it suggests that genetics may be more important than environment. Although adoption studies have been used to study the role of genetics in various disorders and illnesses, this approach has not yet been used in research on social anxiety disorder.

3. **Molecular genetics studies.** In 2003, scientists completed the Human Genome Project, which involved mapping all of the genes in human DNA and determining the sequences of the 3 billion chemical base pairs that make up human DNA. This work has made it possible for scientists to study particular genes that may be involved in the development of social anxiety disorder and many other conditions, using research methods known as *linkage studies* and *association studies.*

So, what do we know about the role of genetics in social anxiety disorder? Most of the studies to date on genetics and social anxiety disorder have been twin studies (for instance, Kendler, Karkowski, and Prescott 1999; Kendler et al. 2001; Stein, Jang, and Livesley 2002), and there has also been a small number of molecular genetics studies (for example, Lochner et al. 2007). Generally, twin studies have found modest to moderate levels of heritability for social anxiety disorder, suggesting that although genetics plays a role, other factors such as a person's environment and experiences are also very important. Molecular genetics studies are just beginning in the area of social anxiety, and over time they should help to uncover which genes are most important in the development of this problem.

Two personality traits closely related to social anxiety appear to be heritable as well, with *heritability estimates* (the extent to which the transmission of a trait across generations is due to genetics) being close to 50 percent across a wide range of studies (Plomin 1989). One of these traits, called *neuroticism,* is a general tendency to feel distressed, anxious, nervous, and worried. The other trait, called *introversion,* is a tendency to be inwardly focused and socially withdrawn. Not surprisingly, shyness and social anxiety tend to be associated with both of these personality styles (Briggs 1988). Recently, researchers have started to use molecular genetics studies to identify specific genes that may contribute to traits such as introversion (Stein, Schork, and Gelernter 2004).

If genetics does play a role in causing social anxiety, does that mean that social anxiety cannot be changed? Not at all. Our genetic makeup affects just about every aspect of who we are, including physical fitness, academic ability, depression, weight, personality, and even our interests and hobbies. Yet we all know that our behavior and experiences still play an important role in determining our behavior and performance in these various domains.

For example, regardless of whether you are genetically predisposed to be athletic, training hard will improve your athletic ability. Furthermore, the environment (for example, the exercise habits that you learn while growing up) may have a profound effect on whether you exercise regularly as an adult. Still, there are differences between people with respect to how hard they must train to become physically fit. For some people, it comes easier than for others—in part, because of their genetic makeup.

The same reasoning holds true for social anxiety. A genetic predisposition to have high levels of social anxiety and shyness simply means that you may have to work harder at overcoming the problem than someone who doesn't have such a tendency.

Effects of the Brain and Neurotransmitters

Compared with other psychological problems, including other anxiety disorders, studies examining the biological factors underlying social anxiety often have failed to obtain significant findings. For example, research examining hormonal factors, sleep patterns, and heart functioning has often failed to find differences between people with social anxiety disorder and people without significant social anxiety.

However, a number of studies have found increased levels of activity in particular parts of the brain during periods of social anxiety. For example, scientists have found that people with social anxiety disorder experience increased activity in a part of the brain called the *amygdala* when looking at pictures of harsh faces (Phan et al. 2006; Stein et al. 2002; Straube et al. 2004). The amygdala is part of the *limbic system* and is activated when we experience the emotion of fear. During public speaking, there also appears to be more activation in the amygdala among people with social anxiety disorder than among people without this problem (Phan et al. 2006).

As reviewed by Britton and Rauch (in press), other areas of the brain that have been found to be activated during social anxiety include the *anterior cingulate cortex* (an area that is involved in controlling emotions, thought, and heart rate, among other functions), the *medial prefrontal cortex* (a section of the brain that is involved in complex cognition, personality expression, and social behavior), the *insular cortex* (a section of the limbic system that is involved in the experience of basic emotions, including fear), and the *hippocampus* (a part of the limbic system that controls memory and spatial abilities). Furthermore, treatment of social anxiety with either cognitive behavioral therapy or medication leads to reductions in activity in the amygdala and hippocampus (Furmark et al. 2002).

Studies examining the role of neurotransmitters (the chemicals responsible for transmitting information throughout the brain) in social anxiety have yielded mixed results (McCabe and Antony, in press). Some studies suggest that the neurotransmitter *dopamine* may be involved in social anxiety, whereas other studies have failed to replicate these findings. Studies regarding the role of serotonin (another neurotransmitter) have also yielded mixed findings. However, medications that work on the serotonin system have consistently been found to be helpful for decreasing the symptoms of social anxiety disorder (more on this in chapter 5).

PSYCHOLOGICAL FACTORS

In addition to biology, people's experiences and beliefs also contribute to whether they develop difficulties with social anxiety and shyness. The ways in which learning and beliefs contribute to social anxiety are discussed in this section.

How Learning Contributes to Social Anxiety

A large number of studies suggests that learning plays an important role in the development of fear. We learn to fear objects and situations through three main routes (Rachman 1976). First, directly experiencing a trauma or some negative consequence in a particular situation can lead to fear. For example, being bitten by a dog can teach a person to be afraid of dogs. Second, observing other people who are afraid of a situation can teach a person to be nervous. So, people may be more nervous behind the wheel of a car if they grew up with a parent who was an anxious driver. Finally, hearing or reading about the dangers of a particular situation can help to cause or maintain a person's fear. For instance, reading about airline crashes can help to strengthen a person's fear of flying.

LEARNING BY DIRECT EXPERIENCE

A history of negative experiences in social situations can increase a person's shyness and social anxiety. For example, in a study from our center, people with social anxiety disorder were more likely to describe a history of severe teasing in childhood than were people with other anxiety problems (McCabe et al. 2003). In addition to teasing, other examples of social traumas include:

- Being bullied by other children while growing up

- Having parents, friends, teachers, or employers who are overly critical

- Doing something embarrassing in a social situation (such as making an obvious mistake, vomiting, having a panic attack, and so on)

In the space below, list examples of negative consequences that you have experienced in social situations that may have contributed to or helped to maintain your social anxiety.

Examples of Negative or "Traumatic" Experiences That May Have Contributed to My Social Anxiety

[space left intentionally blank in the original book]

LEARNING BY OBSERVING OTHERS

Observation is a powerful way of learning to fear specific objects and situations. This form of learning (also called *vicarious learning*) includes developing a fear by observing role models who themselves are anxious in social situations. Another form of observational learning involves witnessing another person experience a trauma in a social situation. Examples of observational learning experiences that could lead to the development of social anxiety include:

- Growing up with family members who are very shy and who rarely socialize

- Watching a classmate be severely criticized by a teacher following a presentation

- Seeing coworkers become very anxious while giving presentations

- Witnessing a friend being teased by other students at school

In the space below, list examples of informational learning experiences that may have contributed to, or helped to maintain, your social anxiety.

Examples of Indirect or Informational Learning Experiences That May Have Contributed to My Social Anxiety

[space left intentionally blank in the original book]

LEARNING THROUGH INFORMATION AND INDIRECT MEANS

People can learn to fear social situations by reading about or being warned about the dangers of making a bad impression on others. Examples of situations that could lead to developing social anxiety through the transmission of information include:

- Being repeatedly told by parents that it is very important to always make a good impression

- Being exposed to messages in magazines and on television that your image is the most important thing about you, and that you are only as attractive as other people think you are

In the space below, list examples of observational learning experiences that may have contributed to or helped to maintain your social anxiety.

Examples of Observational Learning Experiences That May Have Contributed to My Social Anxiety

[space left intentionally blank in the original book]

Why Only Some People Develop Extreme Social Anxiety

Although negative experiences, observational learning, and informational learning are common routes by which people develop fears, they are not enough to explain why some people develop social anxiety and others don't. Almost everyone is exposed to negative experiences in social situations. At one time or another most of us are teased. We are all exposed to anxiety-provoking messages at home, as well as through the media. And yet, not everyone develops a problem with social anxiety. Why is this so?

Most likely, there are other factors that influence whether a particular person develops problems with social anxiety following a history of negative social experiences. These can include biological factors, such as a person's genetic makeup. Previous learning experiences and the ways in which someone deals with his or her negative social experiences may also influence the development of fear. For example, a person who is ridiculed the first time he or she gives a presentation may be more likely to develop a fear of public speaking than someone who is ridiculed on a single occasion after having given many successful presentations previously. Similarly, someone who is severely teased at school may be protected from developing problems with social anxiety if he or she receives support from close friends after the episode.

Finally, avoiding a social situation following a traumatic experience may increase the chances of developing social anxiety. You have probably heard that the best thing to do after falling off a horse is to get back on as soon as possible to avoid developing a fear of horses. The same is true of social anxiety. If you avoid a social situation following a traumatic experience, you may increase your chances of developing a fear of that situation.

HOW BELIEFS CONTRIBUTE TO SOCIAL ANXIETY

As discussed in chapters 1 and 6, people with elevated social anxiety tend to think about social situations in a more negative way than do those people who are less anxious. Anxiety-provoking thoughts, interpretations, and predictions can lead someone to feel fear and anxiety in social situations.

There are numerous studies investigating the role of thinking in social anxiety. There is also evidence that helping people to change their anxious beliefs is an effective way of decreasing their social anxiety. Research on thinking and social anxiety is reviewed elsewhere (Antony and Swinson 2000; Hirsch and

Clark 2004). Some of the highlights of this research include the following findings:

- People who experience high social anxiety rate negative social events as more likely to occur and more costly (in terms of their consequences), in comparison with people who don't have significant social anxiety.

- These people tend to interpret their own performance (such as during a conversation or a speech) more critically than do people who are lower in social anxiety.

- They tend to overestimate the extent to which their physical symptoms (such as blushing) are visible to others.

- They are more likely than less anxious people to assume that others will interpret their physical symptoms (shaking, sweating, and so on) as a sign of a serious problem with anxiety or some mental illness. In contrast, people who are not socially anxious are less concerned about others noticing their physical arousal symptoms. Instead, people without significant social anxiety assume that others will interpret their physical symptoms as normal (perhaps a sign of feeling hot, being hungry, and so on).

- When presented with an ambiguous social situation (for example, a stare from someone else or a phone call that isn't returned), people with elevated social anxiety have a heightened tendency to interpret the situation negatively.

- Social anxiety is associated with a tendency to rate ambiguous or neutral faces as having a more negative expression.

- Compared with people who are less anxious, people with social anxiety disorder tend to pay more attention to information that represents social threat than to nonthreatening information. For example, when asked to look at lists of words, people who are socially anxious spend more time looking at words that are related to social anxiety (words such as "blush" or "party") than do those who are less anxious.

- Social anxiety is associated with a tendency to have a better memory and recognition for other people's faces, particularly if the expression on the face appears to be negative or critical.

Taken together, these studies suggest that social anxiety and social anxiety disorder are associated with thinking styles that may actually make the problem worse. In chapter 6, we'll discuss ways to change your anxious thoughts and replace them with less anxious and more realistic ways of thinking. A number of studies investigating the effects of cognitive behavioral therapy on the negative thinking styles often associ- ated with social anxiety have found that treatment leads to a reduction in negative thinking (Hirsch and Clark 2004).

HOW BEHAVIORS CONTRIBUTE TO SOCIAL ANXIETY

As discussed in chapter 1, avoidance of social situa- tions can have the effect of increasing social anxiety over the long term. In other words, the strategy that people who are socially anxious use most frequently to cope with their fear may actually make the problem *worse.*

In addition, some behaviors that people use to protect themselves in social situations can actually lead to the very outcome that people with social anxiety dis- order fear most—a negative reaction from others. For example, if when talking to other people at a party, you speak very quietly, avoid eye contact, and avoid expressing your views and opinions, people may choose to talk to someone else. They may interpret your behavior as a sign that you're not interested in talking or that you are a difficult person to get to know. See chapters 7 through 9 for a discussion of strategies for confronting feared situations instead of avoiding them and for stopping the safety behaviors that help to maintain your fear over time. And, in chapter 10, we'll discuss strategies for improving communication and social skills.

CHAPTER 3

Getting to Know Your Social Anxiety

WHY CONDUCT A SELF-ASSESSMENT?

The initial step that a psychologist, psychiatrist, or other mental health professional takes in beginning to help an individual with a particular problem is a period of evaluation and assessment. This evaluation process involves collecting information needed to better understand the nature and extent of the problem so that the best possible treatment plan can be formulated. This initial assessment almost always involves an interview and may also include various questionnaires and standard tests. Sometimes, the therapist may ask the person to start keeping a diary to monitor specific thoughts or behaviors.

In the case of social anxiety, a clinician might spend the first session (or even the first few sessions) asking questions about the client's social anxiety, about other difficulties he or she might be experiencing, and about the person's general background and life experiences. The individual also may be asked to answer a series of questionnaires that measure social anxiety and related problems. In addition, the client is often asked to complete diary entries between sessions to measure the person's anxiety in social situations, his or her feelings of depression, and any other aspects of the problem. The assessment process helps the clinician to understand the person's problems and is useful for choosing an appropriate course of treatment. In addition, repeating certain assessments from time to time allows the clinician to measure whether treatment is working (Antony and Rowa 2005).

In the same way, a detailed self-assessment will help you to understand and address your difficulties with social anxiety. We strongly recommend that, before you begin working on changing your own social anxiety, you carry out a careful self-assessment. This assessment process will have the following four main benefits. It will:

1. Allow you to measure the severity of your social anxiety

2. Help you to identify key problem areas

3. Make it easier to choose the most appropriate treatment strategies

4. Provide you with an opportunity to measure your improvement as you use the strategies described in this book

Now we will discuss each of these issues in greater detail.

MEASURING THE SEVERITY OF YOUR SOCIAL ANXIETY

The term "severity" takes into account such variables as (1) the intensity of your fear in social and performance situations, (2) the range of different situations that precipitate your social anxiety, (3) the frequency with which you experience intense social anxiety, (4) the effect of your social anxiety on your day-to-day life, career, and relationships, and (5) the extent to which being socially anxious bothers you. Generally, as the severity of social anxiety increases, typically, so does the intensity of the fear, the number of situations that are affected, the frequency with which anxiety is experienced, the level of interference with day-to-day functioning, and the extent to which a person is bothered by having the fear.

IDENTIFYING WHICH PROBLEMS TO WORK ON

If you're like many people, you probably experience anxiety in a number of different social situations. A comprehensive self-assessment will help you to decide which fears to work on first. First, it will be important to identify which situations you fear and avoid. Next, you will need to identify your priorities—that is, which aspects of the problem you want to begin to address first. When choosing your priorities, here are some suggestions to keep in mind:

- Begin working on problems for which you are likely to see quick changes. Early improvements will help to motivate you to work on more difficult situations.

- Try to work on fears that interfere the most with your day-to-day life. Being able to confront the most disabling fears will have a much bigger impact on your life than working on fears that are less important to you.

- If one of your treatment aims is very important to you but is just too over-whelming to deal with, divide that goal into smaller, more manageable objectives. For example, if you are afraid of dating, you could work on your fear by breaking the situation down into steps such as saying hello to an attractive classmate, sitting beside the classmate for several weeks in a row, speaking with the classmate after class, offering to study with the classmate, and asking the classmate to have dinner with you after class.

CHOOSING THE BEST STRATEGIES FOR CHANGE

A self-assessment also can help you to decide which treatment strategies to use. In many cases, the specific treatment approaches you select will be directly related to factors you identify in your self-assessment. Consider the following examples of how an assessment can help you to select the best approaches for treatment:

- Identifying which situations you fear and avoid will help you to choose which situations to select for exposure practices (as described in chapters 7 and 8).

- Identifying the extent to which you are fearful of the physical feelings that you experience when you are anxious will help determine whether you should practice exposure to uncomfortable physical sensations (as described in chapter 9).

- Assessing those areas in which your social skills can be improved will help you to decide whether to spend time working on the skills involved in assertiveness, public speaking, dating, or general communication. (See chapter 10 for strategies for improving various types of social and communication skills.)

- If you decide to take medications for your social anxiety, the choice of which medication to try will depend on your previous response to medications, possible interactions with other medications you take, medical conditions you may have, side effects that you are willing to tolerate, as well as a number of other factors. If you are considering using medications, thinking about these issues should be part of your self-assessment (see chapter 5).

MEASURING YOUR IMPROVEMENT

Assessment is not only for the initial phase of your treatment. Rather, the process of assessment should continue throughout treatment and even after treatment has ended. Continuing the assessment process throughout treatment will provide you with a way of measuring how much your social anxiety has improved as a result of using the strategies described in this book. Also, conducting occasional self-assessments after treatment has ended will let you know whether your treatment gains have continued over time.

STEP-BY-STEP GUIDE FOR CONDUCTING A SELF-ASSESSMENT

Therapists and clinicians who treat social anxiety use a number of tools to assess clients and patients. The most common of these include the following.

Clinical Interviews

Interviews involve asking a person specific questions about his or her background, anxiety symptoms, and related problems. It is an easy way of getting to know someone and learning about his or her difficulties simply by talking.

Questionnaires

Questionnaires include paper-and-pencil tests that a person completes before beginning treatment, and perhaps again during treatment and after treatment ends. They are used to provide additional information not covered in the interview, as well as to confirm and expand upon the information provided in the interview.

Diaries

Diaries are completed on a day-to-day basis between therapy sessions. They are useful because they provide the individual with an opportunity to record his or her thoughts and feelings as they occur, rather than having to remember all of the details of a complex event later.

Behavioral Assessment

A behavioral assessment involves directly observing a person's behavior or asking the person to perform a specific behavior and then measuring the thoughts and feelings that arise in that situation. The most common types of behavioral assessment for social anxiety are the *behavioral approach test* and *behavioral role-play.* These involve having a person enter a feared social situation (behavioral approach test) or act out a feared situation in a role-play (behavioral role-play) and having the person report his or her fear level, anxious thoughts, and other experiences.

Although these assessments are usually conducted by a psychologist, psychiatrist, or other professional, each can be adapted to be part of your self-assessment. We recommend that your assessment include the following three steps:

- **Conduct a self-interview.** For example, answer important questions about your anxiety and related problems.

- **Complete anxiety diaries.** An example is the Three Components of Social Anxiety Monitoring Form included in chapter 1.

- **Complete a behavioral approach test or role-play.**

Conducting a Self-Interview

Any professional contact with a psychologist, psychiatrist, or other mental health professional typically begins with a clinical interview, during which the clinician asks the client or patient questions about his or her problems. The interview helps the clinician to identify the most important features of the problem and is a first step toward developing an effective treatment plan. To be consistent with this goal, we suggest that you conduct a *self-interview,* in which you answer important questions about your problem.

To help you with this process, we have identified ten basic questions you should try to answer at the start of your self-assessment. The answers to these questions will help you to do the following: decide whether social anxiety is in fact a problem for you; identify the factors that contribute to your social anxiety; and choose the specific situations that you need to work on most. At the beginning of chapter 4, we will suggest additional questions that will help you to develop a treatment plan.

WHICH SOCIAL SITUATIONS DO YOU FEAR AND AVOID?

For each of the following situations (divided into interpersonal situations and performance situations, as defined in chapter 1), record a number ranging from 0 to 100 to rate (1) the extent to which you

78

fear the situation during a typical or average encounter and (2) the extent to which you typically avoid the situation. For example, if you have an intense fear of making presentations but you avoid the situation only about half the time, your fear rating might be an 80 and your avoidance rating might be a 50. If the situation is one that you never encounter, base your ratings on how fearful you *imagine* you would be in the situation and how much you would avoid the situation if it did come up from time to time. Use the following scales to rate your fear and avoidance levels. (Figure 3.1 and 3.2) (Table 3.1 and 3.2)

Fear Scale

0	10	20	30	40	50	60	70	80	90	100
None		Mild			Moderate			Extreme		Very Extreme

Figure 3.1

Avoidance Scale

0	10	20	30	40	50	60	70	80	90	100
Never Avoid		Rarely Avoid			Sometimes Avoid			Often Avoid		Always Avoid

Figure 3.2

Feared Social Situations Worksheet
Interpersonal Situations (interacting with others)

Fear	Avoid-ance	Item
_____	_____	Asking someone out on a date
_____	_____	Starting a conversation with a classmate or coworker
_____	_____	Going to a party

Fear	Avoid-ance	Item
_____	_____	Having friends over for dinner
_____	_____	Being introduced to new people
_____	_____	Talking on the telephone with a friend
_____	_____	Talking on the telephone with a stranger
_____	_____	Expressing a personal opinion (for instance, expressing your views about a movie that you saw recently or a book that you've read)
_____	_____	Being interviewed for a job
_____	_____	Being assertive (such as refusing an unreasonable request)
_____	_____	Returning an item to a store
_____	_____	Sending back food in a restaurant
_____	_____	Making eye contact
_____	_____	Other (specify) _____
_____	_____	Other (specify) _____
_____	_____	Other (specify) _____

Table 3.1

Performance Situations (being observed by others)

Fear	Avoid-ance	Item
_____	_____	Giving a presentation at work
_____	_____	Making a toast at a party or family gathering
_____	_____	Speaking in meetings at work or school
_____	_____	Playing sports or participating in aerobics in front of others
_____	_____	Standing in a wedding party at someone else's wedding
_____	_____	Singing or performing music in front of others
_____	_____	Eating or drinking in front of others

Fear	Avoidance	Item
_____	_____	Using public bathrooms with others in the room
_____	_____	Writing with others watching (such as signing a check)
_____	_____	Making a mistake in public (for instance, mispronouncing a word)
_____	_____	Walking or jogging in a busy public place
_____	_____	Introducing yourself in front of a group
_____	_____	Shopping in a busy store
_____	_____	Other (specify) _____
_____	_____	Other (specify) _____
_____	_____	Other (specify) _____

Table 3.2

WHICH VARIABLES MAKE YOUR ANXIETY BETTER OR WORSE?

An important step in your self-assessment is to become aware of the variables that make your fear better or worse in a given situation. For example, if you are fearful of eating with other people, there are many factors that could influence your fear in this situation, including who you're eating with, where you're eating, and what you're eating. Identifying the variables that affect your level of fear in a particular situation will help you to set up appropriate practices when you begin to use the exposure-based techniques discussed later in this book.

Following is a list of variables that sometimes affect a person's fear and anxiety in social situations. For each item, record a number ranging from 0 to 100 to rate the extent to which the variable listed affects your level of fear or discomfort in the types of social situations that you fear. For example, if you are much more anxious when talking to a woman than when talking to a man, you might rate the effect of the other person's sex on your anxiety at about a 75 or 80. Use the following scale to obtain your rating. (Figure 3.3) (Table 3.3, 3.4, 3.5 and 3.6)

Effect on Your Discomfort Scale

0	10	20	30	40	50	60	70	80	90	100
No Effect		Small Effect			Moderate Effect		Large Effect			Very Large Effect

Figure 3.3

Your Anxiety Variables
Aspects of the Other Person and their Effect on Your Discomfort

Effect on Your Discomfort	Item
_____	Age (whether the other person is older, younger, or the same age as you)
_____	Sex of the other person (same sex, opposite sex)
_____	Relationship status of the other person (married, dating someone, single)
_____	Physical attractiveness of the other person
_____	Nationality or ethnic background of the other person
_____	How confident the other person seems
_____	How aggressive or pushy the other person seems
_____	How interesting the other person appears to be

Effect on Your Discomfort	Item
_____	Whether the person appears to have a good sense of humor
_____	How financially successful the other person seems to be
_____	How well dressed the other person appears to be
_____	Other (specify) _____
_____	Other (specify) _____

Table 3.3

My Relationship with the Other Person and Its Effect on Your Discomfort

Effect on Your Discomfort	Item
_____	How well you know the other person (family member, close friend, acquaintance, stranger, and so on)
_____	How intimate and close you are to the other person
_____	Whether there is a history of conflict between yourself and the other person
_____	The type of relationship between you and the other person (for example, supervisor, coworker, employee)
_____	Other (specify) _____
_____	Other (specify) _____

Table 3.4

Aspects of How You Are Feeling and Its Effect on Your Discomfort

Effect on Your Discomfort	Item
_____	How tired you are overall
_____	General level of stress in your life at the time
_____	How familiar you are with the topic being discussed
_____	How prepared you are before entering the situation (for example, whether you have had a chance to rehearse your presentation)
_____	Other (specify) _____

Effect on Your Discomfort	Item
_____	Other (specify) _____

Table 3.5

Aspects of the Situation and Their Effect on Your Discomfort

Effect on Your Discomfort	Item
_____	Lighting (for instance, the light level is so high that you feel that any sign of anxiety will be visible)
_____	How formal the situation is (for example, eating at a wedding reception vs. a casual dinner with friends)
_____	Number of people involved (such as presenting to a few coworkers vs. presenting to a filled auditorium)
_____	Activity involved (eating, speaking, writing, and so on)
_____	Your physical position (seated, standing, and so on)
_____	Whether you can use alcohol or drugs to feel more comfortable
_____	How long you're stuck in the situation for
_____	Other (specify) _____
_____	Other (specify) _____

Table 3.6

WHAT ARE YOUR FEELINGS AND HOW DO YOU FEEL ABOUT THEM?

Following is a list of physical feelings that people sometimes experience when they are feeling anxious, worried, or frightened. For each item, you should first record a number (from 0 to 100) that reflects the intensity of the feeling during a typical exposure to an anxiety-provoking social situation. A rating of 0 means that, typically, you do not experience the sensation at all, and a rating of 100 means that the sensation typically is extremely intense when you encounter social situations that are a problem for you.

Next, using a scale from 0 to 100, rate the extent to which you are fearful of experiencing the sensation in front of other people. A rating of 0 means that you are not at all concerned about experiencing the sensation in front of others and a rating of 100 means that you are extremely fearful of experiencing the sensation in front of others. (Figure 3.4 and 3.5) (Table 3.7)

Intensity of the Physical Sensations Scale

0	10	20	30	40	50	60	70	80	90	100
Not at All		Mild			Moderate		Extreme			Very Extreme

Figure 3.4

Fear of Having the Physical Sensations in Front of Others Scale

0	10	20	30	40	50	60	70	80	90	100
No Fear		Mild Fear			Moderate Fear		Extreme Fear			Very Extreme Fear

Figure 3.5

Intensity of Sensation	Your Fear of Sensation	Sensation
_____	_____	Racing or pounding heart
_____	_____	Breathlessness or smothering feelings
_____	_____	Dizziness or lightheadedness
_____	_____	Difficulty swallowing, choking feelings, or a "lump" in the throat

Intensity of Sensation	Your Fear of Sensation	Sensation
_____	_____	Quivering or shakiness (in the hands, knees, lips, or whole body)
_____	_____	Blushing
_____	_____	Nausea, diarrhea, or "butterflies" in the stomach
_____	_____	Excessive sweating
_____	_____	Shaky voice
_____	_____	Tearfulness, crying
_____	_____	Poor concentration (forgetting what you're trying to say)
_____	_____	Blurred vision
_____	_____	Numbness and tingling sensations
_____	_____	Feelings of unreality or being detached from your body or from things around you
_____	_____	Tightness, soreness, or weakness in the muscles
_____	_____	Chest pain or tightness in chest muscles
_____	_____	Dry mouth
_____	_____	Hot flushes or chills
_____	_____	Other (specify) _____
_____	_____	Other (specify) _____

Table 3.7

WHAT ARE YOUR ANXIETY-PROVOKING BELIEFS, PREDICTIONS, AND EXPECTATIONS?

As discussed in chapter 1, your beliefs have a big impact on how you feel in social situations. For example, if you expect that others will think you are stupid, weak, or unattractive, you are very likely to feel anxious around other people. On the other hand, if you are not especially concerned about what others think about you in a particular situation, you're much more likely to feel comfortable. Often, our beliefs and predictions are not based on reality. For people who experience elevated anxiety in social and performance situations, beliefs and expectations about these situations are often negative. These thoughts tend to exaggerate the likelihood of danger and lead the person to expect the worst, even when there is no reason to do so.

Cognitive therapy involves teaching people to identify and change their anxious beliefs, predictions, and expectations by considering more realistic alternative beliefs. Before you can change your thoughts, however, you need to be able to observe them and to decide whether they are unrealistic and whether they are contributing to your anxiety.

Chapter 1 lists examples of thoughts and expectations that contribute to social anxiety. Some of these include basic assumptions, such as, "It is important that everyone likes me" and "Nobody will ever think I am interesting." Other anxiety-provoking thoughts may be more focused on a particular situation, such as, "If I arrive at class early, I won't be able to think of anything to say" and "People

will think I am weird if they notice my hands shaking."

To identify your own anxiety-provoking thoughts,
we recommend the following steps. First, review
some of the examples of anxiety-provoking thoughts
listed in chapter 1. These will give you an idea of
the types of thoughts that are often associated with
social anxiety. Next, think of social situations that
you find particularly difficult (for example, talking
to strangers, eating with other people, speaking at
meetings) and try to answer the following questions.
Your answers to these questions will give you an
idea of the types of thoughts, predictions, and expectations that help to maintain your anxiety.

Your Anxiety-Provoking Beliefs

**What am I afraid will happen in the situa-
tion?**

[space left intentionally blank in the original book]

**What might people think about me in the
situation?**

[space left intentionally blank in the original book]

Is it almost always important that I make a good impression? Why?

[space left intentionally blank in the original book]

How will I react in the situation (what symptoms will I exhibit)?

[space left intentionally blank in the original book]

What if my expectations come true? What might that lead to?

[space left intentionally blank in the original book]

Am I aware of any other beliefs or predictions that contribute to my anxiety?

[space left intentionally blank in the original book]

WHAT ARE YOUR ANXIOUS BEHAVIORS?

Anxiety and fear are usually accompanied by a strong urge to do something to reduce these uncomfortable feelings. Are there behaviors that you use to reduce your anxiety? Here are some examples.

Avoidance of social situations. Are there situations that you refuse to enter? For example, do you avoid going to parties, particularly when you won't know people there? When the telephone rings, do you avoid answering it? Do you turn down opportunities to do presentations even when they are important? Avoidance is one of the most common behaviors that helps to maintain your fear and anxiety. Earlier in this chapter you rated the extent to which you fear and avoid various social situations. As part of this review of your anxious behaviors, look over that list again and note which situations you tend to avoid at least some of the time. If there are any other situations that come to mind, list them below.

[space left intentionally blank in the original book]

Overcompensating for perceived deficits. Are there ways in which you try extra hard in social situations to compensate for flaws or faults that you perceive yourself to have? For example, do you overprepare for presentations by putting together too much material, memorizing the presentation, or reading the presentation word for word from your notes? Do you rehearse everything that you are going to say before meeting a friend for dinner, just in case you become overly anxious and lose your train of thought? Do you go out of your way to talk a lot to appear outgoing, just so people won't notice that you're anxious? Each of these is an example of how people sometimes overcompensate to cover up what they perceive to be flaws. If you can think of examples of times when you have overcompensated in social situations for what you thought were flaws or faults, list them below.

[space left intentionally blank in the original book]

Excessive checking and reassurance seeking. Social anxiety, shyness, and performance anxiety sometimes can lead people to engage in frequent checking and reassurance seeking behaviors. Examples include frequently looking in the mirror to make sure that your hair is perfect and continually asking your friends to reassure you that you are interesting or smart.

Although it is helpful to seek reassurance from time to time, constant reassurance seeking can have a negative impact by helping to maintain your fear. By asking for reassurance over and over again, you may strengthen the belief that there is something wrong with you. (Why else would you need to check so often?). Also, you run the risk of never learning to provide yourself with the reassurance that you may need. Finally, constantly asking others for reassurance may cause some of your greatest fears to come true by negatively affecting how others view you. Other people may get tired of always having to provide you with reassurance. Also, if you constantly ask others to make judgments about you (for instance, to tell you how smart, attractive, or interesting you are), you may actually be training them to be more observant and scrutinizing of you than they might otherwise be.

In the space below, list some examples of times when you have engaged in excessive checking or reassurance seeking.

[space left intentionally blank in the original book]

Other subtle avoidance and safety behaviors. Overcompensating for perceived deficits and excessive checking are both examples of *safety behaviors* because they are used to help you feel safer in social situations. Unlike complete avoidance of feared situations, these are more subtle avoidance behaviors, and they can be more difficult to notice. Are there other subtle ways in which you avoid situations or safety behaviors that you use to protect yourself from feeling anxious in social situations?

For example, if you have to give a presentation, do you stand in a particular place? Do you wear certain clothes to hide "defects" that you perceive in your appearance? Do you purposely end the presentation late so that there is no time for questions? Do you use videos or slides during the presentation so the focus won't be on you? Do you avoid making eye contact with the audience? If you're attending a party, do you purposely stay close to someone you know well so that you won't have to talk to other people?

Social Situation	Subtle Avoidance and Safety Behaviors
_____	_____
	_____
_____	_____
	_____
_____	_____
	_____
_____	_____
	_____
_____	_____
	_____

Table 3.8

Do you have a drink or two as soon as you get to the party so that your anxiety doesn't get too high? Do you offer to help in the kitchen so you won't have to talk to the other guests? Do you take frequent bathroom breaks to avoid being with everyone else? When you're talking to other guests at the party, do you ask the other person lots of questions to keep the focus of the conversation off of you?

All of these are examples of subtle avoidance strategies that people sometimes use in social situations. As discussed in chapter 1, these behaviors may decrease your anxiety in the short term by helping you to feel safer. However, in the long term, they typically have the effect of preventing your anxiety from decreasing naturally over time because they prevent you from learning that the situation can be safe and manageable even without relying on subtle avoidance strategies. In the spaces that follow, list examples of subtle avoidance or safety behaviors that you use to manage your anxiety in social situations. Because these behaviors may differ from situation to situation, there is space to record these behaviors for up to five different social situations. (Table 3.8)

Comparing yourself to the "wrong" people. One of the ways in which we evaluate ourselves is to make comparisons with other people. In school, we ask our classmates how they did on their exams to get an idea of how our own work compares to that of others. We are curious about our coworkers' salaries, in part because having that information is a way of knowing whether we are being paid fairly.

Research has consistently found that most people compare themselves to others whom they perceive to be either similar to themselves or slightly better in a particular dimension. For example, an average student is likely to compare his or her grades to those of other average students or to slightly better-than-average students. Similarly, a top athlete tends to compare his or her performance to other top athletes in order to judge the quality of his or her performance. This pattern of social comparison makes sense because it is most likely to provide information you can use to gauge your own performance. Comparing yourself to someone whom you perceive to be much better or much worse than you in a particular dimension will provide information that isn't especially relevant to you. For example, if you are a musician who plays mostly in local clubs, it doesn't make sense to compare your success to that of the most popular and successful musicians in the world. Making such comparisons is likely to cause you to feel inadequate because you will perceive that you can't possibly compete with the best.

Research from our center (Antony et al. 2005) suggests that people who are socially anxious make different types of social comparisons than do those who are less anxious. Specifically, social anxiety is associated with a tendency to make more frequent "upward" comparisons. In other words, people who are socially anxious are more likely to compare themselves to people they perceive as better than they are. The tendency to make upward comparisons increases the likelihood that an individual will feel worse after making the comparison.

Can you think of recent examples of when you have compared yourself to someone whom you perceived to be more attractive, more competent, less anxious, stronger, or smarter than you are? Or, did you make an upward comparison on some other dimension? How did you feel afterward? Do you often tend to compare yourself to people whom you perceive to be ideal or perfect on a certain dimension, rather than people whom you perceive to be typical or average? In the space below, describe an example of a time when you compared yourself to someone who was much "better" than you in some way.

[space left intentionally blank in the original book]

COULD YOU BENEFIT FROM IMPROVING YOUR "PEOPLE SKILLS"?

Everyone has times when they give off the wrong impression simply because they didn't know how to communicate a particular message to another person or group. Generally, this is not a big problem unless it happens frequently or in situations where there is a lot at stake.

In most cases, people who are socially anxious have fine social skills, though they tend to assume that their social skills are much worse than they actually are. Furthermore, as their anxiety decreases and they obtain more practice interacting with others in the situations that they fear, their skills tend to improve over time. Following are some examples of areas where you may want to consider working on improving your skills. This may prove to be particularly helpful for situations that you have tended to avoid over the years and therefore may not have had the opportunity to learn some of the subtleties of navigating your way through the situation. For example, if you have never dated, you may need some practice before knowing how to ask someone out on a date to maximize your chances of a positive response. As you read through the examples, try to identify people skills that you may want to work on. There is space at the end of this section to record your responses.

Assertiveness. Do you have difficulty being assertive? In other words, is it hard for you to say no if someone asks you to do something that you don't want to do? Is it difficult to ask people to change their behavior if they are treating you unfairly or aren't doing their share of the work? Most people sometimes find it difficult to deal directly and assertively with situations like these. However, the more difficulty that you have in situations that call for assertive communication, the more you have to gain from learning assertiveness skills.

Body language, tone of voice, and eye contact. Do you have difficulty making eye contact with other people? Does your tone of voice or body language send the message that you are not open to interacting with others? Behaviors that convey such messages may include speaking very quietly or letting your voice drop off at the end of your sentences, standing far away from other people when you're talking with them, answering questions with very short responses, and displaying a "closed" body posture (such as crossing your arms and legs). Although you may use these behaviors to protect yourself in social situations, they may actually have the opposite effect by turning others away. If you send the message to others that you are unavailable, they will be more likely to leave you alone.

Conversation skills. Do you have difficulty knowing what to say when talking to people at work or school? Is it hard to know how or when to end conversations? Do you find it difficult to know where the fine line is between appropriate self-disclosure and talking too much about yourself? Do you often offend other people with comments that you make? If you have difficulty making small talk or engaging in casual conversations, you may benefit by working on improving these skills.

Meeting new people. Do you have difficulty knowing what to say when you want to initiate contact with new people? Do you have difficulty asking someone out on a date? Are you at a loss for knowing how and where to meet new people? There are lots of different places to meet new people and lots of tricks to making meeting people easier. The first step is identifying whether this is an area that you would like to work on.

Presentation skills. Speaking effectively in public involves a number of complex skills and behaviors. It's not enough to be calm and confident. An effective speaker also knows how to maintain the audience's interest by using humor and effective audiovisual aids and handouts, stimulating audience participation, and conveying an interest in the topic. If you fear making presentations, part of overcoming your fear may include improving your speaking skills.

In the space below, list any social or communication skills that you might like to improve.

Social Skills That I Would Like to Develop or Improve

[space left intentionally blank in the original book]

HOW MUCH DOES YOUR SOCIAL ANXIETY BOTHER YOU OR INTERFERE WITH YOUR LIFE?

As we discussed in chapter 1, social anxiety, shyness, and performance-related fears are only a problem if they interfere with aspects of your functioning or if having the fear is troublesome for you. So, as part of your self-assessment, it's important for you to determine which aspects of your fear trouble you and which don't. Are there particular situations for which you are most interested in overcoming your fear? For example, it may be important for you to overcome your fear of socializing with friends but relatively less important for you to overcome your fear of speaking in front of large groups if that situation never arises.

In the space below, record (1) the ways in which your social anxiety interferes with your functioning (including work or school, social life, relationships, hobbies and leisure activities, home and family life), (2) the specific aspects of your social anxiety that you most want to change, and (3) any aspects of your social anxiety that you are not interested in working on.

Ways in Which Social Anxiety Interferes with My Life

[space left intentionally blank in the original book]

Aspects of My Social Anxiety That I Want to Change

[space left intentionally blank in the original book]

Aspects of My Social Anxiety That I Don't Want to Change

[space left intentionally blank in the original book]

HOW AND WHEN DID YOUR SOCIAL ANXIETY BEGIN?

How old were you when you first had significant anxiety in social situations? What was going on at that time in your life?

[space left intentionally blank in the original book]

How old were you when you first noticed that your social anxiety began to interfere with aspects of your life? What was going on at the time?

[space left intentionally blank in the original book]

What has the course of your social anxiety been over the years? Has it improved, stayed the same, or worsened? Are you aware of factors that may have caused it to change over the years (for example, getting married or moving to a new neighborhood)?

[space left intentionally blank in the original book]

Are there specific events that initially caused you to become more nervous in social situations or made your social anxiety worsen? (Examples may include experiences such as presentations that didn't go well, being teased while growing up, or doing something embarrassing or humiliating in public.)

[space left intentionally blank in the original book]

DOES ANYONE ELSE IN YOUR FAMILY HAVE THIS PROBLEM?

Are you aware of anyone else in your family having problems with shyness, social anxiety, or performance-related fears? If so, do you think that this had an influence on how you feel in these situations? If yes, how?

[space left intentionally blank in the original book]

ARE THERE ANY PHYSICAL CONDITIONS THAT CONTRIBUTE TO YOUR SOCIAL ANXIETY?

For some individuals, certain physical or medical conditions may influence their tendency to experience social anxiety. For example, people who stutter may be more nervous when talking to others compared with people who don't stutter. Often, their fear is exclusively related to a concern that they will stutter and that others will notice. Similarly, people suffering from other medical conditions (for example, shaking due to Parkinson's disease, having to move about in a wheelchair, not being able to write neatly due to severe arthritis) may be self-conscious about having others observe their symptoms.

Other people, although they may not be suffering from a medical condition, may still have a greater tendency than others to have shaky hands, blush easily, or sweat excessively, independent of their fears. For these individuals, these reactions tend to be very intense and may often occur even outside of social situations and when they are not particularly anxious. Although many people who experience these symptoms at such an extreme level are not concerned about others noticing, for some, having these extreme symptoms contributes to their social anxiety.

Do you suffer from any physical conditions or medical illnesses that add to your anxiety around other people? If so, record the details below.

[space left intentionally blank in the original book]

DIARIES

The diaries used to assess social anxiety are usually forms on which individuals record their anxiety-related symptoms, including frequency of exposure to feared situations, anxiety levels (using a numeric scale such as 0 through 100), uncomfortable physical sensations such as blushing or shaking, anxious thoughts and predictions (for instance, "I will make a fool of myself during this presentation"), and anxious behaviors such as avoidance and distraction. An example of such a diary is the Three Components of Social Anxiety Monitoring Form, which you completed in chapter 1. Numerous other forms and diaries are included throughout this book as well. They are designed to be used while you try the specific treatment techniques described in later chapters.

BEHAVIORAL ASSESSMENTS

The most commonly used type of behavioral assessment for social anxiety is the Behavioral Approach Test, or BAT. This assessment method involves physically entering a feared situation and measuring your anxiety and associated symptoms. For example, if you are afraid of public speaking, you might force yourself to speak at a staff meeting. After the meeting, you can record the particulars of the situation (who else was there, how long you spoke for, and so on), your fear level (for example, 80 out of 100), your anxious thoughts (such as, "My words will come out all jumbled"), and whether you engaged in any avoidance behaviors (like avoiding eye contact).

If it is too frightening to try this in a real-life situation, or if it is impossible to do so for another reason, the assessment can be completed in the form of a role-play. In a role-play, the person acts out the feared situation with the therapist or another individual present, instead of being in the real situation. For example, if you are afraid of job interviews, you might try to practice a job interview with another person (friend, family member, or therapist) taking the role of the interviewer. Following the practice, you would again record the particulars of the situation, your fear level, your anxious thoughts, and your avoidance behaviors.

Therapists use behavioral assessments because they have several advantages over traditional forms of assessment, such as interviews and questionnaires. First, they are less likely to be influenced by people's difficulties in remembering the details of their fears. For example, some people may overestimate or underestimate their fear levels if they are asked to describe their fear during past exposures to feared situations. Their memories may be influenced by a particularly negative experience in a feared situation and, as a result, they may report that their fear is actually higher than it typically is. Also, people's memories regarding their reactions in the situations they fear may be poor simply because they typically avoid the fearful situation, making it difficult to know for sure how they feel when they are exposed to the situation.

Another advantage of the behavioral approach test is that it allows the therapist and the individual to directly observe anxious thoughts and behaviors that might otherwise go unnoticed. It also allows the therapist to independently assess the extent to which the client's shaking, blushing, or sweating is actually noticeable to others.

Can you think of a behavioral approach test or role-play that you can set up for yourself? For example, if you are fearful of speaking up in a meeting, try doing it anyway. Immediately after the meeting, record your physical symptoms, anxious thoughts, and the avoidance behaviors that took place while you were conducting the practice. Did it go better than you expected it to go? Was it worse? Was it about what you expected?

TROUBLESHOOTING

You may find that your self-assessment does not go as smoothly as you might like. Here are some common problems that may arise during your self-assessment, as well as some solutions, suggestions, and words of reassurance.

Problem: I didn't know the answers to all the questions.

Solution: That's to be expected. As you progress with the treatment, you will have an opportunity to become better acquainted with your social anxiety. Self-assessment is an ongoing process, and it's not necessary to have all the answers before you start to work on changing your social anxiety. In fact, there may be some questions that you will never know the answers to, and that's okay. The purpose of this chapter is just to help you better understand the areas that are causing you the most difficulty.

Problem: Answering these questions increased my anxiety.

Solution: This is quite common. Conducting a self-assessment forces you to pay attention to the thoughts that contribute to your anxiety. This effect of increased anxiety tends to be temporary. As you progress through the treatment procedures discussed throughout this book, it is likely you will find that focusing on the thoughts and feelings associated with your social anxiety will become less anxiety provoking.nt

Problem: My answers to these questions depend on many different variables, so I find it difficult to come up with a response to certain questions.

Solution: This concern is often raised by people who are undergoing an assessment. Questions are often difficult to answer because the responses depend on so many different factors. For example, the question, "How fearful are you of public speaking?" may depend on such things as the topic of the presentation, the number of people in the audience, the lighting in the room, the length of the presentation, how prepared you are, and many other factors. We suggest that you handle difficult questions by estimating your response based on a typical or average situation. So, if your fear of public speaking ranges from 30 to 70 depending on the situation, you could put down 50. If you prefer, you could just record the range "30 to 70" which would be more precise.

After reading this chapter, you should have a better understanding of the nature of your social anxiety. You should be more aware of the types of social situations that you fear and avoid, the variables that affect your discomfort level, the physical sensations that you experience when you are anxious, the thoughts and behaviors that contribute to your fear, and the ways in which social anxiety interferes with your life. Understanding these aspects of your social anxiety will help you to choose the best strategies for overcoming your fear as you work your way through the rest of this book.

PART 2

How to Overcome Social Anxiety and Enjoy Your Life

CHAPTER 4

Making a Plan for Change

This chapter will help you to consider the range of factors that are important for developing a treatment plan. These factors include deciding whether this is the best time for you to work on your social anxiety, addressing the issue of motivation and readiness for change, selecting treatment goals, trying to understand why treatment may or may not have worked in the past, and understanding your current options for treatment.

IS NOW THE BEST TIME TO START THIS PROGRAM?

In some ways, it may seem as if there is never a good time to begin a new project. There are almost always competing demands that make it difficult to find free time or extra energy to start something new. Work may be unusually busy, you may be getting over a cold, or your children may be a handful right now. Although the time may not be perfect, you will need to decide whether it is even a possibility for you to start this program given your current life circumstances. Your chances of getting the most out of this book will depend on your answering yes to the following questions:

- Are you motivated to become less shy or to decrease your social anxiety? Is this something you really care about?

- Are you willing to feel even more anxious in the short term in order to feel more comfortable in social and performance situations in the future?

- Are you able to put aside, at least to some extent, other major problems and stresses in your life (things such as family problems or work stresses) so that you can focus on learning to manage your social and performance anxiety?

- Are you able to set aside several blocks of time several days per week to practice the techniques described in this book?

Hopefully, after carefully considering these questions, you will make a commitment to work on overcoming your social anxiety. However, you may also decide that this is not the best time for you to work on the problem and that you would rather wait until your life situation changes. If that is the case, you may still find reading this book helpful because it contains strategies that can be used from time to time, as you need them. However, making big changes will require using the techniques described in this book frequently and consistently. The next section will help you further as you decide whether to work on your anxiety at this time.

MOTIVATION AND READINESS FOR CHANGE

Experts have identified five stages that people go through as they contemplate making a change in behavior, such as quitting smoking, losing weight, or improving their work habits (Prochaska, Di-Clemente, and Norcross 1992). The model describing these *stages of change* is often referred to as the *transtheoretical model of change.* These five stages include:

1. **Precontemplation.** At this stage, people are unaware that they have a problem or they have no intention of changing, either because they are unwilling to change or they are convinced that change is impossible. An example would be someone who is very overweight and is convinced that nothing can be done about it. (So why bother trying?)

2. **Contemplation.** At this stage, the individual intends to change sometime soon (for example, in the next six months). The person is aware of the benefits of changing but is also still focused on the possible costs. An example is a

smoker who's thinking about quitting in a few months.

3. **Preparation.** At this stage, the person is ready to change in the near future (for example, in the next month). The benefits of change are much more obvious to the person than the costs of changing. An example is someone who has decided to join a gym in a couple of weeks to become more fit.

4. **Action.** At this stage, the individual actually takes steps to change a problem behavior. For example, an individual who feels depressed might start to see a therapist for depression.

5. **Maintenance.** At this stage, the individual has made the change and is taking steps to prevent the problem behavior from returning. An example would be an individual with a history of problem drinking who has now been sober for six months and has stopped spending time with people who drink excessive amounts of alcohol.

Although this model has been studied mostly in people who are working on changing health habits (for example, exercise, diet, substance abuse, improving medication compliance), it can also be applied to your treatment for shyness and social anxiety. The further along you are with respect to these stages of change, the more likely you will be to benefit from the strategies described in this book. For example, if you are in the action stage, you will likely get more out of this book than if you are at the precontem-plation stage and have no intention of making any changes.

Of course, these stages overlap with one another, and deciding which stage you are in is not always so clean cut. In fact, you may be at a different stage for different aspects of your social anxiety. You may be convinced that it is completely impossible that you will ever be able to date (precontemplation), but you may be thinking about working on finding a better job over the next few months (contemplation). You may also have already signed up for a night class so you can start to meet new friends (action). Fortunately, as you make changes in some areas, you may discover that you become more ready to make changes in other areas as well.

Success at changing your social anxiety will require that you are willing, able, and ready to take action (Miller and Rollnick 2002). Being *willing* means that the change is important to you, and that this is a change you want to make. Being *able* means that you are confident in your ability to make the change (once you have been given the right tools and strategies). Being *ready* means that this is a high priority for you, and that you are prepared to put other priorities aside for now in order to get this done. Use the scale below to rate the extent to which you are willing, able, and ready to make this change. For each rating, you may use any number from 0 to 100. (Figure 4.1)

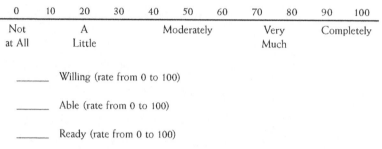

Figure 4.1

COSTS AND BENEFITS OF OVERCOMING YOUR ANXIETY

For the majority of people, the benefits of using the strategies described in this book will far outweigh the costs. If you didn't believe that, you probably wouldn't be reading this book. Still, you may have mixed feelings about changing, and therefore it may be helpful to think about your reasons for change, as well as your reasons for not changing. We will start with a discussion of the potential costs of change.

Costs of Overcoming Your Social Anxiety

In this section, we discuss the costs of changing. As you go through this section, notice that these potential costs are mostly short-term inconveniences that are only present while you are actively working on your anxiety. As your anxiety improves, these costs will fade as well. Also, instead of thinking about these as *costs,* it is helpful to think of them as *challenges.* After all, most of these costs are manageable, and there are often possible solutions available to minimize their impact.

Costs of medication treatments. If you choose to use medications, you will have to remember to take them regularly, and newer medications may be expensive, particularly if they are not covered by your health plan. You may experience side effects. Depending on the medication, side effects may include fatigue, headaches, changes in weight and appetite, and changes in sexual functioning. Of course, as you will learn in chapter 5, many of the side effects associated with medications are worst in the first few weeks, improve over time, and are generally quite manageable. Side effects can also be minimized by adjusting doses, changing medications, or stopping medications altogether.

Costs of psychological treatments. Psychological treatments, such as confronting the situations that you fear, are also associated with costs. First, they are time-consuming. To get the most out of exposure-based treatments, for example, you may need to practice for an hour or more, three to five days per week. Also, psychological treatments can be expensive (especially in the short term), depending on your insurance coverage and the fees charged by the therapist. In addition, conducting exposure practices will probably make you feel anxious and uncomfortable, particularly at the start. Although the exercises are designed so that the discomfort is usually manageable, at times your fear may be intense. In addition to feeling uncomfortable, you may feel more tired, especially on days when you practice confronting situations that make you uncomfortable. You also may feel irritable and perhaps even have anxiety-provoking dreams. Finally, your improvement may not follow a smooth course. It is likely the changes will take time and you may have periods (days, weeks, or even months) during which you feel as though you're slipping backward. For many people this is a normal part of the process of overcoming social anxiety. By continuing to use the strategies described in this book, however, your anxiety should continue to improve over time.

Other possible costs of improving. Overcoming your anxiety may also have an impact on other areas of your life. In most cases, the impact will be positive, but there may be some costs associated with these changes as well. If you are in a long-term relationship, you might find that your partner will need time to adjust to the changes you are making. For example, as you become more comfortable socializing, you may be out more often with friends or coworkers. If your partner is accustomed to having you around most of the time, these changes may require some getting used to. It may be helpful to discuss the changes that you are making openly with your partner, friends, and family members, if appropriate. This will demonstrate to them that you are sensitive to how the improvements in your social anxiety may affect them.

Can you think of other possible costs of overcoming your social anxiety, shyness, or performance-related fears? If so, record them in the following space.

[space left intentionally blank in the original book]

Benefits of Overcoming Your Social Anxiety

Fortunately, there are also benefits of overcoming your social anxiety. As we mentioned in the last section, the costs of overcoming your anxiety are usually just short-term inconveniences. On the other hand, the benefits of change tend to be much more long lasting. What this book challenges you to do is to decide whether you are willing to tolerate some short-term pain, to achieve long-term gains. Examples of potential benefits of overcoming your shyness and social anxiety include the following:

- Learning to feel more comfortable in feared social and performance situations

- Meeting new friends

- Improving the quality of your relationships

- Learning to network more comfortably in situations related to your job or career

- Expanding the possible options for what you can do in your leisure time

- Improving your job prospects (for instance, realizing new opportunities to get a promotion or to seek a higher-paying position)

- Opening up some opportunities for self-improvement by furthering your education

- Learning to increase your enjoyment of life

- Feeling more confident

- Increasing your ability to express yourself

- Learning strategies that you may be able to apply to other problems, such as anger, depression, or a troubled relationship

Based on this list of examples, or others that you can identify, can you think of benefits that would result from overcoming your social anxiety? Focus on benefits that are based on your own *internal values and goals* (for example, "I want to have closer friendships"), rather than the values and goals of others (for example, "My mother wants me to make new friends"). Questions like the ones listed below can be useful as you identify your own reasons for changing:

- How would I like my life to be different in five years?

- What would be better about my life if I felt more comfortable in social situations?

- What type of person would I like to be, and how is my social anxiety preventing me from being that type of person?

- What sorts of things do I miss about my life before social anxiety became as big a problem as it is now?

Record your reasons for changing in the space below.

[space left intentionally blank in the original book]

Now that you have had a chance to consider the costs and benefits of working on your social anxiety, you are in a better position to make a commitment to working on overcoming your fears. Assuming that you have decided to go ahead as planned, the remainder of this chapter will help you to consider the strategies best suited to your individual needs.

SETTING GOALS FOR CHANGE

Without setting specific goals or objectives, it will be impossible for you to evaluate whether you're making the changes that you hope to make. Goals can be described in a number of different ways. First, goals can reflect either *short-term* or *long-term* changes that you would like to accomplish. For example, if you have a fear of public speaking, a reasonable one-week goal might be to ask a single question at a meeting at work, regardless of how anxious you feel. A six-month goal might be to give a thirty-minute presentation without feeling significant anxiety. As you go through the process of overcoming your social anxiety, it is important to identify short-term goals (for example, what you want to accomplish this week), medium-range goals (such as what you want to accomplish over the next few months), and long-range goals (for instance, what you want to accomplish over the next year or two).

Goals also can be described either as *specific* or *general.* A specific goal is more detailed than a general one. Therefore, specific goals are often better suited for guiding you in selecting appropriate treatment strategies, compared with general goals. Also, with specific goals, it is easier to measure whether your objectives are being met. Although it is okay to have a few general goals, you also should try to generate as many specific goals as possible. Examples of general and specific goals are listed below. (Table 4.1)

General Goal	Specific Goal
To be more comfortable during presentations	To have my fear level during presentations at my weekly sales meetings decrease from a level of 100 out of 100 to a level of 40 out of 100
To ask someone on a date sometime	To ask John (or Jane) to have dinner with me by the end of this month
To have more friends	To meet at least three new friends by the end of this year, with whom I can see movies or watch sports
To be comfortable in crowds	To be able to walk through a crowded mall or on a crowded street with my fear below a 30 or 40 out of 100
To cope better with criticism	To be able to tolerate negative feedback on my annual performance review at work without becoming very upset and while still paying attention to all my positive achievements over the year
To ask questions in class	To ask at least one question during each class over the rest of this semester
To deal better with groups	To be able to make small talk at a party while maintaining eye contact and speaking loudly enough for others to hear

Table 4.1

Now, think about what types of changes you would like to make. Specifically, think about aspects of your social anxiety (anxious beliefs, situations that you avoid, and so on) that you would like to change. Try to be realistic. Also, recognize that your goals may change. For example, right now you may not need to make presentations in your daily life. However, if you take a job that involves public speaking, your goals may have to be revised later to reflect this change.

We have included space for you to record your goals for the next month as well as your goals for one year from now. Of course, if you prefer, you may choose other time periods. The main point to remember is that you may have different short-term and long-term goals. Although some goals may be realistic targets for a year or two from now, they may not be realistic goals for one week or one month from now.

One-Month Goals

1. _____

2. _____

3. _____

4. _____

5. _____

6. _____

7. _____

8. _____

9. _____

10. _____

One-year Goals

1. _____

2. _____

3. _____

4. _____

5. _____

6. _____

7. _____

8. _____

9. _____

10. _____

REVIEWING PREVIOUS ATTEMPTS TO TREAT YOUR SOCIAL ANXIETY

This section has two purposes. First, if you've tried to overcome your social anxiety in the past, it will help you review the treatments that worked for you and those that were not especially helpful. Second, this section will help you to identify possible reasons why certain previous attempts to overcome your social anxiety were not useful, if this was your experience. By identifying the reasons for previously successful and not-so-successful treatment attempts, you will be able to make more educated decisions about what types of strategies to try now. If a treatment has worked well in the past, you may want to try it again. If you did not benefit from a particular treatment previously, you may want to try something new. However, you should still consider giving a particular treatment another try if you didn't give it a fair chance the first time.

In the spaces that follow, check off any treatments that you have tried in the past. Also, describe the treatment and record whether the outcome was helpful. (Table 4.2)

Record of Previous Treatments

Yes	No	Treatment
_____	_____	Medications
		If yes, list drug names, duration of treatment, and maximum dosage for each. Also, describe any side effects that you experienced and whether or not each medication helped. Indicate if you took the medication as prescribed.
		[space left intentionally blank in the original book]
_____	_____	Exposure to Feared Situations
		If yes, describe the treatment (including frequency of exposures, duration of treatment, types of situations practiced in, outcome).
		[space left intentionally blank in the original book]
_____	_____	Cognitive Therapy (This therapy is focused on teaching strategies for changing anxious thinking; it usually includes completion of thought records as a component.) If yes, describe the treatment (including duration of treatment, outcome).
		[space left intentionally blank in the original book]
_____	_____	Skills Training (This might include assertiveness training or a public speaking or communications course.) If yes, describe the treatment or course content (including duration of treatment, outcome).
		[space left intentionally blank in the original book]
_____	_____	Insight-Oriented Therapy (This therapy is focused on early-childhood experiences and on helping you to understand the deep causes underlying a particular problem.) If yes, describe the treatment (duration of treatment, outcome).

128

Yes	No	Treatment
		[space left intentionally blank in the original book]
____	____	Supportive Therapy (In this fairly unstructured therapy, the client describes experiences over the past week and the therapist offers support and perhaps suggestions for solving problems that arise from week to week.) If yes, describe the treatment (duration of treatment, outcome).
		[space left intentionally blank in the original book]
____	____	Self-Help Book
____	____	If yes, describe the treatment. (For instance, what book/s did you read? What approach did the book take? Did it help?)
		[space left intentionally blank in the original book]

Table 4.2

Now that you have identified specific treatments you have tried in the past, the next step is to understand why a treatment was ineffective or only partially effective, if that was your experience. Listed below are some of the reasons why psychological treatments and medications are occasionally not helpful.

Why Psychological Treatments Sometimes Don't Help

- The therapy is an ineffective treatment for social anxiety. Many types of psychotherapy have never been studied for the treatment of social anxiety, and others have been found to be of little benefit. (Cognitive behavioral therapy is the best-studied approach and is well supported.)

- The therapist is inexperienced either with the type of therapy being offered or the treatment of shyness and social anxiety, in particular.

- The frequency and intensity of exposure practices is too low. If you practice exposure to social situations too infrequently, you will be less likely to see the desired results.

- The treatment does not last long enough. You may not have benefited from previous therapy if you dropped out of treatment before positive results could be seen.

- An individual expects the treatment to be ineffective. There is evidence that a person's expectations can affect the outcome of psychotherapy (Safren, Heimberg, and Juster 1997).

- The person does not comply with the treatment. If you miss sessions, arrive late for sessions, or don't complete homework, therapy is less likely to be effective.

- There are other problems or stresses in the person's life that interfere with treatment (for example, severe depression, alcohol abuse, stressful job, marital problems, health issues).

Why Medications Sometimes Don't Help

- It is the wrong medication for the problem. Some medications have been shown to be more effective than others for treating social anxiety (see chapter 5). Furthermore, a medication that works for one person may not be the best choice for someone else.

- The medication dosage is not high enough.

- The treatment does not last long enough. Some medications can take up to six weeks to have an effect. Also, stopping certain medications too soon can increase the chances of the anxiety coming back.

- An individual expects the treatment to be ineffective. As with psychotherapy, there is evidence that a person's response to medication is affected by his or her expectations.

- The side effects are too unpleasant to tolerate.

- The person is using drugs, drinking alcohol, or taking other medications that influence the effects of the medication for social anxiety.

- The person doesn't comply with the treatment (for example, misses pills).

If you have tried to overcome your social anxiety in the past, but found treatment to be ineffective or only partially effective, do you have any guesses about why it may not have worked as well as you had hoped it would? Based on your previous experiences with therapy or medication, are there strategies that you want to try again?

1. _____

2. _____

3. _____

Are there strategies that you definitely don't think you should try again?

1. _____

2. _____

3. _____

PROVEN STRATEGIES FOR OVERCOMING SOCIAL ANXIETY

There are hundreds of different approaches that people have used to overcome emotional difficulties, behavior problems, and bad habits. Some of these approaches include psychotherapy, medications, prayer, relaxation training, yoga, hypnosis, distraction, drinking alcohol or using drugs, exercise, changing diet, reward and punishment, herbal remedies, traditional remedies, acupuncture, education and reading about the problem, past-life regression, and so forth. Furthermore, each of these methods can be subdivided into even more categories. For example, there are many different types of psychotherapy and medications, some of which are more useful than others for a particular problem. Given all of the different available options, it can be very difficult for a consumer to select the best approach for overcoming a particular problem.

For most of the methods listed previously, there is almost no controlled research examining their use in treating anxiety in general and social anxiety in particular. The term *controlled* is used to describe studies in which the investigators have examined the effects of a particular treatment while taking steps to ensure that any improvements that occur are, in fact, due to the treatment, rather than to other factors. Note that a lack of controlled research does not mean that a particular treatment is ineffective. It simply means we just don't know whether the treatment works or how well it works.

Even if someone seems to improve after using one of these methods, it can be difficult to know whether it was the treatment that had a beneficial effect or whether other factors contributed to the change. For example, as we mentioned earlier, someone's expectations of improving during treatment can affect his or her improvement. Other reasons why people might improve with a particular treatment may include the passage of time. For some types of problems (such as depression), the symptoms may improve naturally over time, regardless of whether the sufferer receives any specific treatments. Changes in a person's normal routines (for instance, a reduction of stress at work) also can contribute to improvements over and above any treatment effects.

Properly controlled research can help to determine whether the effects of a treatment are indeed due to the treatment rather than to other factors. One strategy used by researchers is the inclusion of a control group. For example, research studies that examine the effects of a medication on a particular problem usually give a percentage of the individuals in the study a *placebo,* which is, essentially, a pill that contains no real medication. This group is called the *placebo control group.* Typically, neither the doctor nor the patient knows whether the person is taking a placebo or the real medication until after the study ends.

The test of whether a medication is helpful depends on how well people who took the medication respond compared with those who took the placebo. Including a placebo control group allows the researcher to directly measure the effects of the medication over and above the effects of the individual's expectations about the treatment. Properly conducted studies examining the effects of psychological treatments also include appropriate control groups to aid in understanding why a particular treatment may appear to work.

In this book, we have chosen to focus on techniques that have been shown in controlled research to be effective for helping people to overcome problems with social anxiety, shyness, and performance-related fears. In other words, these techniques have been shown to be effective compared with no treatment, placebo treatments, other forms of psychotherapy, or other appropriate control groups. The techniques we will focus on include two main groups of strategies: cognitive behavioral therapy and medications.

Cognitive Behavioral Therapy

Cognitive behavioral therapy, or CBT, includes a group of techniques that are usually used together as a package. Numerous studies have shown that CBT is an effective way of overcoming social anxiety (for reviews, see Antony and Rowa 2008; Rodebaugh, Holaway, and Heimberg 2004). Cognitive behavioral therapy differs from other more traditional forms of therapy in the following ways:

- CBT is directive. In other words, the therapist is actively involved in the therapy and makes very specific suggestions.

- CBT's focus is on changing a particular problem. Some other forms of therapy focus on helping the individual develop insight into or understanding of the deep-rooted causes of a problem but do not offer specific strategies for overcoming the problem.

- CBT has a relatively brief duration. The typical course for social anxiety is ten to twenty sessions.

- CBT focuses on current beliefs and behaviors, which are thought to be responsible for maintaining the problem. Some traditional therapies tend to focus more on early childhood experiences.

- In CBT, the therapist and client are partners and work together during treatment.

- In CBT, the client chooses the goals for therapy, with input from the therapist.

- CBT usually includes strategies for measuring progress so that treatment techniques can be adjusted for maximum effectiveness.

- CBT involves changing beliefs and behaviors so that the client is able to better manage anxiety and to navigate anxiety-provoking situations.

Cognitive behavioral therapy for social anxiety includes three main types of strategies. Treatment almost always includes cognitive therapy and exposure to feared situations. In addition, social-skills training is sometimes included.

COGNITIVE THERAPY

The term *cognitive* refers to anything having to do with assumptions, beliefs, predictions, interpretations, visual imagery, memory, and other mental processes related to thinking. The basic underlying assumption of cognitive therapy is that negative emotions occur because people interpret situations in a negative or threatening way. For example, people who are convinced that others will judge them in a negative way or who are overly concerned about the opinions of others are bound to feel anxious or uncomfortable in certain social situations. Cognitive therapy teaches individuals to be more aware of their negative thoughts and to replace them with less negative thoughts. People learn to treat their beliefs as guesses about the way things may be, rather than as facts.

They are taught to examine the evidence supporting their anxious beliefs and to consider the possibility that an alternative belief is true.

For example, if Henry is very hurt and angry because a friend didn't return his call, these negative feelings might stem from Henry's belief that the friend doesn't care about him. In cognitive therapy, Henry would be taught to consider alternative explanations for the friend's behavior, including the possibility that the friend never received the message, forgot to return the call, or is out of town. After all, there are many possible reasons why a caring friend might not have returned Henry's call quickly.

At the beginning of treatment, diaries are used to record anxious thoughts and to counter them with more realistic predictions and interpretations. As people become more comfortable with the methods of challenging their unrealistic negative beliefs, their new ways of thinking become more automatic and the diaries are no longer needed. People learn to manage their anxious thoughts before they get out of control. Cognitive therapy techniques are described in detail in chapter 6.

EXPOSURE

Exposure involves gradually and repeatedly confronting feared situations until they no longer trigger fear. In most cases, exposure is viewed as a necessary component of CBT. In fact, exposure may be even more powerful than cognitive therapy as a way of changing anxious negative thinking. By exposing yourself to situations you fear, you will learn that the risk in these situations is minimal. Through direct experience, many of your anxious predictions and beliefs will be proven incorrect. You will also learn to better tolerate situations in which some of your beliefs actually may be true (for example, when another person actually does judge you negatively). Finally, exposure will provide you with an opportunity to practice your cognitive therapy skills and to improve upon any social or communication skills that may be rusty from having avoided social situations for so long. See chapters 7 through 9 for detailed instructions for designing and implementing exposure exercises.

IMPROVING SOCIAL SKILLS

Social-skills training refers to the process of learning to improve the quality of your communication as well as other social behaviors, so there will be an increased likelihood of obtaining a positive response from others. Note that most people who are socially anxious have better social skills than they think they do. In fact, formal social-skills training is often not included in CBT programs, and people undergoing the treatment still respond quite well. Still, there is evidence that some people can benefit from learning a few new techniques to become more assertive, make small talk more effectively, improve their eye contact, and learn basic skills for dating or meeting new people. Chapter 10 describes strategies for improving social and communication skills.

Medications

Numerous medications have been shown to be effective for treating social phobia (Van Ameringen, Mancini, and Patterson, in press). Mostly, these include certain anti-depressants that also target anxiety (such as paroxetine and venlafaxine) and certain anti-anxiety drugs (for instance, clonazepam). Typically, medications are taken on a daily basis. To varying degrees, all medications are associated with certain side effects. However, for most people, these side effects are quite manageable and most tend to decrease over time.

Other Treatments

There are a number of other therapies that have preliminary or limited research support for treating social anxiety. Some of these treatments are quite new, and all of them have only been investigated in one or more studies for social anxiety (most of which are not controlled studies). Though it is too early to know if these therapies are as effective as CBT and medications, here are some brief descriptions of these approaches:

MINDFULNESS TRAINING

Mindfulness training involves learning to focus on one's present experiences (for example, thoughts and feelings) without judging them or trying to change them and without dwelling on the past or anticipating the future (see Orsillo and Roemer 2005). Meditation is often a component of mindfulness training. Preliminary evidence supports the use of mindfulness for treating general worries (Roemer and Orsillo 2007) and for preventing relapse in depression (Williams et al. 2007). Evidence from a recent pilot study suggests that mindfulness training may be useful for treating social anxiety (Bögels, Sijbers, and Voncken 2006).

ACCEPTANCE AND COMMITMENT THERAPY (ACT)

ACT is a relatively new form of therapy that is related to mindfulness training in that a goal of this treatment is to teach people to accept their experiences (including emotions, thoughts, imagery, and other experiences) rather than trying to control, fight, or change them (Hayes and Smith 2005). Mindfulness training is used as part of ACT, but other strategies are used as well. In addition to acceptance, people receiving ACT are also encouraged to make a commitment to live a life that is consistent with their own values and goals, which typically involves changing behaviors. Though ACT is often presented as an alternative to CBT, it actually overlaps with CBT quite a bit. For example, ACT for anxiety and CBT for anxiety both use exposure as a component (Eifert and

Forsyth 2005). A preliminary, uncontrolled study suggests that ACT may lead to reductions in social anxiety (Ossman et al. 2006).

APPLIED RELAXATION TRAINING

Applied relaxation involves the combination of learning to relax the muscles of the body with exposure to increasingly challenging situations. A few studies suggest that applied muscle relaxation may be useful for social anxiety (Jerremalm, Johansson, and Öst, 1980; Osberg 1981). However, it is difficult to know whether this approach is effective because of the relaxation component, the exposure to feared situations, or both. There are no studies investigating whether relaxation training adds any benefit over and above the effects of exposure alone.

INTERPERSONAL PSYCHOTHERAPY (IPT)

IPT is a brief therapy that focuses exclusively on interpersonal aspects of a person's problem, such as problems in the individual's relationships with others. IPT has been studied primarily in people who are depressed, and it's been shown in a number of well-controlled studies to be an effective treatment for depression, as well as certain other problems (Weissman, Markowitz, and Klerman 2007). Because of the interpersonal focus of IPT, some researchers have wondered whether it might also be effective for treating social anxiety. A preliminary, uncontrolled study (Lipsitz et al. 1999) suggests that IPT may be

142

useful for treating social anxiety, though more research is needed.

CHOOSING AMONG TREATMENT OPTIONS

If you decide to try medications, you will probably need to get a prescription from a physician—usually your family doctor or a psychiatrist. However, note that in some states other professionals (for example, nurse practitioners) may be able to prescribe medications. In fact, two states (New Mexico and Louisiana) now allow psychologists with appropriate training to prescribe medications as well. For most people, a visit to your family doctor is a good place to start if you are interested in trying medications. He or she can make a referral to a psychiatrist or other professional if needed. If you are interested in trying a psychological treatment such as CBT, you have the option of trying to overcome the problem on your own or seeking professional help.

Self-Help or Professional Help?

For some people, a self-help approach such as that described in this book may be sufficient. In fact, a study by Moore, Braddock, and Abramowitz (2007) found that most people who used the first edition of this book achieved significant reduction in their social anxiety, even without any additional therapy.

However, for others, a self-help book alone is not enough, and many people find that the added structure and support provided by a therapist is important. If you decide to seek professional help, this book can still help to reinforce what you learn in therapy. An important part of CBT involves educating the client (often using self-help readings) and encouraging the client to practice the various CBT techniques between sessions. In other words, CBT conducted with a therapist often includes a self-help component. Combining a self-help book with your therapy may even reduce the number of therapy sessions needed (Rapee et al. 2007). For more information on finding a therapist, see the section on seeking professional help that appears later in this chapter.

Cognitive Behavioral Therapy or Other Psychotherapy?

In almost all cases, we recommend cognitive therapy and exposure as the psychological treatment of choice for social phobia. Adding social-skills training to the program may be useful for some individuals as well. As for other psychological therapies, although they certainly have a place for treating certain types of problems, they are not sufficiently proven when it comes to treating social phobia and other anxiety-related conditions.

Some people with whom we have worked have reported benefits from combining CBT with another form of
psychotherapy. In these cases, typically they have
seen one therapist for CBT and another for dealing
with other issues (for example, marital problems,
coping with childhood abuse). Although this approach
sometimes works well, we recommend that your two
therapists stay in close contact with each other so
that they can ensure they are not giving you contradictory messages during therapy.

Medication or CBT?

A number of studies have investigated whether CBT,
medications, or their combination work best (Antony
and Rowa 2008). Although there are some differences
across studies, the overall pattern of findings has been
that all three of these approaches are about equally
effective, at least in the short term. For example, in
the largest study conducted to date, CBT, fluoxetine
(an antidepressant), and a combination of fluoxetine
and CBT were all found to be about equally effective
and were all more effective than placebo (Davidson
et al. 2004).

Although these approaches are about equally effective
in the short term, CBT tends to be a more effective
treatment than medications over the long term
(Liebowitz et al. 1999). In other words, once all
treatments have stopped, people who have been only

taking medications are more likely to experience a return of symptoms than people who had CBT.

Also, just because these three approaches are about equally effective *on average,* that doesn't mean that they are equally likely to be effective *for you.* Some people seem to do better with medications, whereas others seem to do best with CBT or a combination of these approaches. The approach we usually recommend is to start with either CBT or medication, and then introduce the other treatment after several months, if needed.

Group or Individual Therapy?

Cognitive behavioral therapy can be delivered either individually or in groups. Both approaches work well. Although most studies have found group and individual therapies for social anxiety to be about equally effective, some have found an advantage for individual therapy (for a review, see Bieling, McCabe, and Antony 2006).

Regardless of which approach you choose, you should be aware of the advantages and disadvantages of each. Group treatment gives people an opportunity to meet other people with the same problem. This allows people to learn from the mistakes and successes of others and reminds them that they are not the only ones suffering from this problem. Group treatment also provides clients with opportunities to interact with other individuals who can participate in exposure exercises and role-play practices. For example, group members can be an audience during exposures that involve giving presentations.

The cost is another advantage of group therapy. Because you are sharing the therapist's time with other people, the cost per session is often lower than for individual therapy. If you decide to enter group treatment for social anxiety, we recommend that you try to find a group that focuses exclusively on anxiety problems, and ideally on social anxiety (rather than a group that includes people who suffer from a wide range of different problems). You are most likely to find a specialized social anxiety group at an anxiety disorders specialty clinic.

Individual therapy also has advantages. First, it can be less scary than group therapy, particularly at the beginning. As you can imagine, people with social phobia are often quite terrified of starting group treatment, although anxiety about speaking in front of the group usually diminishes after the first few weeks. Furthermore, with individual therapy, you don't have to share your time with other group members. And, because there is more time to focus on you, the program can be individually tailored to suit your personal needs. Individual therapy also has advantages from a scheduling perspective. If you miss a session due to illness or vacation, usually you can just reschedule an individual appointment. In contrast, if you miss a group session, catching up on the material that you missed may be more complicated.

Whether you decide to seek group or individual treatment should depend on a careful weighing of all of these factors. Keep in mind, however, that you may not have a choice. Although the availability of CBT is increasing, this form of therapy is still hard to find in some places, either in a group or individual format. We would like to emphasize that, in choosing a therapy, the most important factor is finding a therapist who has experience in providing CBT for social anxiety. Whether you choose group or individual therapy should be a secondary issue, since both seem to work well.

THE IMPORTANCE OF REGULAR PRACTICE

Although simply reading about how to overcome social phobia may be helpful, to make big changes in your social anxiety, it will be necessary for you to actually practice the techniques described throughout this book. For example, you will get more out of the cognitive strategies described in chapter 6 if you complete the monitoring forms and diaries and frequently take advantage of opportunities to challenge your anxious beliefs.

To get the most out of exposure practices, it will be important to enter feared situations as frequently as possible and to stay in the feared situations until your fear has decreased, or until you learn that your feared consequences don't occur. Many of your exposure practices can be conducted during the course of your everyday life (for instance, having lunch with coworkers instead of eating alone), but other practices may require you to set aside time just for the exposure exercises.

INCLUDING A HELPER OR CO-THERAPIST

It may be helpful to involve a helper or "co-therapist" in your treatment, for example, a friend, coworker, or family member. Your helper can provide you with opportunities to practice role-play exposures, such as presentations, simulated job interviews, making small talk, or asking another person out on a date. In addition, he or she can provide you with honest feedback about your performance and offer suggestions for improvement.

When choosing other people to help you out, we suggest that you select people whom you trust. The person should be someone who is supportive and unlikely to become frustrated or angry if things move slowly or if you are finding a particular situation difficult or anxiety provoking. If possible, your helper should read relevant sections of this book so that he or she has a better understanding of the treatment and how it works. If this is not practical, an alternative option would be to have you describe to your helper what his or her role will be during the practices.

DEALING WITH ADDITIONAL PROBLEMS

Many people who suffer from social anxiety also experience other problems, including other anxiety disorders, depression, alcohol or drug use problems, and relationship difficulties. In most cases, these other problems tend not to interfere with the treatment of social anxiety. However, if you are currently suffering from problems in addition to your shyness, there are two questions that you should consider. First, is your social anxiety the most important problem to focus on currently? If not, you should probably focus on the problem that is interfering the most with your life. For example, if your depression is more severe than your social anxiety, it may be important to deal with your depression first and then turn your attention to the social anxiety when your depression is under control. Second, are your other problems so severe that they are likely to get in the way of your social anxiety treatment? If so, you should work on the other problems first. For example, if you are drinking alcohol so frequently that you're unlikely to follow through with the exercises in this book, then dealing with your drinking before working on your social anxiety is a good idea.

SEEKING PROFESSIONAL HELP

If you are interested in seeking professional help for your social anxiety, here are some additional suggestions to keep in mind.

How to Find a Therapist or Doctor

One of the most difficult aspects of finding a therapist or doctor is knowing where to look. A good place to begin is with your family doctor, who will likely be aware of psychiatrists, psychologists, and anxiety specialty clinics in your area. You may also want to call nearby hospitals and clinics to see if they have programs that offer either CBT or medication for social anxiety. The Internet is also a great source of information about treatment options in your area. Check with your insurance company about the rules regarding coverage for treatment of psychological conditions. Your plan may have restrictions regarding who you can see and the number of sessions that are covered.

Another way to find help is to contact a national organization that focuses either on anxiety-related problems or CBT. For example, the Anxiety Disorders Association of America (www.adaa.org) offers information about treatment options and self-help groups across the United States and Canada (the ADAA has both consumer and professional members). The Association for Behavioral and Cognitive Therapies (www.abct.org) is a professional organization that also provides information on practitioners who treat anxiety-related problems. Full contact information for these and other organizations is provided in the resources section at the back of this book. You may also contact your state psychological or psychiatric associations to get information about psychologists or psychiatrists in your area.

When choosing a professional, don't be afraid to ask questions. Before making a commitment, here are some issues that you should clarify:

- The type of treatment being offered. For example, if you are interested in a psychological treatment, you should ask whether the person is experienced in providing CBT for social and performance anxiety.

- The typical number of sessions recommended for treating this problem, recognizing that it is often difficult to know this before conducting a thorough assessment. In many cases, ten to twenty sessions is enough.

- The length of each session. One-hour sessions are typical, though longer time periods are sometimes needed for exposure sessions.

- The frequency of sessions. Weekly sessions are typical.

- The cost per session and preferred method of payment. Are the fees flexible?

- The location and setting. For example, is the treatment conducted in a private office? A hospital? A university clinic? A community clinic? A research center?

- The availability of group vs. individual treatments for social anxiety. Either approach is likely to help.

- Who provides the treatment? A psychologist? Psychiatrist? Psychology student or psychiatric resident? How experienced is the person? Where was he or she trained? If it is a student therapist, how closely is he or she supervised? How experienced is the supervisor? Can you meet with the supervisor if you wish?

Types of Professionals

If you are interested in receiving a psychological therapy, like CBT, your therapist can be a psychologist, physician, nurse, social worker, or professional from any of a number of other backgrounds. However, keep in mind that most practicing clinicians, regardless of their background, do not have extensive experience in providing CBT for anxiety-related problems. It is much more important that you find someone who is familiar with treating social anxiety using cognitive and exposure-based treatments than what degree the person has. Currently, psychologists are the most likely to have this background, but other professionals are increasingly being trained in providing cognitive and behavioral treatments.

Understanding the differences between types of therapists often can be confusing. A brief description of some of the main professionals who often provide CBT and related treatments follows:

Psychologist. In most places, psychologists who specialize in treating psychological disorders usually have a doctoral degree in clinical or counseling psychology. Often, this degree is a Ph.D. (which includes significant training in both research and in providing clinical care), although it may also be a Psy.D. (indicating a primary training focus on providing clinical services and relatively less emphasis on research) or an Ed.D. (indicating training that stems from an educational psychology perspective). Typically, the training of a psychologist includes an undergraduate bachelor's degree (four years), followed by an additional five to eight years of graduate training. In some states and provinces, psychology practitioners with a master's degree (usually two years of graduate training) can also call themselves psychologists, whereas in other places, master's level clinicians are called by other terms (for example, psychological associate, psychotherapist, psychometrist).

Psychiatrist. A psychiatrist is a physician who has specialized in treating mental health problems after completing four years of medical school. Typically, this specialty training includes a five-year residency and also may include additional fellowship training. Psychiatrists are more likely than other types of professionals to understand and treat anxiety from a biological perspective, although increasingly, psychiatric training programs are requiring training in CBT. Advantages of being treated by a psychiatrist over other types of professionals include the opportunity to obtain medications in addition to other forms of therapy, as well as the opportunity to be assessed by a physician who is uniquely qualified to recognize medical conditions that may be contributing to the problem.

Social worker. Social workers are trained to do many different things including helping people to deal better with their relationships, solve their personal and family problems, and learn to cope better with day-to-day stresses. They may help people to deal with the stresses of inadequate housing, unemployment, lack of job skills, financial distress, serious illness or disability, substance abuse, unwanted pregnancy, and other hardships. Most social workers specialize, and some end up providing psychotherapy either in a private practice or a hospital or agency setting. Although CBT is seldom a formal part of social-work training programs, some social workers obtain specialized training in CBT following their formal schooling.

Other professions. Professionals from a variety of other groups may be trained to provide CBT or other forms of psychotherapy. These include some family physicians, nurses, occupational therapists, clergy or other religious leaders, and even psychotherapists without any formal degree in a mental-health related field. As mentioned earlier, it is more important to know whether the person you're seeing has the experience and expertise in treating social anxiety using strategies that have been proven to be useful than whether the person is a nurse, family doctor, psychologist, psychiatrist, occupational therapist, social worker, or a student in one of these fields.

FINAL QUESTIONS REGARDING TREATMENT OF SOCIAL ANXIETY

Here are some answers to a few additional frequently asked questions.

How long does treatment take? As mentioned earlier, cognitive behavioral treatment for social and performance anxiety typically takes between ten and twenty sessions. Sometimes a person may make significant gains after just three or four sessions, particularly if the fear is very mild. Other times, treatment may last many months or even years. If you are being treated with medication (particularly antidepressants), it is usually recommended that you stay on the medication for six months to a year or more before slowly decreasing the dosage and eventually discontinuing the medication. If the symptoms return, it may be necessary to resume taking the medication or to try a different form of treatment.

Are the effects of treatment long lasting? As we discussed earlier, the effects of CBT tend to be relatively long lasting, although you may experience some bad days occasionally. In contrast, stopping medication treatment suddenly is more likely to lead to a return of the anxiety. You can protect against this to some degree by staying on the medication for a longer period (perhaps at a reduced "maintenance" dosage) and by stopping the medication very gradually. Also, stopping certain types of medications is more likely to lead to a return of symptoms than stopping other medications, as reviewed in chapter 5. It is advisable to discuss reducing or stopping medication with the professional who is prescribing it for you before you change the dose you're taking.

Will you be completely "cured"? A small percentage of people who have significant social anxiety are able to reach a point at which they rarely experience any social anxiety at all. Similarly, a small percentage of people do not obtain any benefit from either CBT or medications. For most people, however, the result of treatment is somewhere in between these two extremes. It is realistic to expect that proper treatment is likely to lead to a significant decrease in your social anxiety, avoidance behaviors, and impairment of day-to-day life. However, it is also likely that there will remain some situations that will still be anxiety provoking, at least to some extent. This outcome may not seem too bad if you remember that most people experience social and performance anxiety from time to time.

What if you don't like your therapist or doctor? Although it is unrealistic to expect to be feeling better after only a few weeks, you should know after one or two meetings whether you are comfortable working with your therapist or doctor. If you are not pleased with how things are going, consider trying someone else. Within six to eight weeks after beginning either CBT or medication, you should begin to see changes. If changes have not occurred after two months, you should talk to your doctor or therapist about the possible reasons for the lack of improvement and consider other treatment options.

MEASURING CHANGE DURING TREATMENT

In chapter 3, we emphasized the importance of monitoring your progress throughout your treatment program. We recommend that periodically (every few weeks) you reflect on your progress by considering what types of changes you have made and what changes remain to be accomplished. Depending on your progress, you may decide to revise your treatment plan. You may also decide to update your treatment goals. We recommend that you occasionally complete some of the forms in chapter 3 as a way of assessing whether your social anxiety is improving.

DEVELOPING A COMPREHENSIVE TREATMENT PLAN

In chapters 1 and 2, you learned about the nature and causes of social anxiety. In chapter 3, you completed a thorough assessment of your own anxiety symptoms. Then, you continued the self-assessment process throughout this chapter, as you reviewed your previous attempts at treatment and developed your treatment goals. You are now ready to develop a treatment plan. By now, you should have a good idea of what you need to work on and whether you will try to overcome your social anxiety on your own or with the help of a professional therapist or physician.

If you are considering trying medication, we recommend that you read chapter 5 next. Chapter 5 reviews the various medications that have been shown to be useful for treating social and performance anxiety. If you are interested in trying cognitive behavioral techniques, we suggest that you develop a treatment schedule for the next few months. The following list is one example of such a schedule:

- In the next week, read chapter 6 and begin to work on changing your negative thinking patterns. Chapter 6 includes a number of effective cognitive strategies as well as diaries that you should complete several times per week.

- Continue to practice the cognitive strategies for two to three weeks before moving on to exposure-based techniques (chapters 7 through 9).

- When you are ready to begin exposure practices, begin reading chapters 7 and 8. As you read these chapters, you will have the opportunity to plan exposures designed specifically for your own pattern of fear and avoidance. We recommend that you practice the situational exposure strategies for five or six weeks before moving on to chapter 9.

- At the same time that you are practicing exposures, you should continue to practice using the cognitive strategies that you will learn in chapter 6. By using the cognitive strategies and practicing exposures to feared situations, you should notice your fear beginning to decrease.

- After five or six weeks of practicing exposure to feared situations, read chapter 9 to learn more about how to expose yourself to feared physical sensations. If you are frightened of feeling certain sensations when you are anxious, we recommend that you spend two to three weeks practicing the strategies described in chapter 9. At the same time, continue to practice the cognitive and exposure techniques from the earlier chapters.

- If there are social skills that you would like to improve, this will be the time to use the exercises described in chapter 10. Again, we recommend that you do not stop using the skills that you learned earlier, particularly the cognitive and exposure-based strategies.

At this point, several months will have passed and your anxiety will be likely to have improved significantly. We recommend that you read chapter 11 at this point, which discusses ways of maintaining the gains you have made so far.

If you are curious and you want to read later sections in the book now, that's fine. However, it's important that you go back and practice the strategies in each chapter before moving on to the next set of techniques. These strategies are the building blocks that eventually will lead to an improvement in your social anxiety.

After completing this chapter, a number of issues should be clearer to you. First, you should have a better idea of whether this is the best time for you to work on overcoming your social anxiety. Second, you should have formulated a number of treatment goals, both for the short term and the long term. Finally, it is likely that you will have considered the various treatment options and identified your own treatment preferences. The remaining chapters in this workbook provide more detailed instructions in how to take advantage of particular strategies for managing social anxiety.

CHAPTER 5

Medications for Social Anxiety and Social Anxiety Disorder

DECIDING TO TAKE MEDICATION

As discussed in earlier chapters, two approaches have been shown to be useful for overcoming social anxiety: medications and cognitive behavioral therapy (CBT). Chapter 4 reviewed the key points to keep in mind when deciding whether to use drug treatments to overcome your symptoms of social anxiety. Medications and CBT have been shown to be about equally effective in the short term for treating social anxiety. Still, each approach has advantages and disadvantages.

Advantages of Medications Compared with CBT

- Medications are often easier to get. Any physician (for example, family doctor or psychiatrist) can prescribe medications, as can certain other professionals. In contrast, therapists who have specialized training in providing CBT are often more difficult to find.

- Drug treatments are easy to use and don't take up much time. You just need to remember to take your pills. In contrast, CBT requires a lot of hard work and can be time consuming.

- Medications often work more quickly than CBT. Depending on the type of drug, changes in anxiety can be observed in as little as an hour for treatment with anti-anxiety medications, and in as little as two to four weeks for treatment with antidepressant medications. Typically, CBT takes several weeks to months before significant changes take place.

- Medications are often less expensive in the short term. Visits to your doctor can be infrequent once a stable dosage is reached. At that point, the only cost is the medication itself. In contrast, CBT usually requires regular visits to a therapist throughout the treatment and therefore can be costly, especially if you have limited coverage through your health insurance.

Disadvantages of Medications Compared with CBT

- Anxiety is more likely to return after stopping medication than after stopping CBT. In other words, the effects of CBT are often longer lasting.

- Medication may be more expensive than CBT over the long term. Because medication is typically used for a longer period (often years), the costs are likely to add up to more than the cost of CBT, which generally lasts only several months.

- Many people experience side effects when taking medications. Although these are usually manageable and improve after the first few weeks, some people experience more severe side effects, making treatment with medication unpleasant or impossible. The main side effect of CBT is an increase in anxiety during exposure to feared situations, and this anxiety resolves quickly.

- Medications for social anxiety may interact with alcohol and with other medications. They may also cause problems in people who have certain medical illnesses. CBT does not interact in the same ways with alcohol, medications, or medical illnesses.

- Some medications are difficult to stop taking because they may cause uncomfortable symptoms during discontinuation. This is particularly a problem with anti-anxiety medications, as well as with a few specific anti-depressants. Medications with the potential for dependence should be discontinued slowly, under supervision from your doctor. In contrast, physical dependence and withdrawal problems are not associated with CBT.

- Some medications (in particular, monoamine oxidase inhibitors) require a restricted diet. CBT does not require any food restrictions.

- Many medications must be either used with caution or avoided completely during pregnancy or if you are breastfeeding. CBT can be used safely in either of these situations.

In deciding whether to try medications, you should consult with your doctor. Keep in mind, however, that your doctor's advice regarding this issue is likely to be influenced by his or her own expertise and preferences (for example, family doctors are often much less familiar with research on CBT than with medication options). In reality, it's very difficult to predict who is most likely to respond to CBT or vs. medication, vs. a combination of these two approaches. We generally recommend that people try CBT initially, if it is available, because the benefits tend to be longer lasting than those of medication. In cases where CBT alone is not effective or is only partially effective, the addition of medications can be considered.

CHOOSING AMONG MEDICATIONS

If you decide to try medications, there are two general classes of drugs that have been found to be effective for social anxiety: antidepressant and anti-anxiety medications. There is also evidence that beta-adrenergic blockers (also called "beta-blockers") may help with focused performance fears (for example, fears of public speaking), as well as some preliminary research supporting the use of certain anticonvulsant medications (these are drugs that are usually used to treat seizures). We will discuss each of these approaches in this chapter, and we will also review what is known about the use of herbal remedies for treating social anxiety.

When selecting among these medications, you and your doctor should take into account the following factors:

- **Research findings on available medications.** Treatment guidelines recently published by the Canadian Psychiatric Association recommended antide-pressant treatments as the first medications to try for social anxiety disorder, based on the most recent research (Swinson et al. 2006). In particular, venlafaxine, escitalopram, fluvoxamine, paroxetine, and sertraline had been investigated in the largest number of studies at the time the guidelines were published. These medications are discussed later in this chapter.

- **Your particular social anxiety symptoms.** For example, although people with focused performance fears (like public speaking or performing music) may benefit from treatment with beta-blockers, people with more generalized forms of social anxiety tend not to benefit from these medications.

- **Side effect profile of the medication.** For instance, if you're already struggling with your weight, you might want to choose a medication for which weight gain is not a likely side effect.

- **Previous response to medications.** If you or a family member has previously responded to a particular medication, that drug might be a good option for you to try now. On the other hand, if there is a drug that didn't work for you in the past (despite a long enough trial at an adequate dosage), this might be a time to try something new.

- **Additional psychological disorders that are present.** For example, if you are experiencing depression, it might make more sense to try an antidepressant than an anti-anxiety drug. The antidepressant would likely lead to an improvement in both problems.

- **Cost.** Older medications tend to be less expensive than newer medications, often because older drugs are available in generic forms.

- **Interactions with other medications and herbal remedies.** If you are already taking certain medications or herbal products, you should choose a drug that will not interact with the products you are already taking.

- **Interactions with certain foods.** Medications such as phenelzine can be dangerous if taken with certain foods (those containing tyramine, such as aged cheese and draft beer). Other medications may also interact with foods. For example, grapefruit juice appears to decrease the metabolism of certain selective serotonin reuptake inhibitors (such as sertraline and fluvoxamine), increasing the likelihood that they will accumulate in the body.

- **Interactions with medical conditions.** If you have a particular medical condition (for example, high blood pressure), you should choose a drug that will not worsen the symptoms of your illness.

- **Substance-use issues.** If you enjoy drinking alcohol or if you use other drugs, you should choose a medication that is unlikely to interact with these substances.

- **Discontinuation issues.** Medications that leave the body quickly (in other words, those with a short half-life) are more likely to cause withdrawal symptoms and are often harder to discontinue. Therefore, drugs with a longer half-life are usually easier to discontinue. If you and/or your doctor are concerned about your ability to discontinue a medication, this should be factored into your decision regarding which drug to take. (The term *half-life* refers to the time that it takes for half of the amount of drug in your body to be metabolized or broken down. For example, a drug with a half-life of twelve hours would be 50 percent broken down in twelve hours and 75 percent broken down after another twelve hours. Drugs with a longer half-life are broken down more slowly, giving the body time to adjust to stopping the drug).

STAGES IN MEDICATION TREATMENT

Treatment with medication involves the following five different stages:

1. The first stage is the *assessment.* During this phase, your doctor will ask you the necessary questions to help choose the best medication for your needs.

170

2. The second stage is *initiation of the drug.* In most cases, medications are started at relatively low dosages to give your body a chance to adapt gradually to the new drug.

3. The third stage is *dose escalation.* During this stage of treatment, the dosage is gradually increased until the individual's symptoms start to improve. The goal of dose escalation is to find the lowest dosage that is effective for a particular person. Throughout the process, care is taken to minimize any side effects that may be present.

4. The fourth stage is called *maintenance.* During maintenance, the individual continues to take the medication for an extended period of time. For anti depressants, it is usually recommended that treatment continue for at least a year, minimizing the chances of symptoms returning following discontinuation.

5. The fifth and final stage of medication treatment is *discontinuation.* Some time after a person has improved on a medication, the individual may be encouraged to decrease the amount of the medication to assess whether he or she is ready either to lower the dosage or to stop the medication completely. If a person is also receiving CBT, it may be helpful to have regular CBT sessions during the discontinuation phase. In some cases,

your doctor may recommend that you continue to take a medication that is working for you.

TREATMENT WITH ANTIDEPRESSANTS

Antidepressants are the most frequently recommended medications for social anxiety. These drugs are called "antidepressants" because they were initially marketed for treating depression. However, don't be fooled by their name. These drugs are useful for a wide range of psychological problems, including social anxiety disorder. In fact, they appear to work for this problem regardless of whether an individual is depressed. There are several classes of antidepressant medications that are thought to be useful for treating social phobia. Each of these is described in this section. In addition, a table of recommended dosages is included at the end of this section.

Note that we also indicate which of these drugs is officially approved by the United States Food and Drug Administration (FDA). Although FDA approval typically indicates that a medication is safe and effective when used properly, there are many medications that are safe and effective for social anxiety that are not approved by the FDA or regulatory bodies in other countries. This is because it is very expensive and time consuming for pharmaceutical companies to obtain official FDA indications for their products, and they therefore tend to limit the number of problems for which they apply for approval.

Selective Serotonin Reuptake Inhibitors (SSRIs)

SSRIs are often the first choice for treating social phobia. In fact, the SSRI paroxetine (Paxil) was the first drug to receive an FDA indication for treatment of social anxiety disorder. Paroxetine is also available in a continuous release formula, marketed under the name Paxil CR. Another SSRI that is FDA approved is sertraline (Zoloft). Although only two SSRIs are officially approved for treating social anxiety disorder, there is no evidence that either of these medications works any better or worse than most other SSRIs for this problem. In practice, any of the SSRIs can be used to treat problems with social anxiety. Other SSRIs that have been found to be effective for social anxiety disorder include fluvoxamine (Luvox), citalopram (Celexa), and escitalopram (Lexapro in the United States, Cipralex in Canada). Fluoxetine (Prozac) has been found to be effective in some studies, but not others (Hedges et al. 2007; Swinson et al. 2006).

Although the side effects vary slightly across the SSRIs, some of the most common ones include nausea, diarrhea, headache, sweating, increased anxiety, tremor, sexual dysfunction, weight gain, dry mouth, palpitations, chest pain, dizziness, twitching, constipation, increased appetite, fatigue, thirst, and insomnia. Don't be discouraged by the long list of side effects. Most people experience only a very small number of these, and some individuals experience no side effects at all. Side effects are generally quite manageable. They tend to be worse during the first few weeks of treatment and can be managed by keeping the dosage low until the person becomes used to the medication. Certain side effects (for example, medication-related weight gain and sexual dysfunction) tend not to decrease over time, unless the drug is stopped or the dosage is decreased.

SSRIs typically take two to four weeks before they start working. They are believed to work by altering serotonin levels in the brain. *Serotonin* is an example of a *neurotransmitter,* which is a chemical involved in the transmission of information from one brain cell to the next. Serotonin is thought to be involved in the regulation of emotion and other aspects of psychological functioning.

Most SSRIs are relatively easy to discontinue, although paroxetine is more likely than the others to cause withdrawal symptoms during discontinuation because it is metabolized more quickly by the body. Therefore, paroxetine should be stopped more gradually than the other SSRIs. Common withdrawal symptoms during discontinuation of paroxetine include sleep disturbances, agitation, tremor, anxiety, nausea, diarrhea, dry mouth, vomiting, sexual disturbances, and sweating.

Selective Serotonin and Norepinephrine Reuptake Inhibitors (SNRIs)

Venlafaxine XR (Effexor XR) is currently the only available SNRI that has been found in large studies to be effective for treating social anxiety disorder—in fact, it is approved by the FDA for this purpose (the "XR" stands for "extended release"). Unlike the SSRIs, venlafaxine acts both on the serotonin and norepinephrine neurotransmitter systems, both of which appear to be related to problems with anxiety and depression. A number of well-controlled studies suggest that venlafaxine is useful for treating social phobia (Swinson et al. 2006), although, like the SSRIs, it takes several weeks to have an effect. The most commonly reported side effects of venlafaxine include sweating, nausea, constipation, loss of appetite, vomiting, sleepiness, dry mouth, dizziness, nervousness, increased anxiety, and sexual disturbances. When discontinued too quickly, the most common withdrawal symptoms include: sleep disturbances, dizziness, nervousness, dry mouth, anxiety, nausea, headache, sweating, and sexual problems. Duloxetine (Cymbalta) is another recently introduced SNRI that has been shown to be useful for depression and some forms of anxiety. However, with the exception of published case studies (Crippa et al. 2007), this drug has not yet been studied for social anxiety, and it is too early to recommend it for this problem.

Noradrenergic/Specific Serotonergic Antidepressants (NaSSAs)

Currently, the only NaSSA available is a drug called mirtazapine (Remeron). Like the SNRIs, mirtazapine works by affecting levels of both norepinephrine and serotonin. This drug is newer than the other antidepressants discussed so far. Nevertheless, some initial studies suggest that mirtazapine is an effective treatment for social anxiety disorder (Muehlbacher et al. 2005; Van Veen, Van Vliet, and Westenberg 2002). The most common side effects of mirtazapine include sleepiness, weight gain, dry mouth, constipation, and blurred vision.

Monoamine Oxidase Inhibitors (MAOIs)

MAOIs affect three neurotransmitter systems in the brain: serotonin, norepinephrine, and dopamine. The most studied MAOI for treating social phobia is phenelzine (Nardil). This drug has consistently been found to alleviate the symptoms of social phobia (Swinson et al. 2006). Like the other antidepressants, phenelzine takes several weeks to have a therapeutic effect.

Despite their effectiveness, MAOIs are rarely used in clinical practice because of necessary dietary restrictions and because the side effects tend to be worse than those from other medications. When taking MAOIs, you must avoid foods containing a substance called tyramine. These include aged cheeses, meat extracts, overripe bananas, sausage, tofu, soy sauce, draft beer, and many other foods. MAOIs are also dangerous when combined with certain other medications, including SSRIs. The most commonly reported side effects of MAOIs include dizziness, headache, drowsiness, sleep disturbances, fatigue, weakness, tremors, twitching, constipation, dry mouth, weight gain, low blood pressure, and sexual disturbances.

Reversible Inhibitors of Monoamine Oxidase (RIMAs)

Reversible inhibitors of monoamine oxidase are a type of MAOI that tend to have fewer side effects than traditional MAOIs. In addition, they are less likely than traditional MAOIs to interact with other medications and with foods containing tyramine. The only RIMA that is available is moclobemide (Manerix in Canada, Aurorix in several other countries), though this drug is not currently marketed in the United States. Findings from studies on moclobemide for social anxiety disorder have been mixed. Early studies found that this medication was helpful for treating social anxiety, whereas more recent studies have found only modest effects. In some studies, moclobemide was no better than placebo (Swinson et al. 2006).

The most commonly reported side effects for people taking moclobemide include fatigue, constipation, low blood pressure, decreased sex drive, dry mouth, difficulties ejaculating, insomnia, vertigo, and headache. Like the other antidepressants, moclobemide takes several weeks to have a therapeutic effect. (Table 5.1)

Dose Ranges for Antidepressants in the Treatment of Social Phobia

Generic Name	Brand Name	Therapeutic Dose Range (mg)*
SSRIs		
citalopram	Celexa	10–60
escitalopram	Lexapro/Cipralex	10–20
fluoxetine	Prozac	10–80
fluvoxamine	Luvox	50–300
paroxetine	Paxil	10–60
paroxetine CR	Paxil CR	12.5–75
sertraline	Zoloft	50–200
Other Antidepressants		
mirtazapine	Remeron	15–60
moclobemide	Manerix/Aurorix	300–600
phenelzine	Nardil	45–90
venlafaxine XR	Effexor XR	75–375

Table 5.1: *Dosages are based, in part, on recommendations by Bezchlibnyk-Butler, Jeffries, and Virani 2007.

TREATMENT WITH ANTI-ANXIETY MEDICATIONS

The most frequently prescribed anti-anxiety medications are the benzodiazepines. These are sedatives that include drugs such as clonazepam (Klonapin in the USA; Rivotril in Canada), alprazolam (Xanax), diazepam (Valium), and lorazepam (Ativan). To date, only clonazepam and alprazolam have been investigated in controlled studies for the treatment of social anxiety disorder (Swinson et al. 2006). Although neither is officially approved by the FDA for treating social anxiety, both of these medications have been found to be useful for this problem. The typical starting dose for alprazolam and clon-azepam is .5mg per day, with a maximum daily dose of 1.5 to 3mg for alprazolam and 4mg for clonazepam (Swinson et al. 2006).

When taken on a regular basis, these medications tend to be effective for treating social anxiety. The most common side effects include drowsiness, light-headedness, depression, headache, confusion, dizziness, unsteadiness, insomnia, and nervousness. These drugs may affect a person's ability to drive safely and they tend to interact strongly with alcohol. In addition, they should be used with caution by older people because higher dosages have been associated with a greater likelihood of falling.

There are several advantages to taking benzodiazepines compared with antidepressant medications. First, they work very quickly (within a half hour) and therefore can be used on an "as needed" basis to deal with particularly stressful situations. They also may be used during the first few weeks of antidepressant treatment, while the individual waits for the antidepressant to take effect. In addition, the side effect profile of benzodiazepines is quite different from that of antidepressants, and these drugs may be more easily tolerated by some people.

Despite these benefits, benzodiazepines have fallen out of favor in recent years, mostly because they can be difficult to discontinue. Stopping these drugs can cause temporary (but sometimes intense) feelings of anxiety, arousal, and insomnia. In rare cases, abrupt discontinuation can cause seizures. Given that discontinuation from these medications can cause intense anxiety, it is not surprising that some individuals have difficulty stopping these drugs. The symptoms of withdrawal can be minimized by discontinuing these drugs very gradually. Benzodiazepines are a potentially effective option for treating social anxiety, particularly over brief periods. However, they are typically not recommended as a first-line treatment (Swinson et al. 2006).

TREATMENT WITH BETA-ADRENERGIC BLOCKERS

Beta-blockers are normally used for treating high blood pressure. In addition, they are effective for decreasing some of the physical symptoms of fear such as palpitations and shakiness. A number of early studies suggest that beta-blockers are useful for managing intense fear in certain performance situations (Hartley et al. 1983; James, Burgoyne, and Savage 1983). In particular, they are often used by actors, musicians, and other performers to manage stage fright. However, beta-blockers are ineffective for treating more generalized forms of social anxiety and shyness. The most commonly used beta-blocker for treating performance fears is propanolol (Inderal). This medication is normally taken in a single dose of 5 to 10 mg, about twenty to thirty minutes before a performance.

ANTICONVULSANTS

Anticonvulsants are used to treat seizures, as well as pain, anxiety, and certain mood problems. Recently, there have been a number of preliminary studies finding that certain anticonvulsants such as gabapentin (Neurontin), pregabalin (Lyrica), and topiramate (Topamax) may be useful for treating social anxiety disorder (Swinson et al. 2006). At this point, however, it is too soon to recommend these treatments for social anxiety. Additional research is needed.

NATURAL AND HERBAL REMEDIES FOR SOCIAL ANXIETY

In recent years, herbal preparations have become popular for treating a wide range of health problems. For the treatment of anxiety and related problems, commonly used herbal preparations include St.-John's-wort, kava kava, inositol, Rescue Remedy, and various other products. Generally, there have been very few studies on these products in people with anxiety-based problems, and we are aware of only one study that has specifically tested the effects of an herbal remedy for treating social anxiety disorder (Kobak et al. 2005). In this study, 600 to 1800mg per day of St.-John's-wort (also known as hypericum) was compared to an inactive placebo in forty people with social anxiety disorder. No differences were found in the effectiveness of St.-John's-wort vs. placebo, despite the fact that some studies have found St.-John's-wort to be an effective treatment for depression.

In addition to the lack of studies on the *effectiveness* of herbal treatments, very little is known about the *safety* of many of these remedies or the extent to which they interact with conventional medications. Be sure to tell your doctor if you are taking any herbal products, just in case there are any known interactions with medications you may also be taking.

Although little is known about the effects of herbal treatments on social anxiety, there are a few studies on the use of herbal products for other anxiety problems (Connor and Vaishnavi, in press). Still, more studies are currently under way. In the coming years, additional information regarding the safety, interactions, and effectiveness of these treatments will be available.

COMBINING MEDICATIONS

Your doctor may recommend combining several medications for treating your social anxiety. In most cases, there is very little research on the benefits of combining different medications. However, one combination that has been studied for the treatment of anxiety is the combination of an antidepressant (for example, paroxetine) with a benzodi-azepine (for example, clonazepam). Ideally, both drugs are started at the same time. The benzodiazepine helps to keep the anxiety under control during the first few weeks while the person waits for the antidepressant to start working. Then, once the antidepressant kicks in, the benzodiazepine is discontinued gradually.

A limited number of studies have investigated whether it is useful to combine an SSRI with a benzodiazepine.

Whereas some studies of anxiety problems other than social phobia suggest that this combination is useful for reducing anxiety symptoms more quickly than an SSRI alone (Pollack et al. 2003), a study of people suffering from social phobia did not find any added benefit of combining medications on the rate of recovery (Seedat and Stein 2004).

COMBINING MEDICATION WITH PSYCHOLOGICAL TREATMENTS

Studies comparing medications to CBT have generally found both approaches to be very effective for reducing anxiety. In addition, a number of researchers have begun to study the benefits of combining CBT and medications (Antony and Rowa 2008). Overall, there do not appear to be any consistent benefits of combining these treatments. That is, medication, CBT, and a combination of these approaches all tend to be about equally effective on average, based on the available evidence (for instance, Davidson et al. 2004). However, that doesn't mean that one approach or another is not likely to be more effective for any one person (including you). In other words, it is often the case that some people do best with CBT, some do best with medication, and some do best with a combined treatment. If you decide to try combining CBT with medication, it is helpful if both treatments are delivered by the same person, or if the professionals providing you with CBT and medication are in contact with one another. Treatment is most likely to be helpful when multiple treatments are delivered in a coordinated fashion.

COMMON QUESTIONS ABOUT MEDICATION

Question: Is taking medication a sign of weakness?

Answer: Taking medication for social phobia is no more a sign of weakness than taking medication for any other problem, such as physical illnesses like high blood pressure.

Question: What level of improvement can I expect?

Answer: A small percentage of people obtain no benefit at all from medications for social phobia. Another small group of people obtain almost complete improvement. However, most people with social phobia experience moderate improvements with medications. They tend to feel less anxious overall and are more comfortable in a broader range of situations. However, there may still be areas in which the social anxiety is a problem for them.

Question: Are medications for social anxiety dangerous?

Answer: When taken as prescribed, medications for social phobia are generally safe. When side effects cause problems, as a rule they are easy to manage by decreasing the dosage or switching to a different drug.

Question: Is it dangerous for me to stop taking my medication?

Answer: Medications should always be stopped gradually and in close consultation with your doctor. If done properly, discontinuation is generally safe.

Question: What happens if my medication doesn't work for me?

Answer: If your medication doesn't work, it is important to first make sure you have been taking it for a long enough time and at an adequate dose. If your medication still is not effective despite an appropriate duration and dosage, you may still benefit from trying a different medication or from receiving CBT.

Question: How long should I try a medication before assuming that it isn't going to work?

Answer: Most antidepressants will start to have an effect within four to six weeks, if not earlier. If you haven't experienced any benefit after eight weeks at a high enough dosage, it may be worth discussing the possibility of trying a different treatment with your doctor.

Question: If I go off my medication and my anxiety returns, am I likely to benefit again if I resume taking the same medication?

Answer: Often, when a previously effective medication is tried for a second time (following a break), it will work again. However, sometimes a particular medication is less effective the second time, in which case a different medication may be prescribed.

In summary, medications can be an effective method of managing severe social anxiety. Certain anti-anxiety medications (for example, clonazepam) and a number of different antidepressants (for instance, paroxetine, venlafaxine) have consistently been shown to help reduce symptoms of social anxiety. If you decide that you would like to try medication, a first step is to contact your family doctor or psychiatrist. Your doctor will be able to recommend a specific medication that is likely to work for you.

CHAPTER 6

Changing Your Anxious Thoughts and Expectations

The word *cognition* refers to the ways in which we process information, including experiences such as thought, perception, interpretation, attention, memory, and knowledge. The word *cognitive* is simply the adjectival form of the term cognition. For example, cognitive science is the science concerned with the ways in which we think. *Cognitive therapy* is a type of psychotherapy that is designed to alter negative and unrealistic beliefs, thoughts, and interpretations.

This chapter provides an overview of strategies that have been shown to be useful for decreasing social anxiety by changing negative or unrealistic patterns of thinking. Many of the cognitive techniques and principles discussed in this book have been presented and expanded upon elsewhere by authors such as Aaron T. Beck (Beck, Emery, and Greenberg 1985), David Burns (1999), David M. Clark (Clark and Wells 1995), Richard Heimberg (Heimberg and Becker 2002), Christine Padesky (Greenberger and Padesky 1995), and others. Over the years, strategies similar to those discussed in this chapter have been adopted by the majority of therapists who practice cognitive therapy.

THE ORIGINS OF COGNITIVE THERAPY

Cognitive therapy was proposed in the 1960s and 1970s as an alternative to traditional *psychodynamic psychotherapies,* which were the most prevalent forms of therapy at the time. The original (and most influential), form of psychodynamic psychotherapy is *psychoanalysis,* which Sigmund Freud developed in the early 1900s. Psychodynamic psychotherapies, including psychoanalysis, are concerned with helping individuals understand deep-rooted unconscious conflicts that are presumed to cause or contribute to their psychological problems. For example, Freud proposed that depression can occur as a response to having unconscious aggressive thoughts or feelings toward a loved one. Because such feelings are viewed as unacceptable by the individual, he or she is very motivated to keep such thoughts and feelings outside of conscious awareness. According to Freud, rather than allowing the aggressive thoughts to surface, the individual may turn those angry feelings inward, leading to feelings of self-hatred and worth-lessness, which are often features of depression.

There are many newer forms of psychodynamic therapy (most psychodynamic psychotherapists no longer accept all of Freud's ideas), though the focus of these treatments often remains on recounting early childhood experiences, interpreting unconscious experience (such as dreams), and helping individuals to understand the unconscious motivations for their behavior. Although psychodynamic psychotherapies remain popular, they have gradually lost ground to other forms of therapy, including cognitive and behavioral therapies. Some reasons for the decline of psychodynamic psychotherapies include the relative lack of research supporting many of the underlying theoretical assumptions, as well as a lack of research demonstrating the effectiveness of this form of treatment for many specific problems, including social anxiety.

Despite these criticisms, psychoanalysis and the psychodynamic psychotherapies have made considerable contributions to the understanding and treatment of psychological problems. For example, these were the first treatments based on the assumption that simply talking to another person can lead to psychological changes. In addition, these treatments highlighted the importance of nonconscious information processing. Although there is little evidence to prove the existence of many of the unconscious motivations proposed by Freud, there is evidence that suggests people are frequently unaware of the perceptions and interpretations that contribute to their understanding of their environment. Finally, although many specific aspects of his theory were probably misguided, Freud highlighted the importance of early experience in determining psychological functioning later in life.

The Birth of Cognitive Therapy

In the 1960s and 1970s, a number of psychologists and psychiatrists, disenchanted with psychodynamic psychotherapies, began to explore other ways of helping their patients and clients. Working independently, psychiatrist Aaron Beck (1963; 1964; 1967; 1976) and psychologists Albert Ellis (1962; 1989) and Donald Meichenbaum (1977) each developed new forms of therapy based on the premise that people's difficulties with depression, anxiety, anger, and related problems stem from the ways in which they think about themselves, their environment, and the future.

For example, fear was assumed to stem from a belief that a particular situation was threatening or dangerous. Beck, Ellis, and Meichenbaum each developed treatments designed to help individuals recognize how their beliefs and assumptions contribute to their negative emotions, and to overcome psychological suffering by changing these negative thoughts. Ellis called his form of treatment *rational emotive therapy* and later renamed it *rational emotive behavior therapy* (REBT, 1993). Meichenbaum referred to his form of treatment as cognitive-behavior modification (CBM). It was Aaron Beck, however, who first used the term *cognitive therapy* to describe his treatment. Each of these three new treatments was developed at about the same time, and they were quite similar with respect to their underlying assumptions and some of the treatment strategies used.

Over the years, Beck's form of treatment has become more popular and prominent than either Ellis's or Meichenbaum's approaches. Furthermore, Beck's cognitive therapy has been subjected to more rigorous study than either REBT or CBM for the treatment of social anxiety. Therefore, the methods discussed in this chapter are based on those proposed by Beck and his collaborators, as well as others who adapted and expanded upon Beck's methods for treating social anxiety and related problems.

ASSUMPTIONS OF COGNITIVE THERAPY FOR SOCIAL ANXIETY

Here are some of the basic assumptions of cognitive therapy, particularly as related to the treatment of shyness, social anxiety, and performance fears.

1. Negative emotions are caused by negative interpretations and beliefs. People who interpret a given situation in different ways are likely to experience different emotions. For example, imagine that a friend of yours has cancelled a dinner date at the last minute without providing a reason. Below is a list of possible

emotional reactions you might have depending on your beliefs and interpretations.

Situation: Friend cancels dinner date at the last minute and gives no reason (Table 6.1)

Interpretation	Emotion
"My friend has been hurt or is ill."	Anxiety or worry
"My friend isn't treating me with the respect I deserve."	Anger
"My friend doesn't care about me."	Sadness
"Thank goodness the dinner has been cancelled; I am always so nervous when I have to eat with others."	Relief
"I guess something else came up. Everyone changes plans from time to time, including me."	Neutral

Table 6.1

2. Anxiety and fear result when a person interprets a situation as threatening or dangerous. Although fearful predictions and interpretations are sometimes accurate, they are often exaggerated or inaccurate. Chapter 1 provided a list of thoughts and assumptions that can contribute to social anxiety. These include beliefs about one's performance (such as, "People will think that I am an idiot"), as well as beliefs about the anxiety itself (for instance, "It's important for me not to appear anxious in front of other people"). Beliefs

such as these help to maintain a person's anxiety in social and performance situations.

3. You are the expert regarding your own thoughts and feelings. Unlike some other forms of therapy, which assume that the therapist is the expert, cognitive therapy assumes that the patient and therapist have unique areas of expertise, and the best way to work on a problem is to take advantage of the skills and expertise that each brings to the therapeutic situation. The therapist is assumed to be an expert on the principles and methods of cognitive therapy. The patient is assumed to be an expert regarding his or her own experiences, assumptions, and beliefs. In most cases, the therapist and patient decide together whether a particular belief is exaggerated or unrealistic, and together they generate strategies for changing negative patterns of thinking.

4. The goal of cognitive therapy is to be able to think more *realistically* rather than simply to think *positively.* There are occasions where your anxious beliefs are realistic and are quite consistent with the actual threat in a given situation. In these cases, anxiety may be a good thing because it helps you stay on guard and protect yourself from possible danger. For instance, being a bit nervous while interacting with an authority figure

(for example, your boss, a police officer) may protect you from seeming overly confident, demanding, or aggressive. Cognitive therapy focuses on situations where your beliefs, predictions, and interpretations are exaggerated when compared with the actual level of danger in the situation.

5. People naturally tend to seek out and pay attention to information that confirms their beliefs. In the case of social anxiety, people pay more attention and give more weight to evidence that others are judging them negatively (such as a history of being teased in high school) than to evidence that contradicts the anxious beliefs (for instance, a history of very positive performance appraisals at work). Cognitive therapy aims to help people to consider all the evidence before making any assumptions.

TYPES OF ANXIOUS THINKING

Anxious thinking begins and persists when people make incorrect assumptions about what is likely to happen in a given situation, about the quality of their own performance, and about what other people are thinking of them. This section includes descriptions of some of the most common styles of thinking that often seem to play a role in social and performance anxiety. Note that there are additional examples of negative and exaggerated thinking that other authors have highlighted (see, for example, Burns 1999) that we have chosen not to include in this section. In most cases, these were omitted either because they were not especially relevant to social anxiety or because they were very similar and overlapped considerably with those examples that we have included. In fact, even the various thinking styles on this list overlap to some extent. As you may notice, a particular anxious thought (something like, "Other people will think that I am boring") may easily fit into more than one category (probability overestimation, mind reading).

Probability Overestimations

A *probability overestimation* is a prediction that a person believes is likely to come true, even though the actual likelihood is relatively low. For example, someone who is fearful of giving presentations might predict that the next presentation is likely to go poorly, even though her presentations usually go well. Similarly, a person who is nervous about dating might assume that other people will find him unattractive, even though many people have found him to be attractive in the past. If your thoughts are similar to those listed below, you may have a tendency to overestimate the likelihood of negative events.

Examples of Probability Overestimations

- I will be overwhelmed with panic.

- Everyone at the party will think I'm stupid.

- My presentation will be a disaster.

- I will never be in an intimate relationship again.

- I will have nothing to say if I phone my cousin.

- I will lose my job if I make a mistake.

- If I go out, everyone will stare at me.

Can you think of recent instances when you assumed that things were going to work out badly, without any evidence for that assumption? If so, list your own examples of probability overestimations below:

[space left intentionally blank in the original book]

Mind Reading

Mind reading is actually just an example of a probability overestimation. It involves making negative assumptions about what other people are thinking, particularly what they might be thinking about you. If social anxiety is a problem for you, it is likely that you assume that others think negatively about you. Although it is true that people sometimes make negative judgments about others, the chances are that this occurs much less often than you think. In many cases, your assumptions about what others are thinking are probably exaggerated or even completely untrue. Each of the following kinds of thoughts represents mind reading:

Examples of Mind Reading

- People find me boring.

- My boss will think I'm an idiot if he sees my hands shaking.

- When people look at me, they are thinking I am strange or weird.

- Most people see anxiety as a sign of weakness.

- My friends think I am awkward or stupid when I lose my train of thought.

- People always know when I am feeling anxious.

Can you think of recent examples of times when you have made assumptions about what other people are thinking about you? If so, list your own examples of mind reading below:

[space left intentionally blank in the original book]

Personalization

Personalization is the tendency to take more responsibility for a negative situation than you should, rather than acknowledging all of the different factors that may have contributed to the situation. Here are some examples of personalization, followed by examples of other factors that in reality may have contributed to the situation. (Table 6.2)

Examples of Personalization	In Reality
At a friend's birthday party, I was talking to another guest and we ran out of things to talk about very quickly. I think the conversation ended so fast because I am so boring and can't think of things to say.	In reality, other factors that may have contributed to the situation include (1) the other person couldn't think of anything to talk about, (2) I had nothing in common with the other guest, even though neither of us is actually boring, and (3) it is normal for many conversations at parties to end fairly quickly. Nobody was at fault.
The fact that my boss got angry at me for making a mistake is proof that I am incompetent.	In reality, other factors that may have contributed to the situation include (1) my boss is always getting angry at people, so I shouldn't feel singled out, (2) my boss's expectations are too high (I know that not every boss in the world would have yelled at me for making a mistake; part of why my boss became angry had to do with his own expectations, rather than me making a mistake), and (3) there are many reasons why people make mistakes besides incompetence.

Examples of Personalization	In Reality
People were falling asleep during my presentation, proving once again that I am a really boring speaker.	In reality, other factors that may have contributed to the situation include (1) the topic was somewhat dry and would have been difficult for any speaker to make exciting, (2) the presentation was late in the day, and the audience was feeling tired, and (3) it is normal for some people to feel bored at a talk; other people probably found it interesting.
I was in an elevator and a woman was looking at me. She was probably thinking that I looked strange.	In reality, other factors that may have contributed to the situation include (1) she was staring at me because she liked the way I look or what I was wearing, (2) she was looking in my direction but wasn't really looking at me (maybe she was staring into space or daydreaming), and (3) she noticed me but was thinking of other things.

Table 6.2

Can you think of recent examples of times when you engaged in personalization? If so, list your own examples of personalization in the space below:

[space left intentionally blank in the original book]

"Should" Statements

"Should" statements are incorrect or exaggerated assumptions about the way things *ought* to be. Statements that include words like "always," "never," "should," and "must" are often "should" state-

ments. Sometimes, the tendency to use words such as these is a sign of having overly rigid and perfectionistic expectations for yourself or for others. Here are some examples:

Examples of "Should" Statements

- I should never feel nervous around other people.

- I must never let my anxiety show.

- I should never make mistakes.

- I must never inconvenience other people.

- Others should never think badly about me.

- I ought never to do anything to draw attention to myself.

- Others must never tease me or laugh at something that I have done.

- I should always be interesting and entertaining to others.

- I must do things perfectly so everything is just right.

In the space below, list examples from your own life of unreasonable expectations ("shoulds") that you hold for yourself or others:

[space left intentionally blank in the original book]

Catastrophic Thinking

Catastrophic thinking (also known as *catastrophizing*) is the tendency to assume that if a negative event were to occur, it would be absolutely terrible and unmanageable. From time to time, we all make mistakes, offend others, or look foolish. One difference between people who are socially anxious and those who are not particularly anxious is how they deal with these unfortunate social events. People who have very little social anxiety are often able to say to themselves, "Who cares what this person thinks? I have the right to make a mistake from time to time." Or, "I feel sorry that I upset that person, but everyone puts their foot in it at times." In contrast, people who feel anxious around others are more likely to think, "It would be a disaster to have others think badly of me." Below are more examples of catastrophic thinking:

Examples of Catastrophic Thinking

- It would be terrible if my anxiety showed during my presentation.

- I would not be able to handle making a fool of myself.

- It would be terrible to be unable to think of things to say during my date on Saturday night.

- If someone shows signs of not liking me, it feels like the end of the world.

- It would be terrible to lose my train of thought during a presentation.

- It would be a disaster if I blushed while answering a question in class.

In the space below, list examples of times when you have catastrophized or exaggerated how bad a particular outcome would be if it actually were to occur:

[space left intentionally blank in the original book]

All-or-Nothing Thinking

All-or-nothing thinking (also called *black-and-white thinking*) is the tendency to judge any performance that falls short of perfection as being completely unacceptable. People who engage in this style of thinking tend to categorize their behavior as being either perfect or awful, without acknowledging all of the possibilities that lie between these two extremes. As with "should" statements, all-or-nothing thinking is associated with excessive perfectionism and a tendency to hold unrealistic standards. Following are several examples of all-or-nothing thinking:

Examples of All-or-Nothing Thinking

- If I lose my train of thought even once, I will blow the entire presentation.

- Even one person thinking I look nervous is too many.

- If I don't get an A on my exam, my teacher will think I am stupid.

- It is unacceptable if my boss makes any negative comments or suggests even one area for improvement during my annual performance review.

- Showing any signs of anxiety is almost as bad as falling completely apart.

In the space below, list examples of the times when you engaged in all-or-nothing thinking:

[space left intentionally blank in the original book]

Selective Attention and Memory

Selective attention is the tendency to pay more attention to certain types of information than to other types. *Selective memory* is the tendency to remember certain types of information more easily than other types. As discussed earlier, people are more likely to attend to and remember information that is consistent with their beliefs. Therefore, people with social anxiety are more likely than others to remember times when they were criticized or teased by another person or when they performed poorly in a social situation. When performing in social situations or interacting with others, individuals with social phobia are more likely to notice people who appear to be bored or disapproving. Some other examples of selective memory and attention are provided below:

Examples of Selective Attention and Memory

- Ignoring positive feedback from a teacher or boss (in other words, discounting positive feedback as if it doesn't matter), yet taking negative feedback very seriously (for example, letting negative feedback ruin your day)

- Focusing on the one low grade on your report card and ignoring all the high grades

- Remembering being teased in high school, while forgetting about the good times spent with friends after school

- Focusing on audience members who seem bored during your presentation and ignoring those in the crowd who appear to be enjoying your talk

- Focusing on the moment during a conversation when you stumbled over your words and lost your train of thought, while ignoring the fact that the rest of the conversation was fairly smooth

Can you think of ways in which you selectively pay attention to events or information that confirm your anxious beliefs and selectively ignore information that is inconsistent with those beliefs? In the space below, list examples of times when you have engaged in selective attention or memory:

[space left intentionally blank in the original book]

Negative Core Beliefs

In addition to paying attention to your negative thinking in particular situations that trigger your anxiety, it may also be useful to become more aware of any deeper, more central, and long-standing assumptions that contribute to your feelings of anxiety. These assumptions are called *core beliefs* and they can include negative assumptions that people hold about themselves (for example, "I am incompetent"), other people (for instance, "Other people cannot be trusted"), and the world (such as, "The world is a dangerous place"). The more strongly held these core beliefs are, the more difficult they may be to change.

One technique for uncovering core beliefs involves continually asking about the meaning of each fearful belief you have until the core beliefs underlying your anxious interpretations are revealed. This process is illustrated in the following conversation between Liam and his therapist:

Liam: I am terrified to ask my coworker Cindy out on a date.

Therapist: What are you afraid might happen if you ask her out?

Liam: Mostly, I'm afraid she will say no.

Therapist: Why would that be a problem?

Liam: If she rejects me, it will probably mean that she doesn't find me attractive.

Therapist: What would be so bad about that?

Liam: It will confirm my own belief that I am unattractive.

Therapist: What if that's true?

Liam: Well, if I really am unattractive, that means nobody will ever think I'm attractive or want to date me. It would mean that I am unlovable.

Therapist: What would be bad about being unlovable?

Liam: If I am unlovable, I am bound to be alone forever.

Therapist: So, to summarize, you seem to be saying that (1) if another person turns down your invitation for a date, it means that she finds you unattractive, (2) if another person finds you unattractive, then everyone will find you unattractive, (3) being turned down for a date means that you are unlovable and destined to be alone forever. Do you think of yourself as unlovable?

Liam: I think I do. Part of me knows it isn't true, but much of the time I just can't shake that belief.

HOW TO IDENTIFY YOUR ANXIOUS THOUGHTS AND PREDICTIONS

In chapter 3, we discussed strategies for identifying your anxious thoughts. We suggest that you review the relevant passages in chapter 3 on identifying anxious thoughts before trying to use the techniques discussed in the remainder of this chapter. There is no point trying to change your anxious beliefs unless you are clear about the content of these beliefs. In addition to reviewing the anxious thoughts recorded in chapter 3, identifying your anxious beliefs, predictions, and assumptions should be an ongoing process. Whenever you find yourself in an anxiety-provoking situation, try to identify the specific thoughts and beliefs that contribute to your discomfort. In most cases, you can identify your anxious predictions and assumptions by asking yourself a series of questions such as the following:

- What am I afraid will happen in this situation?

- What do I fear that the other person will think about me?

- What will happen if my anxious thoughts are true?

Sometimes it may be difficult to pinpoint your fearful thoughts. Chances are that social anxiety has been a part of your life for so long that your negative thoughts are well-rehearsed, very quick, and almost automatic (like habits). Also, the fact that you probably avoid the situations you fear makes it that much more difficult to remember exactly what thoughts tend to occur when you are actually in the situation.

If you have difficulty identifying your anxious beliefs, we suggest that you try to engage with the situations you fear and attempt to identify your assumptions and predictions while you are still in the situation. With practice, it should get easier to recognize your anxious beliefs. In fact, even if you are unable to identify the specific thoughts that contribute to your anxiety, practicing being in the situation will likely lead to a decrease in your fear, as discussed in chapters 7 and 8.

STRATEGIES FOR CHANGING ANXIOUS THINKING

This section provides an overview of seven different techniques for changing the beliefs and predictions that contribute to your social anxiety. These include (1) examining the evidence for your beliefs, (2) challenging catastrophic thinking, (3) remembering your strengths, (4) seeing yourself as others do, (5) examining the costs and benefits of your thoughts, (6) creating rational coping statements, and (7) conducting behavioral experiments. Along with a description of each strategy, we include exercises to provide opportunities to try each technique. Near the end of the chapter, we offer some suggestions for tying together all the pieces and for integrating the cognitive therapy techniques into your larger treatment plan.

Examining the Evidence

The fact that you are anxious about being judged by others in a particular situation doesn't mean that your fearful predictions and thoughts are true. In fact, what we assume others are thinking is often completely different than what other people actually think of us. How many times have you heard someone say, "My hair looks awful" or "I am such a loser" and thought to yourself that the individual was just fine? If you are consistently assuming you're inferior in the eyes of others, you are probably exaggerating or misinterpreting other people's reactions to your appearance, behavior, or performance.

The first step toward changing your thoughts is to recognize that your beliefs are not facts. Rather than assuming that your beliefs are true, it is important to treat your anxious thoughts as guesses or hypotheses. By examining the evidence, you will be able to assess the extent to which your beliefs are true. Remember, your natural tendency may be to seek out only information that confirms your negative beliefs about yourself. Examining the evidence involves trying to achieve a more balanced view by looking at all the evidence, especially information that contradicts or disproves your anxious thoughts and predictions.

In order to examine the evidence for your beliefs, we recommend you get into the habit of asking yourself questions such as the following:

- How do I know for sure that my prediction will come true?

- What does my past experience tell me about the likelihood of my thoughts coming true?

- Have there been times when I have experienced anxious thoughts that didn't come true?

- Are there facts or statistics that can help me to decide whether my prediction is likely to come true?

- Are there other possible interpretations for this situation?

- How might another person interpret this situation?

You may find it useful to type these questions on a small index card and carry that card as a reminder in your pocket or wallet. Essentially, examining the evidence involves four basic steps: identifying your anxious beliefs, generating alternative beliefs, weighing the evidence supporting and contradicting your beliefs, and choosing more realistic beliefs. Asking questions similar to those listed above will help you to identify alternative beliefs and to evaluate the evidence concerning your anxious and alternative beliefs. An illustration of how to use this strategy to combat a fear of shaking during a presentation appears below:

Steps for Examining the Evidence

1. Identify the Anxious Thought

   • The audience will think I am incompetent if they see my hands shaking during my talk.

2. Generate Alternative Beliefs

   • Nobody will notice my shaking.

   • Only a small number of people will notice my shaking.

   • People who notice my shaking will think I am tired or that I have had too much coffee.

   • People who notice my shaking will think I am feeling a bit anxious.

- It is normal to shake sometimes, so people will think nothing of it if they notice my shaky hands.

3. Examine the Evidence

Evidence Supporting Your Anxious Belief

- I believe that my shaking is very extreme.

- A few people have commented on my shaky hands over the years.

- I tend to notice when other people shake.

Evidence Supporting Your Alternative Beliefs

- I know others with shaky hands, and people don't seem to think they are incompetent.

- When I notice other people shaking, I don't think they are incompetent.

- Often people seem not to have noticed me shaking when I asked them if it was noticeable.

- When people have noticed my shaking, they haven't tended to treat me differently.

• The people in the audience know me well. I can't imagine that their opinions of me would change dramatically based on whether my hands shook during a single presentation.

4. Choose a More Realistic Belief

• Some people may notice my shaky hands, but it's unlikely that they will think I'm incompetent.

The following form can be used as you begin to work on examining the evidence supporting and contradicting your anxious beliefs. You may want to make copies of this form so that you can continue to use it whenever you encounter a feared situation.

Form for Examining the Evidence
Situation

[space left intentionally blank in the original book]

Anxious Beliefs, Predictions, and Interpretations

[space left intentionally blank in the original book]

Alternative (Non-Anxious) Beliefs, Predictions, and Interpretations

[space left intentionally blank in the original book]

Evidence Supporting My Anxious Beliefs, Predictions, and Interpretations

[space left intentionally blank in the original book]

Evidence Contradicting My Anxious Beliefs, Predictions, and Interpretations

[space left intentionally blank in the original book]

Choosing a More Realistic Way of Thinking

[space left intentionally blank in the original book]

To further illustrate the process of examining the evidence, here is an example of a discussion between Stephen and his therapist demonstrating how to first identify anxious beliefs and then challenge those beliefs based on your past experiences.

Therapist: What are you afraid will happen if you attend your company picnic next week?

Stephen: I am nervous that I won't be able to come up with anything to say to anyone. Everyone else will be talking about their children. I'm not in a relationship, and I have no kids, so I will have nothing in common with any of them.

Therapist: How sure are you that you will have nothing to say?

Stephen: Probably about 90 percent.

Therapist: What that means is that nine out of ten times that you attend an event such as this one, you have nothing to say. Is this really true? What happened at last year's company picnic?

Stephen: When I first arrived, it was difficult. I stood off to the side and didn't say much to others. After a while, people started to include me in their conversations and it got easier. I think it was especially difficult last year because I had just started at the company and didn't know anyone very well.

Therapist: Were you able to think of things to say?

Stephen: At first, I struggled. I think it was harder for me than it was for the others, but I was able to think of a few things to talk about, especially later in the afternoon.

Therapist: Did everyone at last year's picnic bring a partner or spouse? Did they all talk about their children?

Stephen: No. In fact, there are a few other single people at work. Last year, lots of people ended up talking about work.

Therapist: Thinking back to last year's company picnic, do you still think that you won't have anything to say at this year's picnic?

Stephen: Well, I may not be as talkative as some other people, but I suppose I will probably find something to talk about. Maybe it will be easier this year because I've worked with these people for over a year, so I know them much better.

Challenging Catastrophic Thinking

Challenging catastrophic thinking requires shifting the focus of your thoughts from how terrible a particular outcome would be to how you might manage or cope with the situation if it were to occur. One of the most effective ways of overcoming your catastrophic thoughts is to ask yourself questions like the following:

- So what?

- What if my fears actually come true?

- How can I cope with _____ if it were to occur?

- Would _____ really be as terrible as I think?

- Does this really matter in the big scheme of things?

- Will I care about this a month from now? A year from now?

In many cases, you will realize that even if your fear does come true, it won't be the end of the world. You will cope with the situation, and your discomfort will pass. Below you will see a discussion between Aimee and her therapist illustrating how to use this technique to challenge catastrophic thoughts related to asking someone out on a date.

Aimee: I am terrified of asking anyone out on a date for fear of rejection.

Therapist: Is there a particular person whom you have considered asking out?

Aimee: There is a guy in one of my classes. I've sat with him a few times. The class ends just before lunch, so I've thought of asking him to have lunch with me.

Therapist: What's stopping you? What do you think might happen if you ask him to join you for lunch?

Aimee: Mostly, I am afraid he won't be interested in me. I will put him on the spot and he'll have to come up with an excuse for rejecting my offer. I'm afraid he'll think I'm stupid, or even worse, he'll feel sorry for me.

Therapist: As we've discussed previously, there are many different possible reactions that he could have. Thinking you're stupid or feeling sorry for you are just two of many possibilities. Nevertheless, let's assume for a moment that your fears actually are true. What if he does think you are foolish and pathetic?

Aimee: I don't know. I hadn't really thought beyond that. I would feel terrible.

Therapist: Would it mean that you really are pathetic and stupid?

Aimee: I suppose not.

Therapist: Would it mean that all other people also think you are stupid and pathetic?

Aimee: Not really.

Therapist: Why not?

Aimee: Well, his opinion doesn't reflect that of other people. I know my friends don't think I'm pathetic. At least I hope not.

Therapist: If you're not stupid or pathetic, why else would he reject you?

Aimee: Perhaps he might have other lunch plans. Or, maybe he already has a girlfriend.

Therapist: Those are both possibilities, but let's come back to your original thoughts. What if he really thinks you're pathetic and that's why he isn't interested in spending time with you?

Aimee: I guess it wouldn't matter. Over the past few weeks, I've come to recognize that not everyone has to like me. Perhaps it would mean that we're just not a good match.

Therapist: If he declines your offer for lunch, do you think you will be able to cope with the feelings of rejection?

Aimee: I think so. It will feel bad at first, but I think I can stop myself from getting too down on myself.

Overcoming catastrophic thinking also involves combating the tendencies to concentrate only on the immediate consequences of some negative experience (for example, "People will think badly about me during my presentation") and to forget that your discomfort will pass after a short time. In reality, the consequences of making a mistake or of embarrassing yourself are usually minimal and almost never last very long. Even if people notice that you have made a mistake or that you appear to be anxious, they are likely to forget about it after a few minutes.

We have included a Decatastrophizing Form toward the end of this chapter to help you challenge your catastrophic thoughts in social situations. The form includes three columns. In the first column, you should describe the situation that led you to feel anxious. In the second column, describe your anxious thoughts and predictions. Now, ask the questions provided in the previous bulleted list (such as, "So what?") and record your noncatastrophic responses in the third column. Following are some examples.

Column 1 (Examples of Situations)

- Giving a presentation

- Having difficulty thinking of things to say during a conversation

- Attending a party

- Asking someone out on a date

222

- Walking through a busy mall

Column 2 (Examples of Anxious Thoughts)

- _____ will think I am stupid.

- My hands will shake.

- I will look weak or incompetent.

- _____ will feel sorry for me.

- My anxiety will be noticed by _____.

Column 3 (Examples of Noncatastrophic Responses)

- Even if _____ thinks I'm an idiot, it doesn't mean I really am one. His opinion doesn't reflect that of everyone else.

- It wouldn't be the end of the world if _____ noticed my anxiety. Everyone feels anxious from time to time.

- Who cares if my hands shake? I have the right to have shaky hands. Probably no one will even notice. Even if they notice, they probably won't care. My boss has shaky hands and nobody seems to care.

- If I am ridiculed or laughed at, it would be manageable. Most people get teased and ridiculed from time to time. I certainly laugh at other people sometimes. Other than the temporary discomfort or embarrassment, it wouldn't really matter in the big scheme of things.

Remembering Your Strengths

If you tend to focus on small mistakes and perceived flaws in your personality or appearance, you will likely continue to feel anxious. For example, if you assume that everyone is judging you based on whether your hands shake, you are more likely to be nervous when your hands are shaking. Similarly, if you assume that everyone else is criticizing you based on ten seconds during your presentation when you lost your train of thought, you will probably continue to be nervous when giving presentations. Although it is true that we all judge and criticize other people from time to time, it is unlikely that people are noticing and judging the specific behaviors that you assume are being criticized.

People's judgments of one another are based on many different dimensions, including appearance (for example, height, weight, hair color and style, facial features, clothing, shoes, and so on), intelligence (for instance, verbal abilities, problem-solving skills, knowledge of trivia, and so on), competence (such as abilities to do one's job well, computer skills, ability to fix things around the house), work habits (for example, tendency to arrive on time, work hard, and not take overly long breaks), athletic abilities (like the ability to play tennis, fitness level, strength), creativity (for instance, musical or artistic ability), health habits (such as diet, exercise, smoking, drinking), health status (presence of medical problems), social status (type of home, income, type of job), mood (happy, excited, sad, angry, fearful), and personality (generosity, empathy, confidence, politeness, arrogance), to name just a few.

Most of us are far above average on some dimensions, far below average on some other dimensions, and well within average range on most dimensions. The extent to which a person criticizes you about a particular dimension probably depends on whether that person believes that particular domain is important. Although some people may criticize you for appearing nervous, it's likely that most people couldn't care less. If you assume others are focusing only on those dimensions in which you judge yourself to be inferior, you will continue to feel anxious and fearful around other people.

Because your natural tendency may be to focus on those areas in which you feel you don't measure up to others, it may take some practice to recognize dimensions in which you excel or in which you are similar to most other people. As a start, it may be helpful to list some of your strengths in the space provided below.

Areas of Strength

[space left intentionally blank in the original book]

Seeing Yourself as Others Do

One powerful method for challenging the overly harsh standards that you may hold for yourself is to try to see anxiety-provoking situations through another person's perspective. What if the tables were turned and a close friend came to you for advice and support after giving a presentation? What if your friend expressed many of the same thoughts that you experience when you are in a feared social or performance situation? What might you say?

For example, what if your friend said to you, "I totally blew my presentation. My voice was trembling, and at one point I even lost my train of thought. I'm sure I looked like a complete idiot." How would you respond to your friend? Most likely you would say something like, "You probably did better than you think. Even if you did look anxious, people probably didn't care." Or, perhaps you would say something like, "I also feel very anxious during presentations. It feels very uncomfortable in the moment, but eventually it passes."

It is often much easier to challenge someone else's anxious thoughts than it is to challenge your own. Therefore, we suggest that you try coping with your own anxious thoughts by mentally "stepping out" of the situation for a moment. Imagine that it is someone else (perhaps a close friend or family member) who is experiencing the anxiety. What might you tell him or her? Taking the perspective of a close friend may help you to challenge your own anxious thoughts.

Another helpful method of shifting perspectives is to imagine how you might judge someone else who exhibits the same anxious behaviors that you do. For example, if you are worried that others might criticize you if your voice become shaky, you might ask yourself, "Am I critical of other people when I notice their voice shaking?" Most likely, you would not assume someone else to be incompetent, stupid, or weak just because he or she seems a bit shy or anxious in a particular situation. Well, the same is true of other people. It is unlikely that they will make such harsh judgments of you, even if they do notice that you're anxious.

A third strategy for shifting perspectives is to ask yourself how someone who isn't anxious might interpret the situation you fear. For example, if you believe that it's important to avoid parties if there is any risk at all of looking anxious, you can ask yourself how someone who isn't anxious might view that situation. You can even imagine how a particular person (for example, a friend, relative, spouse, or therapist) might view the situation.

To summarize, shifting your perspectives involves asking yourself three types of questions:

- What might I say to a close friend or relative who was having the same thought as me?

- How might I view someone else who was exhibiting the same behavior as me (shaking, sweating, making a mistake, and so on)?

- How might someone without an anxiety problem view this situation?

Examining the Costs and Benefits of Your Thoughts

As we have discussed throughout this chapter, anxious thoughts about social and performance situations are often untrue. However, sometimes they may be true (at least partially true) and still be a problem. In addition to establishing whether your thoughts are true, it's useful to consider whether your thoughts and behaviors are helping you. If they are helpful, then they may be worth holding on to. If not, it may be time to let them go.

Almost everyone wants to make a good impression and probably no one would choose to be thought of as incompetent, stupid, boring, or weak. In fact, many of the anxiety-provoking beliefs held by individuals with excessive social anxiety are similar in content to those held by people who don't have problems with social anxiety. Beliefs such as "It is important to be liked by other people" and "It is important to make a positive impression" are often helpful beliefs that most of us develop early in life. Making a good impression on others helps us to develop friendships, get promoted at work, and impress our teachers. In fact, many rewards in life depend on being able to influence others in a positive way.

However, excessive social anxiety is usually associated with a tendency to be overly concerned with the opinions of others—so much so that it interferes with your life and may actually lead to a more negative impression on others, particularly if you avoid important social events. The problem with the beliefs and thoughts associated with social anxiety is not necessarily that they are untrue (although sometimes they are), but rather that they are held in an exaggerated and inflexible way. For example, if the belief "I should make a good impression on others" motivates you to do a good job at work, that's great. If, on the other hand, the same belief makes you feel paralyzed and unable to get any work done, that's a problem.

In addition to establishing the accuracy of your anxious beliefs and predictions, it may also be helpful to consider whether your thoughts and behaviors are helping you. Following is a form that you can use for this exercise. If you are unsure about whether a particular anxiety-provoking thought is true or false, try examining the costs and benefits of constantly dwelling on the thought. How would the quality of your life improve if you didn't have the thought?

Describe Your Anxious Thought or Prediction

[space left intentionally blank in the original book]

List the Benefits of Having That Anxious Thought or Prediction

[space left intentionally blank in the original book]

List the Costs of Having That Anxious Thought or Prediction

[space left intentionally blank in the original book]

Rational Coping Statements

At the height of your fear, it may be difficult to challenge your anxious thoughts using some of the techniques described in this chapter. You may find that your attention is completely focused on trying to get through the situation, and it may seem impossible to think logically. Rational coping statements are relatively easy to use and don't require the same level of logical analysis as other techniques, such as examining the evidence and evaluating the costs and benefits of your anxious thoughts. Rational coping statements are short "nonanxious" sentences that may help to combat your anxious thinking. Examples include the following:

- It would be manageable if _____ didn't like me.

- It's okay to blush in front of others.

- Panic attacks are uncomfortable but not dangerous.

- It is okay to look anxious during a presentation.

- People don't seem to notice my shaky hands.

You may find it helpful to write or type several coping statements on an index card and carry the card with you as a reminder. When you are in an anxiety-provoking situation, you can take the card out of your wallet or purse and remind yourself of one or more of these statements, thereby combating your anxious thoughts. Choose statements that are most relevant to you. Also, choose statements that are believable. For example, there is no point telling yourself, "I am not going to be anxious" if you always feel anxious when giving speeches and you are about to give a speech. A more believable alternative is, "It's not the end of the world if I become anxious."

In the following spaces, record five rational coping statements that are relevant to your own particular anxious beliefs.

1. _____

2. _____

3. _____

4. _____

5. _____

Behavioral Experiments

Cognitive therapy involves examining the validity of your beliefs and thoughts in the same way that a scientist examines the validity of a scientific theory or hypothesis. In fact, the experiment is the most

232

powerful strategy scientists have to test their own beliefs. In cognitive therapy for social anxiety, experiments involve challenging anxious beliefs by setting up small behavioral tests to see whether a belief is in fact valid. Through a series of repeated behavioral experiments, it is likely that you will disprove many of the beliefs and predictions that contribute to your fear and anxiety. Some examples of specific experiments that can be used to test the validity of various anxiety-provoking thoughts are listed below. (Table 6.3)

Anxiety-Provoking Thought	Example of Behavioral Experiment
It would be terrible to have my hand shake while I hold a glass of water.	Purposely shake your hand while you hold a glass of water. For a true test of your beliefs, let the water spill all over you! Then see if it really is so terrible.
I will make a fool of myself at my job interview tomorrow, so why bother going?	Go to the job interview and see what happens.
I can't cope with being the center of attention.	Do something to draw attention to yourself. For example, arrive to class late, drop your keys, wear your shirt inside out, or knock over some unbreakable items in a supermarket.
It would be terrible to seem stupid or incompetent.	Line up at a store and after your items have been rung up, explain to the cashier that you have forgotten your money.
I will be rejected if I ask a coworker to have dinner with me.	Invite your coworker for dinner and check out his or her reaction.

Table 6.3

When selecting possible experiments, try to choose practices in which you have little to lose. For example, don't tell your boss how much you hate him, just to see what happens! Try to select experiments in which the worst that will happen is possible discomfort or temporary embarrassment. Remember that the more social risks you take, the more often they will pay off. Along the way, however, you will also experience rejection from time to time. If you don't take risks, you will never be rejected—but you will also never experience the benefits of taking social risks, including improved relationships, a better job, and other possible rewards.

In the spaces below, imagine and record some experiments you could try in order to test out your particular anxious thoughts. In the first column, write down your anxious belief. In the second column, design a small experiment that will provide a good test of whether your belief is true. (Table 6.4)

Anxious Thought	Behavioral Experiment
_____	_____
_____	_____
_____	_____
_____	_____

Table 6.4

The next few chapters discuss strategies for confronting the very situations and feelings that you fear. As you will see, exposure to feared situations is actually a type of behavioral experiment. By repeatedly exposing yourself to situations that make you anxious, you will learn that your fears often don't materialize.

USING A THOUGHT RECORD OR COGNITIVE DIARY

Throughout this chapter, we have included various forms and diaries to be used for challenging anxious thoughts. In this section, we now provide a more general Social Anxiety Thought Record that can be used whenever you experience anxiety in a social situation. Unlike the other forms in this chapter, which are each designed for use with a particular technique (examining the evidence, overcoming catastrophic thinking, and so on), the Social Anxiety Thought Record is designed to be used with any of the cognitive strategies. At the end of this chapter is a blank form, as well as a completed sample.

It really doesn't matter which form you use to record and change your thoughts. You can use the forms provided in this chapter, or you can design your own. The diaries in this chapter are only suggestions. The main point of these diaries is to get you into the habit of paying attention to your thoughts and actively trying to change them. Once the new patterns of thinking become second nature, it will no longer be necessary to record your thoughts on paper. In the meantime, we recommend that you use some type of diary or form several times per week after encountering feared social or performance situations. The best times to complete the forms are either before entering the situation (as a way of preparing for the encounter) or immediately afterward (as a way of challenging any anxious thoughts that occurred while you were in the situation).

Instructions for Completing the Social Anxiety Thought Record

Column 1: Date and Time

Record the date and time.

Column 2: Situation

Describe the situation or trigger for your fear. Typical examples might include the following:

- Gave a presentation

- Went to a meeting

- Person was watching me on the subway

- Ate lunch with a coworker

- I was blushing

- My hands shook in front of my boss

- Went to a party

- Had to do an oral book-report for class

- Was introduced to my sister's new boyfriend

- Went on a blind date

Column 3: Anxiety-Provoking Thoughts and Predictions

In the third column, list any anxious thoughts that occur in response to the situation and triggers reported in column 2. Usually these thoughts will be predictions of danger, embarrassment, and so on. Often these thoughts will be automatic or almost unconscious. It will take practice to identify them. Try to come up with very specific thoughts. A thought such as, "Something bad will happen" is too vague. Typical examples of specific anxious thoughts include the following:

- People will notice my blushing and think I am strange

- People will notice that I am nervous

- I will make a fool of myself

- People will think I am stupid

- People will see me for the idiot I really am

- People will think I'm ugly

- I will have to leave the situation

- I am incompetent and clumsy

- I need an alcoholic drink to feel comfortable

- People can always tell how I am feeling

- Anxiety is a sign of weakness

- I'll be viewed as boring

- People will not like me

- I will have nothing to say

Column 4: Anxiety Before (0–100)

Rate your anxiety level before countering your anxiety-provoking thoughts. Use a 0 to 100 point scale, where 0= no anxiety and 100= extreme anxiety.

Column 5: Alternative Thoughts and Predictions

Record examples of alternative thoughts and predictions. For example, if you believe that people will think you are strange if you blush, alternative predictions might include such thoughts as (1) nobody will notice my blushing, (2) people who notice my blushing will think I am hot or not feeling well, and (3) people who notice my blushing will think nothing of it.

Column 6: Evidence and Realistic Conclusions

Consider the evidence for your anxiety-provoking thoughts as well as your alternative thoughts. For example, if you fear blushing, you might record your observations that most people don't mention that they notice your blushing, and that even when people do notice that you are blushing, they still seem to enjoy your company and they still treat you well. In this column, you should also record a realistic conclusion based on the evidence. For example, you might record, "Many people don't seem to notice my blushing, and even when someone does notice it, there are no real consequences other than my temporary embarrassment."

Column 7: Anxiety After (0–100)

Rate your anxiety level after countering your anxiety-provoking thoughts. Use a 0 to 100 point scale, where 0= no anxiety and 100= extreme anxiety.

INTEGRATING COGNITIVE STRATEGIES INTO YOUR TREATMENT PLAN

The cognitive techniques described in this chapter are not meant to be used on their own. Rather, they should be used as part of a comprehensive treatment plan that includes exposure to feared situations. Exposure-based treatments are discussed in chapters 7 through 9. We recommend that you first practice the cognitive techniques for a few weeks before formally beginning exposure practices. Learning to manage your anxiety by changing your thinking will help you when confronting the situations that you fear. In addition to exposure and cognitive therapy, your treatment may also include medication (see chapter 5) and social-skills practices (see chapter 10), depending on your own personal needs and preferences.

A WORD TO SIGNIFICANT OTHERS, FRIENDS, AND FAMILY MEMBERS

If you are working with a loved one who is trying to overcome his or her social anxiety, you can help him or her to change anxiety-provoking thoughts into more realistic thoughts by engaging in calm, logical discussions about the situations he or she fears. This process should always be done in a supportive way, and you should be careful not to put your loved one down for having anxiety-provoking beliefs (after all, we all have irrational thoughts from time to time). You should also be careful not to tell your loved one what he or she *should* be thinking. Rather, your loved one should draw his or her own conclusions based on the evidence. Finally, remember that your role is to be supportive—not to nag or pressure your loved one into making changes or to argue about how to interpret anxiety-provoking situations. You and your loved one should discuss what role he or she would like you to have, and how you can best facilitate the process of change.

TROUBLESHOOTING

Problem: I have difficulty identifying my anxious thoughts.

Solution: Ask yourself questions such as, "What might _____ think about me?" and "What do I think will happen in this situation?" If, after trying to answer these questions, you are still unable to identify your anxious beliefs, try to detect your thoughts while you are actually in the situation you fear. If you are unable to identify specific thoughts and predictions, don't worry. You can still benefit from the exposure-based strategies discussed in chapters 7 through 9.

Problem: I have difficulty believing the alternative, nonanxious, rational thoughts.

Solution: Sometimes the cognitive techniques seem superficial when a person first starts to use them. Over time, the new nonanxious thoughts should become more believable. If not, the exposure-based strategies (chapters 7 through 9) are among the most powerful methods for changing anxious thoughts and will likely help. Sometimes, changing thoughts through firsthand experience in a feared situation is more effective than trying to change thoughts by simply trying to think differently.

Problem: When I am in a social situation, I am too anxious to think clearly, so I can't use the cognitive strategies.

Solution: Try using the cognitive strategies before you enter the situation. If this is not practical, try using them after you have been in the situation for a while (your fear should decrease over time) or even after leaving the situation.

Problem: I can't be bothered completing the monitoring forms. They are confusing, and they take too long to complete.

Solution: There are many different ways to learn the techniques described in this chapter. The forms and diaries are designed to make the process easier. However, if they are getting in the way of using the strategies, try developing a simpler form (for example, you may want to use a two-column form—with one column for recording your anxious thoughts and another column for recording your new nonanxious thoughts). Alternatively, you can even forget about the forms and diaries and simply use the techniques in your head.

A SUMMARY GUIDE TO CHALLENGING THOUGHTS

This chapter includes a large number of suggestions and strategies for identifying and changing your anxious thoughts. Now that you have had a chance to read through the chapter and complete some of the exercises, we encourage you to continue using the cognitive techniques to cope with your social and performance anxiety. Generally, using the cognitive strategies will involve the following steps:

1. Identify your anxious thoughts, predictions, and interpretations.

2. Examine the validity of your anxious predictions using some of the techniques described in this chapter (such as examining the evidence, taking the perspective of others, examining the costs and benefits of your thoughts, conducting behav-

ioral experiments). Are your predictions realistic? For example, will others really think _____ about you?

3.   Examine the validity of your catastrophic thoughts by asking the question, "So what if my anxious thoughts are true?" For example, "What if a few people in the audience really think my presentation is awful? How might I cope with that?"

4.   Use the Social Anxiety Thought Record to identify and challenge your anxious thoughts on paper. (Table 6.5, 6.6, 6.7 (a) and 6.7 (b))

Decatastrophizing Form

Situation	Anxious Thoughts and Predictions (What do I think will happen?)	Noncatastrophic Responses (What if my thoughts come true?)

Table 6.5

Social Anxiety Thought Record

Date and Time	Situation	Anxiety-Provoking Thoughts and Predictions	Anxiety Before (0–100)	Alternative Thoughts and Predictions	Evidence and Realistic Conclusions	Anxiety After (0–100)

Table 6.6

Social Anxiety Thought Record—Completed Sample

Date and Time	Situation	Anxiety-Provoking Thoughts and Predictions	Anxiety Before (0–100)	Alternative Thoughts and Predictions	Evidence and Realistic Conclusions	Anxiety After (0–100)
April 3, 2 PM	Meeting at work	I will say something stupid, people will think I'm an idiot.	90	I will say something intelligent. I will say something that is neither stupid nor intelligent. Some people will think I'm smart, some people may think I am of average intelligence. Whatever I say won't change what my coworkers already think about my intelligence.	My boss asked me to speak at the meeting, so she must think I have something worthwhile to say. Everyone says stupid things from time to time, and there is no reason to think that I shouldn't also say dumb things sometimes. Nothing terrible will happen if I say something stupid. Everyone in the room already knows me. Even if someone thinks I am stupid, it won't be the end of the world.	50
April 5, 7 PM	Eating dinner with a friend, my hands are shaking	My shaking hands will be noticeable. My friend will think that I am nervous and will see that as a weakness.	70	Maybe my friend won't notice my hands shaking. Even if he notices, he may not think it is due to anxiety. Even if he thinks it is due to anxiety, he may not see it as a weakness.	I have known my friend for years. He knows that I get nervous sometimes, and he still wants to spend time with me. He gets nervous in situations that don't bother me (he is afraid of flying). I have the right to have shaky hands sometimes!	45

Table 6.7(a)

| April 7, 3 PM | Returning an item to a store | 70 | The cashier will think I'm stupid for buying this item in the first place. I won't be clear when trying to explain what I want to do. The cashier won't let me return the item, and I won't know how to respond. | The cashier will not think I am stupid. I will be able to explain what I want to do. The cashier will allow me to return the item. Even if I am anxious, I will be able to cope with this situation. | 20 | I have returned items to stores before, and it always seems to work out. Chances are that it will work out this time, too. Returns are allowed within 30 days, so I have the right to return this item. Even if I seem nervous, the cashier doesn't have the right to turn down my request. If I can't think of the right words, I can just take my time until the words come to me. |

© 2008 Martin M. Antony

Table 6.7(b)

CHAPTER 7

Confronting Your Fears Through Exposure

Chapter 6 provided a detailed overview of cognitive strategies that have been shown to be useful for changing anxious patterns of thinking. Almost all of the cognitive techniques involve learning to think differently about social and performance situations by (1) broadening the possible range of interpretations and beliefs that you can hold for a particular social situation, and (2) considering all the evidence before assuming that a specific thought is true.

This chapter provides an introduction to a number of techniques that are useful for changing the behaviors that maintain your anxious beliefs and feelings. Essentially, these strategies involve confronting your fears directly by exposing yourself to the situations and the feelings that you currently fear and avoid. This chapter starts with a review of the behaviors that contribute to social anxiety and a summary of the strategies that can be used to change these behaviors. The remainder of the chapter provides more detailed descriptions of the underlying principles of exposure and the best ways of conducting exposure-based therapy.

Chapters 8 and 9 build directly on the content of this introductory chapter by providing more in-depth instructions for exposure to social situations (chapter 8) and exposure to feared sensations (chapter 9). The exercises described in chapters 7 through 9 should be used after you have had a chance to practice some of the cognitive methods described in chapter 6. We recommend that you begin to learn about exposure by reading chapters 7 and 8 and that you practice the situational exposure exercises for at least three to five weeks before moving on to chapter 9. Then, we suggest that you read chapter 9 and make some attempts to expose yourself to feared sensations, if these exercises are relevant to you. As reviewed in chapter 9, exposure to physical sensations may be useful if you are fearful of experiencing particular feelings (for instance, sweating, shaking, blushing, racing heart) associated with being anxious or nervous. If you are not fearful of these behaviors, then the strategies described in chapter 9 will not be as important.

BEHAVIORS THAT CONTRIBUTE TO SOCIAL ANXIETY

All organisms try to avoid situations that cause fear, pain, or discomfort. Avoidance is a method of protecting oneself from possible danger. In the short term, staying away from perceived threats is a very effective way of decreasing or preventing these uncomfortable feelings. Your experience has probably taught you that confronting feared situations causes you to feel overwhelmed and that avoiding or escaping from feared situations leads to a sense of relief. However, avoiding the situations, objects, and feelings that make you anxious is also a guaranteed way to ensure that your fear will continue over the long term. The likelihood of threat in the social situations that you avoid is probably very low. Avoidance can actually do more harm than good, particularly in the long term.

By avoiding the situations that make you uncomfortable, it may seem as though you prevent your feared negative consequences from occurring. Just as a person who fears flying may believe that avoiding a flight has protected him or her from experiencing a possible plane crash, you may believe that avoiding social or performance situations protects you from experiencing various social catastrophes, such as being humiliated or criticized by others. Of course, statistically, the risk of dying in a plane crash is close to zero (about one in ten million, according to some sources). In other words, the risk of being in a plane crash is almost identical (close to zero) whether you fly or not! The same may be said of public speaking, attending parties, and other social situations. The risk of actual threat or danger is significantly less than socially anxious individuals usually assume. In fact, the long-term consequences of avoiding social situations are often far greater than the risks of confronting these situations.

Exposure to feared situations and feelings is a very powerful method of learning that avoidance is neither necessary nor helpful in the long run. By confronting your fears, you will discover that many of your anxiety-provoking beliefs and interpretations are untrue or exaggerated. In addition, your interpersonal skills will improve as you will have more opportunities to practice various types of social interaction and performance. In other words, not only will you become more comfortable making small talk, giving speeches, or dealing with conflict situations, you will also become more effective and competent at mastering these challenging situations.

There are three main types of anxious behaviors that we will review here. Each of these is a potentially harmful habit because it prevents your fear from decreasing over the long term. These behaviors include (1) avoiding feared social and performance situations, (2) avoiding feared sensations and feelings, and (3) subtle avoidance strategies and safety behaviors.

Avoidance of Social Situations

Avoiding social situations such as public speaking, making conversation, attending meetings, dating, and working out at the gym prevents you from learning that these situations are safe and that your fears are generally unwarranted. Escaping early from these situations (for instance, leaving a party after a few minutes) can also have a negative impact on your fear by reinforcing your experience that being in the situation makes you uncomfortable, and leaving the situation provides relief and a reduction in fear. In reality, staying in a situation despite the fear that it arouses also leads to a reduction in fear. Fear may take longer to decrease when you stay in the situation, but the long-term benefits will be greater. By staying until your fear decreases, you will learn that you can be right in the middle of the situation and feel relatively comfortable. Strategies for overcoming avoidance of feared situations are discussed throughout this chapter, as well as in chapter 8.

Avoidance of Feared Sensations

As we discussed previously, in addition to avoiding certain situations, you may also avoid feeling certain sensations or feelings, particularly in social situations. Perhaps you avoid eating hot foods that cause you to feel flushed when you're dining with friends or relatives. Alternatively, you may avoid wearing warm clothes while speaking in public, in case they cause you to sweat. Avoiding sensations such as sweating and blushing reinforces your beliefs that these sensations and feelings are dangerous. If you are fearful of experiencing particular symptoms in the presence of others, you will likely find that exposing yourself to these feelings can help you to become more comfortable with them. The goal is to reach a point at which sensations, like shaking or a racing heartbeat, are, at worst, mildly uncomfortable but not frightening. The general principles discussed throughout this chapter will be relevant to overcoming your fear of physical symptoms. However, specific exercises for overcoming these fears are discussed more thoroughly in chapter 9.

Subtle Avoidance Strategies and Safety Behaviors

Subtle avoidance behaviors (also called *safety behaviors*) are not-so-obvious strategies that people often use to cope with anxiety-provoking situations. Unlike completely avoiding a feared situation, subtle avoidance strategies involve partial avoidance of the situation. Often these behaviors are not noticeable to others. In fact, they may be so subtle that even you are not aware of them. As is the case with more obvious types of avoidance, learning to let go of your subtle forms of escape will help you to overcome your fear, just as removing training wheels is an important step in learning to ride a bicycle, and letting go of crutches is an important step in relearning to walk after an injury. We will now discuss some examples of subtle avoidance strategies.

Distraction. Distraction involves escaping from anxious thoughts and feelings by focusing on thoughts or images that are more pleasant or by keeping yourself busy with distracting activities. For example, while attending a party, you might offer to help serve food or drinks so that you are constantly busy with some activity and your mind is distracted from the anxious feelings that you might otherwise be experiencing. Or, while traveling on a bus or train, you might always be sure to bring a book or portable radio to distract yourself from feeling anxious about making eye contact with others or from thinking about what others might be thinking about you. Such distractions may help you to feel comfortable while in social or performance situations, but in the long term they prevent you from learning that you can manage the situation without having to rely on subtle avoidance.

Overprotective behaviors. Overprotective behaviors are small things that you may do to feel safer in the situations that you fear. Examples may include the following:

- Wearing extra makeup or a turtleneck sweater to hide blushing

- Finding out who else will be at a party before deciding whether to attend

- Wearing gloves to hide shaking hands

- Sitting down or leaning against a podium while giving a presentation

- Eating in a dimly lit restaurant so your date won't notice your anxiety

- Wearing sunglasses to help avoid making eye contact

- Always attending social events with a friend so you can avoid talking to people who you don't know well

When designing exposure practices, it is important that you also try to eliminate these subtle safety behaviors.

Overcompensating for perceived deficits. Overcompensating involves working extra hard to make sure that your fearful predictions don't come true. For example, if you are afraid of looking foolish during a presentation, you may spend days rehearsing and memorizing what you will say. If you're fearful of making small talk, you may spend hours preparing topics of conversation and rehearsing what you might talk about. If you are afraid of looking unattractive, you may put too much effort into fixing your hair, choosing your clothes, or building your muscles at the gym. In many cases, these situations might be managed with less effort, leaving time and energy for other things. Exposure practices should be designed to eliminate any tendencies to overprepare or overcompensate for flaws that may not even be present. For example, instead of spending hours memorizing a presentation, try giving your talk with only minimal (but still adequate) preparation.

Excessive checking and reassurance seeking. Excessive checking involves spending too much time and effort trying to find out whether you are perceived by others in a positive light. We all engage in occasional checking (for example, looking in the mirror at a party, asking a coworker whether she enjoyed your presentation). In fact, we recommend that you occasionally continue to check on other people's reactions to you and your actions. Checking and receiving reassurance are helpful ways of testing out your beliefs. However, if you ask for reassurance or check too frequently, this may be a behavior you want to decrease. The key is moderation. Occasional checking is helpful, but constant checking can be a problem. Constantly obtaining reassurance about your performance is like constantly checking with your doctor whenever you experience an unusual sensation. Never going to the doctor may cause you serious health problems that might otherwise have been detected early or prevented. But going to the doctor several times a week to check out every ache and pain can backfire; your doctor may stop taking your concerns and complaints seriously. Constant requests for reassurance can also backfire, having the exact effect that you are trying to avoid—namely a negative response from others.

Substance use. Substance use can undermine the effects of exposure by artificially lowering your level of fear in social and performance situations. For exposure to be effective, it's important for you to experience some degree of fear. It is also important for you to learn that your fear will usually decrease naturally if you stay in the situation. Drinking alcohol or using other drugs whenever you are in a situation that makes you anxious will prevent you from learning that your anxiety will decrease even without the drug or alcohol. When designing exposure practices, we recommend that you not drink alcohol or use drugs during the practice. If you want to have a glass of wine or a beer at a party, try to wait until after your fear has decreased somewhat.

A STEP-BY-STEP OVERVIEW FOR CONDUCTING EXPOSURE-BASED TREATMENTS

The main steps involved in any exposure-based treatment program are initial assessment, planning appropriate practices, carrying out the practices, and taking steps to maintain the improvements over the long term.

Initial Assessment

We discussed the issue of assessment in chapter 3. To plan effective exposure practices, you will need to know the situations and sensations that you fear and avoid as well as becoming aware of the different variables that affect your fear level. When you completed the exercises in chapter 3, you probably identified a number of variables that affect your fear level when you are in a social or performance situation that causes you to feel uncomfortable. You should review the relevant sections of chapter 3 before beginning your exposure practices.

Planning Appropriate Practices

Planning your exposure practices starts with developing an *exposure hierarchy.* An exposure hierarchy is a list of feared situations ranked in order of difficulty, from least fear provoking at the bottom, to most fear provoking at the top. Chapter 8 provides examples of hierarchies and includes instructions on how to develop your own hierarchy for situational exposure. Chapter 9 provides sample hierarchies and instructions for developing a hierarchy for exposure to feared sensations. Developing an exposure hierarchy will provide a structure that will allow you to begin with easier exercises and work your way up to more difficult ones.

Carrying Out the Practices

Once you've identified some practices likely to be helpful, the next step is to begin carrying them out. Generally, exposure begins with more manageable situations and works up to more and more difficult situations. As confronting the situations becomes easier, you should begin to let go of the subtle forms of avoidance that were discussed earlier. Later, after practicing situational exposure for several weeks (as described in chapter 8), it may be useful to add exercises involving exposure to feared feelings and sensations (as described in chapter 9).

Exposure practices should be structured, planned in advance, and carried out frequently. The ways in which exposure practices are carried out affect whether the practices are helpful or not. Exposure can actually increase your fear if not done properly. The remaining sections of this chapter provide suggestions for the best ways to conduct exposure to maximize the chances of decreasing your fear.

Maintaining Your Improvements

In order to maintain your improvements, it's important that you continue occasional practices even after your fear has decreased. These strategies are explored in greater detail in chapter 11.

TYPES OF EXPOSURE

This section discusses three different dimensions that should be taken into account when planning exposure practices. They are (1) exposure to social situations vs. feared sensations; (2) imagined vs. live exposure; and (3) gradual vs. rapid exposure.

Exposure to Social Situations vs. Feared Sensations

Situational exposure involves exposing oneself to places and situations that produce anxiety. Overcoming social and performance anxiety almost always includes situational exposure as a component. In other words, to become more comfortable with public speaking, meeting strangers, or lunching with your coworkers, you will need to practice these activities.

Some people with social and performance anxiety may also benefit from exposure to sensations. This form of exposure is sometimes called *interoceptive exposure,* and it involves practicing exercises that trigger particular physical sensations. For example, spinning in a chair can be used to induce dizziness, and running up and down the stairs will make your heart race. Exposure to sensations is useful for people who are fearful of experiencing uncomfortable physical feelings.

If you are not afraid of the physical sensations that you experience when anxious, there is no need to practice these exercises. However, if you are frightened by the physical sensations you experience in social situations, you may find it helpful to practice experiencing these feelings purposely until they no longer frighten you. Exposure to sensations can be combined with situational exposure so that feared physical feelings are purposefully brought on during the course of the exposure to feared situations. Chapter 9 provides a detailed description of how to use interoceptive exposure to reduce your fear of sensations.

Imagined vs. Live Exposure

Exposure can be conducted in your imagination (imagining being in a feared situation) or in real life (actually entering the feared situation). Generally, whenever possible, we recommend that live exposure (also called *in vivo exposure*) be used rather than imagined exposure. Although both approaches can lead to a reduction of fear, live exposure has two big advantages. First, some people have difficulty imagining feared situations in a way that actually arouses their fear; and, second, there is evidence that live exposure is more effective at reducing fear (Emmelkamp and Wessels 1975).

Nevertheless, under certain circumstances, imagined exposure may be helpful. If you are too fearful to enter a situation in real life, you can use imagined exposure as a stepping-stone to the real situation. For example, if you are planning to ask someone out on a date, you might consider using an imagined exposure to the situation at first. Once you have become more comfortable imagining the situation, trying the real thing might become easier. Also, imagined exposure can be helpful when the situation is impractical or impossible to practice in real life. For example, if you must give a presentation to a group of 200 people, you may not be able to practice it in front of a large group. Instead, imagining a large group in your mind's eye might be a good way to practice for the actual presentation when you are preparing your talk.

Situational role-play is a compromise between imagined exposure and live exposure. Role-play involves rehearsing being in a particular situation with the help of a friend, family member, or therapist. For example, before exposing yourself to a real job interview, you could practice mock interviews with other individuals posing as the interviewers. Or, you could ask your family or friends to act as the audience while you practice a presentation. These various forms of situational exposure (imagined, in vivo, and role-plays) are discussed more thoroughly in chapter 8.

Gradual vs. Rapid Exposure

Exposure may be conducted gradually or rapidly. Rapid exposure involves taking steps very quickly, skipping steps, and sometimes trying more difficult situations before you have completely mastered easier situations. For example, rapid exposure to public speaking might have you start off with talking in front of large groups of unfamiliar people instead of to small groups of familiar people.

Gradual exposure tends to begin with easier practices and progresses to the more difficult practices much more slowly. Compared with rapid exposure, a person who is working on gradual exposure may spend more time practicing each step before moving on to the next level of difficulty. In addition, gradual exposure is less likely to leave out intermediate steps, compared with rapid exposure. With gradual exposure, by the time you get to the top steps of your hierarchy, you will be better prepared and less likely to feel overwhelmed by the practice.

Gradual exposure is similar to progressing through school one grade at a time. If you had to jump from ninth grade to twelfth grade, you would likely find the increase in difficulty overwhelming. By progressing through high school one grade at a time, you find each grade to be just slightly more difficult than the previous grade. By the time you get to twelfth grade,

264

the increase in difficulty is only a small step compared with your work in eleventh grade.

Gradual exposure to public speaking might begin by presenting small speeches in front of a close friend or family member or by asking questions at meetings. After those practice situations become easier, you might try speaking for longer periods of time during meetings or practicing a speech in front of a small group of friends or family members. This could then progress to practicing your speech in front of several coworkers. With gradual exposure, you might not actually speak in front of large groups of unfamiliar people until many earlier steps have been mastered.

Gradual and rapid exposure are both effective ways of reducing fear, and the end result of each is usually the same. However, each approach has advantages and disadvantages over the other. With rapid exposure it is likely you will see changes more quickly, which will save you time. Also, these quick results may motivate you to work even harder at overcoming your fear, just as seeing quick changes in your weight or fitness level can motivate you to stick to an exercise and healthy-eating plan. However, compared with gradual exposure, rapid exposure is associated with higher levels of discomfort and fear. Rapid exposure requires a strong commitment from you to tolerate higher levels of discomfort.

The differences between these two forms of exposure can be compared to the difference between jumping into a cold swimming pool and entering the pool slowly. Jumping into the pool quickly causes more initial discomfort, but you get used to the water more quickly. On the other hand, getting into the pool slowly and gradually may be less shocking to your system, but it will take you longer to get used to the water.

We recommend that you practice exposures as quickly as you are willing to. If you are able to take steps more quickly, you will overcome your anxiety more quickly. If you prefer a more gradual approach, that's fine, too. Sometimes, you may find it difficult to judge whether a particular step is too difficult. Remember, there is no harm in taking steps too quickly. If an exercise ends up becoming too overwhelming, you have the option of continuing to practice it until it becomes easier or stepping back, trying a less difficult exercise, and working your way up to the difficult practice more gradually. Either approach is likely to be helpful. The decision is a matter of personal preference and how much discomfort you're willing to tolerate.

HOW EXPOSURE WORKS

Many cognitive-behavioral researchers and therapists believe that exposure works by providing individuals with an opportunity to test the validity of their fearful thoughts, assumptions, and interpretations. In chapter 6, we discussed the use of behavioral experiments for challenging anxious beliefs and predictions. Repeated exposure may be thought of as a form of behavioral experiment. By entering feared situations and exposing yourself to feared sensations repeatedly, you will discover whether your beliefs about social and performance situations are true or false.

Why Exposure May Not Have Worked in the Past

People who are about to begin exposure-based treatments often wonder why they should expect exposure to work now if it hasn't worked in the past. In all likelihood, you've already been exposed to anxiety-provoking social situations from time to time and, in many cases, your fear has probably not decreased. In fact, your anxiety may have increased with repeated exposures. Given such previous experiences with exposure, you may be skeptical about whether simply exposing yourself again to feared social situations will lead to a decrease in your fear.

It's important to acknowledge that exposure is not effective under all circumstances. For example, unpredictable exposure can lead to an increase in fear, particularly if it involves a negative event or consequence. Imagine this situation: You are afraid of dogs and a dog unexpectedly runs out from behind a tree and starts growling at you. That kind of exposure would only make your fear worse. On the other hand, if you are gradually exposed to your neighbor's friendly dog, at your own pace, your fear of dogs might decrease.

In everyday life, exposure to feared situations is often unpredictable. In addition, such everyday exposures tend to be brief and infrequent. All of these factors make exposure in everyday life less likely to lead to a decrease in fear, compared with the type of exposure that is used in cognitive-behavioral therapy. A summary of the main differences between the type of exposure you may have experienced in the past (previous exposure) and the type that has been shown as useful for helping people overcome fear (therapeutic exposure) appears below. (Table 7.1)

Typical Previous Exposures	Typical Therapeutic Exposures
These are often unpredictable and uncontrollable (e.g., you "end up" in the middle of an unexpected conversation; you are "forced" to go to a party that you would rather not attend).	These are predictable and under your control (e.g., you make a decision to enter an anxiety-provoking situation specifically so that you can learn to be more comfortable in the situation).

Typical Previous Exposures	Typical Therapeutic Exposures
These have a brief duration (e.g., you get into the situation, feel anxious, then leave. This teaches you that when you are in the situation you feel frightened, but when you leave you feel better).	These are prolonged (e.g., you decide to stay in a situation until the anxiety comes down on its own or until you learn that your feared consequence doesn't occur. Here, you learn that you can be in the situation, nothing bad happens, and your anxiety eventually subsides).
These are infrequent (e.g., because you usually avoid when anxious, you are not in the feared situation very often. Each time you are in the situation, it's like starting over).	These are frequent (e.g., you practice your exposures over and over again and close together. The benefits of exposures start to add up).
These usually involve anxious thinking (e.g., "People think I'm an idiot," "People will think I'm incompetent if they notice my shaky hands").	These include (e.g., you ask yourself questions to counter or challenge the anxious beliefs and predictions).
These include subtle ways of avoiding the situation countering of your anxious thoughts (e.g., by distracting yourself, using alcohol, bringing someone with you, sitting in a certain "safe" location).	These do not include subtle avoidance strategies (e.g., you make a decision to not use these strategies so that you teach yourself to master the situation on your own).

Table 7.1: Adapted from Antony, M.M. and R.P. Swinson. 2000. Phobic Disorders and Panic in Adults: A Guide to Assessment and Treatment. Washington, DC: American Psychological Association. Used with permission.

OBSTACLES TO COMPLETING EXPOSURE PRACTICES

There are many different reasons why people sometimes don't follow through on exposure practices. We suggest that you anticipate the possible obstacles in advance and try to think of ways to overcome them. There are always going to be reasons not to practice. To combat the excuses you will undoubtedly come up with, you will need to remind yourself of your reasons to continue to practice despite lack of desire, lack of time, or being overwhelmed with the idea of confronting situations that make you anxious and uncomfortable. Here is a listing of some of the most common reasons why people procrastinate when it comes to doing exposure exercises. We've also offered some possible solutions to these problems.

Obstacle: My practices are never planned in enough detail, so I am not sure exactly what I am supposed to do.

Solution: At the beginning of each week, plan your exposure practices thoroughly. You should know exactly what you're going to do, where you're going to do it, and when you're going to practice (dates and times).

Obstacle: Although I have good intentions, my plans never seem to work out. For example, when I plan to have lunch with a friend, I often find that my friend isn't available when I call.

Solutions: Make sure you make plans early. Leaving things for the last minute will make it much more likely that your plans won't work out.

Be sure to have a backup plan. For example, if you're planning to have lunch with a coworker, make sure you have an alternative second plan and, sometimes, even a third plan, just in case your friend isn't available for lunch.

Obstacle: I always forget to practice.

Solutions: Plan your practices the way you would any other activity in your day. Set aside blocks of time to practice and record them in your appointment calendar just as you would for any other appointments, so you don't forget.

Set an alarm (e.g., on your wristwatch or a small clock) as a reminder to practice.

Ask other people to remind you, if necessary.

Obstacle: The idea of doing therapeutic exposure work seems overwhelming. I am just too scared.

Solutions: Start with an easier practice. The activity that you choose should be challenging but not completely overwhelming. If a particular task seems impossible, start with an easier task that does seem possible.

Use the cognitive strategies discussed in chapter 6 to challenge your anxious thoughts before entering a feared situation.

Obstacle: I'm too busy. There never seems to be enough time to do the work.

Solutions: Put aside small blocks of time to be used exclusively for your social anxiety exposure practices. If time is reserved just for this purpose, you will be less likely to feel as if your practices are getting in the way of your other important activities. This is something you want to do for yourself. If you really want to deal with your social anxiety, you know you can find the small blocks of time to reserve for the practices. Think of practice times as taking a class. You may not always want to go to a class, but if you want to learn what is being taught there, you find the time to go.

Choose practices that can be completed during the course of your regular routine. For example, you need to eat every day—you might as well eat some of your meals with other people instead of always eating alone.

Set aside a large block of time (e.g., clear a week-long vacation from work) and spend the whole time practicing exposure nonstop.

Obstacle: I am not convinced that exposure practices will be helpful.

Solutions: Begin with a smaller exposure practice in which you have little to lose, but in which you can still test whether exposing yourself to the situation leads to a decrease in your fear.

The belief that exposure won't work is probably just an example of a negative thought that isn't necessarily true. Examine the validity of your beliefs regarding exposure. For example, can you think of reasons why exposure may not have worked in the past? After you finish reading this chapter, you may have some new ideas about how to ensure that exposure will be more likely to work now.

Obstacle: My feared situations are difficult to create. For example, I can't think of any places to practice public speaking.

Solutions: Chapter 8 contains a large number of possible situations in which to practice exposure. Reading chapter 8 should help you to generate ideas.

Talk to family members and friends. They may be able to help you to come up with some ideas for practices.

HOW TO CONDUCT EXPOSURE PRACTICES

This section provides suggestions for getting the most out of your exposure practices. These include instructions for how to prepare for practices, suggestions to keep in mind when planning practices, what to do during a particular practice, and what to do following the practice. Some of the most important suggestions are summarized in a checklist following this section.

Preparing for Exposure Practices

As much as possible, it's important to plan your exposure practices in advance. As discussed earlier, planning involves making decisions at the beginning of the week about particular practices that you intend to try, as well as coming up with backup practices in case your original plans don't work out. It is very likely that planning will involve setting aside specific times during which to practice. You should also have an idea of how a practice fits in with your short-term and long-term goals. For example, if your long-term goal is to be able to give a presentation to a large group of coworkers, practicing speaking to smaller groups may be an important step in your plan.

Before beginning any particular practice, we suggest that you make some very specific predictions about what might happen during the practice. Once you are aware of your anxiety-provoking thoughts and predictions, use the cognitive strategies described in chapter 6 to challenge your thoughts. Challenging your anxious thoughts before entering into the situation will help you to manage your fear and discomfort.

Importance of Predictability and Control

As we discussed earlier, exposure works better if it is predictable and if you have a sense of control over what's happening in the situation. Therefore, it's best to start with exposure practices in which you have a pretty good idea of what is likely to happen. Some situations, however, are inherently unpredictable. For example, if you decide to ask another person out on a date, it may be impossible to know how the other person will respond. In these cases, you can make the situation somewhat more predictable by considering in advance all of the possible outcomes that could occur. For example, the person might accept your invitation, turn it down, or put off responding for the time being (for example, by not returning your call or saying, "I'm not sure, let me get back to you"). The person may be warm or may come across as cold or uninterested. By anticipating as many outcomes as possible (as well as how you might cope with each outcome), you will be less likely to be surprised.

Duration of Exposure

Exposure works better if it lasts long enough for you to learn that your feared outcome doesn't occur. We suggest that you try to stay in the situation for as long as possible. For example, if you are at a party, try to stay for at least a couple of hours. If you're giving a presentation and have the option of making it longer, try to take advantage of the opportunity to speak for a longer time. Ideally, you should stay in the situation until your anxiety decreases to a mild or moderate level. However, even if your anxiety doesn't decrease during a particular practice, exposure will still likely be helpful, especially if you don't leave the situation too quickly.

If you are practicing being in a situation that is naturally very brief (something like asking a stranger for the time or directions), you can prolong the anxiety-provoking situation by repeating the exposure over and over for a longer period. For example, instead of asking one person for information while walking through a shopping mall ("Where is the food court?"), you can ask twenty or thirty different people for the same information over the course of an hour or more. The chances are good that your fear will decrease over time.

Frequency of Exposure

Exposure works better if practices are repeated close together. For example, giving a speech once a week is more effective than giving a speech once a month. Daily speeches will decrease your fear more effectively than once a week, even if the number of practices is the same. In other words, giving a presentation five days in a row will likely lead to a greater decrease in fear than giving a presentation once per week for five consecutive weeks. So, try to schedule practices as frequently as possible. We recommend that you set aside at least an hour to practice exposure on most days. Once your fear has begun to decrease considerably, it is a good idea to gradually spread out the practices to every few weeks or even to every few months, depending on the situation and how often it arises in your day-to-day life. Occasional practices will help to maintain the improvements you have made in decreasing your fear.

Practice in a Variety of Situations

To some extent, working on decreasing your fear in a particular social or performance situation will help you to feel more comfortable in other social situations as well. This process is called *generalization,* and research has shown that generalization often occurs as a result of exposure. For example, if you learn to feel comfortable asking questions in class, some of that success may "spread," or generalize, to other situations, making it easier for you to speak up at meetings at work. However, generalization will not cause your success to spread to every situation you fear. Therefore, to get the most out of exposure, it's best to practice in a variety of different contexts, places, and situations. For example, if you want to be more comfortable making small talk, we recommend that you practice with your coworkers, family members, strangers in the elevator, at parties, and in as many other situations as possible.

Choose Practices That Are Challenging but Not Impossible

You may feel discouraged if while trying a particular practice, you become anxious or uncomfortable. There is no need to feel discouraged. In fact, it is helpful for you to feel some discomfort during exposure practices. That's why you are doing the practices in the first place. Over time, you will begin to feel less anxious. A successful practice is one that you complete, regardless of how anxious you feel.

On the other hand, it's not necessary to choose practices that are completely terrifying or for which you find it impossible to stay in the situation. If a situation seems too difficult, we encourage you to try something easier. But do try something.

Choose Practices with Minimal Risk

Choose practices in which the likely consequences are minimal, except for a period of feeling anxious. For example, if you want to be more comfortable with the possibility of seeming foolish or being the center of attention, there are lots of safe practices that you can try (for example, walking around with your shirt inside out, telling the cashier that you have forgotten your wallet when you reach the front of the grocery line). There is no need to take unnecessary risks, such as telling your boss what a jerk he is or yelling out a dirty joke at your best friend's wedding. If you're not sure about the realistic risks associated with a particular practice, ask someone whose judgment you trust (perhaps a friend or family member).

Measure Your Improvement

It will be helpful to assess your anxiety from time to time using the forms and suggestions in chapter 3. Evaluating your improvement periodically will remind you of how far you have come and will also let you know when it is time to move on to new situations.

Include a Helper or Coach

Consider including a friend, coworker, or therapist to act as a coach during exposure practices. This individual can help you with role-play practices (for instance, a mock job interview, practicing making small talk) and can provide you with feedback following your practices. If you choose to include a helper during some exposure exercises, that person should be familiar with the basic principles of exposure. Either you should instruct the person about what their role as helper or coach entails, or you should have the person read the relevant sections of this book. In fact, some combination of both approaches may work best. In addition, the person you choose to work with should be supportive and unlikely to become frustrated if things don't work out as planned.

Keep Your Expectations Realistic

Don't expect your anxiety to change overnight. It will likely take weeks or months for it to improve. Also, you won't be able to follow your improvement like a straight line on a graph. You may find that in some situations your anxiety decreases fairly quickly, whereas in other situations success takes longer. Also, you may find that some exposure practices don't lead to any improvement in your fear. You may even have weeks during which your fear and anxiety worsen. A good rule of thumb is to expect one step back for every two or three steps forward.

Don't Fight Your Feelings

For years, you have probably been trying to control your anxiety, to prevent it from occurring, and to get rid of it as soon as possible—no matter what the cost. By now, you have probably discovered that trying to control your emotions doesn't work. In fact, attempts to control your anxiety are likely to make it worse rather than better. Fighting your fear is like lying in bed trying hard to fall asleep by a particular time, telling yourself, "I must fall asleep!" Often, the more you try to sleep, the harder it becomes. In fact, for some people who have trouble sleeping, trying to stay awake is a productive strategy. As soon as they stop *trying* to sleep, they fall asleep quite quickly.

When you can allow yourself to become anxious without fighting the feelings, eventually you will become much more comfortable in social and performance situations. This sounds contradictory, but it really works this way. Instead of fighting your feelings, just let them happen. Instead of evaluating your experiences (for example, "sweating in front of others is unacceptable"), accept them. When practicing exposure, you should observe your responses and experiences without evaluating them. Your fear will likely pass more quickly if you are not trying so hard to get rid of it. Remember, the worst thing that can happen is that you will feel uncomfortable for a while. Being anxious is not dangerous, and anxiety always passes.

As reviewed in chapter 4, variations of cognitive behavioral therapy have recently been developed that emphasize the importance of accepting one's experiences rather than trying to change them. Examples include mindfulness meditation and a form of psychotherapy called acceptance and commitment therapy (Hayes and Smith 2005). These treatments have been found to be effective for treating certain types of anxiety problems, as well as for preventing depression from returning in people who have recently overcome an episode of depression (Eifert and Forsyth 2005; Orsillo and Roemer 2005; Williams et al. 2007). Learning to accept your uncomfortable feelings rather than fight them will ultimately help you to feel more comfortable in the situations you fear.

Eliminate Subtle Avoidance Behaviors

As discussed earlier in this chapter, it is important that you stop the subtle avoidance strategies you use to feel safer in social and performance situations. For example, if you tend to sit on your hands so people won't notice them shaking, try letting your hands show. If you avoid talking about yourself when conversing with others, purposely try to talk about your own interests and opinions. For example, mention a book that you've recently read or a movie that you've seen, and share your opinions. If it's a best seller or a big hit, and you liked it, try to convey your enthusiasm to the person with whom you're talking; if you didn't like it, don't hide your opinion. Express yourself and take a chance on engaging in an exciting dialogue.

Eliminating safety behaviors such as overpreparing for presentations, drinking alcohol at parties, and wearing makeup to hide blushing will help you to learn that social situations can be managed, even without using these strategies and behaviors.

Ending a Practice and Moving On to the Next One

Ideally, an exposure practice should not end before your fear has decreased to a mild or moderate level (such as 20 to 40 on a 0- to 100-point scale). Sometimes, this will take a few minutes; other times, it may take several hours. If possible, try to stay in the situation until you feel more comfortable. However, even if your fear doesn't decrease within a practice, you will still likely benefit from the practice over the long term.

In reality, you may not always have control over when an exposure practice ends. For example, if you're practicing eating lunch with coworkers during a half-hour lunch break, you may not have the option of stretching the lunch into two hours just to give your anxiety a chance to decrease. If the situation ends before your anxiety has decreased, try to practice the same situation again as soon as possible. Continue to repeat the practice until it becomes easier. At that point, you can move on to another practice.

Using Exposure Records and Diaries

To get the most out of your exposure practices, we suggest that you use the diaries and forms provided in chapters 8 and 9 to monitor your progress.

The Aftermath of Exposure: Processing What Happened

Chances are that you will feel good following your exposure practices. Although you may be tired, you likely will also feel relieved to have completed the practice and proud of your accomplishments. Nevertheless, some people tend to analyze their every move and criticize their performances during the practice (for example, "People surely noticed my anxiety," "I came across like a bumbling idiot"). If you tend to dwell on what happened during your practices, we suggest that you try to put a more positive spin on the experience.

Remember that the main reason you are practicing exposure is to *eventually* feel more comfortable in social and performance situations. However, for now, expect to feel uncomfortable during practices. Expect that your performance won't be perfect (in fact, the goal isn't perfection anyway). Rather than dwelling on what happened or didn't happen, try to use the cognitive techniques from chapter 6 to challenge your negative thinking. Also, try to take something positive from the experience. Even if things didn't go the way you had hoped they would, you can still use the experience to plan future practices and to generate ideas for what you might do differently the next time.

A WORD TO SIGNIFICANT OTHERS, FRIENDS, AND FAMILY MEMBERS

If you are reading this book in order to help a loved one, here are a few suggestions to keep in mind. First, your loved one must be on board with this treatment. Treatment is not something that can be forced on someone who isn't willing to make the necessary changes. In addition, you should avoid the temptation to trick, force, bribe, or coerce a person into doing exposure practices. In order to get the most out of treatment, it's important that the decision to do exposure comes from the individual.

Your role in exposure therapy is to help brainstorm possible exposure practices, to provide support, to participate in exposure role-plays (for example, a simulated job interview), and to be involved in actual exposure practices when you're asked to do so. For example, if your loved one fears attending parties, he may ask you to attend a party with him. If your loved one fears eating in restaurants, she may ask you to join her for a meal. In advance of any exposure practices, discuss with your loved one what he or she would like you to do in the situation (for example, provide reassurance, provide company, probe for anxiety-provoking thoughts, and so on).

SUMMARY OF EXPOSURE GUIDELINES

This chapter described a long list of guidelines for how to get the most out of your exposure practices. Following is a list of the most important suggestions, in summary form.

- Plan practices in advance. Set aside time to practice exposure.

- Exposure practices should be predictable and under your control (particularly early in treatment).

- Exposure should be frequent (almost daily), especially at the start.

- Exposure should be prolonged. Try to stay in the situation until your fear has decreased.

- Use cognitive strategies to challenge anxious thoughts before entering the situation.

- Use cognitive strategies to challenge anxious thoughts during the practice.

- Use cognitive strategies to challenge anxious thoughts after leaving the situation.

- Don't fight your anxious feelings in the situation. Just let the feelings happen.

- Eliminate subtle avoidance strategies like distraction, alcohol use, and over-protective behaviors.

- Practice in a number of different situations.

- Choose practices in which the actual risk is minimal, especially at first.

- Choose practices that are challenging, but not impossible.

- Complete exposure records (see chapters 8 and 9) with each practice.

TROUBLESHOOTING

Problem: My fear does not decrease during my exposure practices.

Solutions: This is normal to some extent. Although anxiety and fear usually decrease during the course of a particular exposure practice, most people experience occasional practices in which their anxiety doesn't decrease. Here are some suggestions for dealing with this situation.

Make sure that you are staying in the situation long enough. Sometimes it can take several hours for a person's fear to diminish.

Make sure that you are not using subtle avoidance strategies. The normal pattern during exposure is for fear to increase and then gradually to decrease. Using subtle avoidance strategies such as distraction may cause the fear to go up and down repeatedly over the course of the practice, because most people are not very good at distracting themselves for long periods.

Negative thinking can sometimes interfere with the effects of exposure. If your fear does not decrease during a particular exposure practice, challenge your anxious thoughts using the techniques described in chapter 6.

If all else fails, just keep practicing. Sometimes it takes repeated exposure practices before a person's fear begins to lessen.

Problem: My fear returns between exposure practices.

Solution: This is normal for most people. With more and more practice, your fear will decrease more quickly during practices and will not return as intensely between them. One way of preventing your fear from returning between exposures is to increase the frequency of your practices, particularly early in treatment.

Problem: My physical symptoms (for instance, stuttering, shaking, sweating) are very noticeable.

Solution: Remember that, despite how it seems to you, the chances are good that your symptoms are not as noticeable to others as you think they are. Furthermore, as your anxiety decreases, the intensity of these symptoms will likely decrease. If you are concerned about people noticing your symptoms, use the cognitive techniques from chapter 6 to challenge your anxious thinking. Remember that there are lots of people who blush, shake, or lose their train of thought and who couldn't care less about what other people think. The problem is not that you experience these symptoms, but rather your beliefs about the consequences of having these symptoms.

Problem: I am just not good at _____ (making small talk, public speaking, and so on).M

Solution: Your social skills are likely much better than you think they are. As discussed in earlier chapters, people who are socially anxious tend to be overly critical of their social and performance skills. Nevertheless, there may be ways in which certain skills can be improved. It is likely that exposure alone will contribute to an improvement of your skills. For example, practicing making small talk will help you to learn what works during a casual conversation and what doesn't. In addition, we suggest that you read chapter 10, which includes specific strategies for improving social and communication skills.

Problem: My fear is too high to benefit from exposure.

Solutions: Ideally, you should choose practices that arouse a fear level of 70 to 80 out of 100, although it is also okay if your fear reaches even higher levels. One method for keeping your fear in check is to use the cognitive strategies from chapter 6 to challenge your anxious thoughts before entering the situation.

At times, however, even using the cognitive techniques beforehand won't prevent your fear from becoming very intense.

If you find that your fear is completely overwhelming, you have three options. First, you can try to wait a while longer to see if your fear decreases. Alternatively, you may consider taking a short break and then trying the same exercise again. Finally, you can try switching to a less difficult practice. Any of these approaches is usually fine. The main point is not to give up completely.

Problem: The situations that I fear are very brief in duration, so there isn't enough time for my fear to decrease.

Solution: This issue was discussed earlier in the chapter, but it's worth highlighting again here. Ideally, if an exposure practice is brief, you should try to find creative ways to lengthen the duration of the practice, if possible. For example, if you are fearful of chatting with the cashier at the front of a supermarket line, try lining up repeatedly over the course of an hour or two and buying only a few items at a time. This approach will give you more opportunities to talk to the cashiers, compared with paying for all your groceries at once.

Problem: I just had something terrible happen during an exposure practice (for example, my boss criticized my presentation). How can I ever try exposure again?

Solutions: Although rare, it is possible that an unexpected negative event will occur during an exposure practice. For example, you could experience a bad panic attack during a job interview, or you may be laughed at during a presentation. If something bad does happen during an exposure practice, it's natural for some of your fear to return. It may be helpful to "rethink" the meaning of the negative event using the cognitive techniques described in chapter 6. In addition, we recommend that you resume your exposure practices. If necessary, you can return to a previous item in your hierarchy and work your way back to where you were when the unfortunate incident took place.

Problem: I don't avoid the situation, and yet my fear persists.

Solutions: Although exposure usually leads to a decrease in fear, occasionally people report having intense fear in social situations despite almost never avoiding these situations. For example, a person may eat with others on a regular basis but still get anxious in the situation. If you continue to experience fear, despite never avoiding the feared situation, you may find it difficult to come up with appropriate exposure exercises. Here are three strategies to consider.

First, if you fear experiencing arousal symptoms while in social situations, try the interoceptive exposure exercises discussed in chapter 9. Second, assess whether you are engaging in subtle avoidance strategies, overprotective behaviors, alcohol or drug use, or other strategies that may be undermining the effects of the exposure. If so, try to discontinue these behaviors. Finally, a special effort should be used to identify and challenge the anxious predictions and beliefs that continue to maintain your fear (see chapter 6).

CHAPTER 8

Exposure to Social Situations

In chapter 7, we provided an overview of the basic principles underlying exposure-based treatments for social anxiety. In this chapter, we'll present additional information about how to use these strategies to confront the social and performance situations that make you anxious or uncomfortable. You should be very familiar with the material in chapter 7 before moving on to this chapter. As noted earlier, we suggest that you use the cognitive strategies described in chapter 6 to combat anxious thinking before, during, and after exposure practices. During practices, you should refrain from using subtle avoidance techniques such as distraction, drugs or alcohol, and safety behaviors (for example, eating in a dimly lit restaurant so people don't notice your blushing). Finally, a reminder that exposure works best when practices are:

- Frequent (daily, if possible)

- Prolonged (until the anxiety decreases)

- Predictable and controllable

- Planned in advance

- Conducted in a variety of different situations

SITUATIONAL EXPOSURE PRACTICES

This section provides suggestions for exposure practices involving different types of social and performance situations, including public speaking, making small talk, meeting new friends and dating, situations involving conflict with others, being the center of attention, eating and drinking in public, writing in front of others, job interviews, being in public, and talking to people in authority. In addition to the suggestions provided here, there is space in each section for you to record additional ideas for practices that might be relevant to your own social and performance anxiety.

At first, many of the items suggested in this section may seem overwhelming. However, as suggested in chapter 7, you should begin with challenging but manageable practices. Over time, you will become more comfortable and most likely you will be able to try some of the more difficult practices. In addition, some of these practices may seem very easy to you. If you have no trouble with a particular type of social or performance situation, there is no need to practice confronting it. Instead, focus on the situations that are anxiety-provoking for you.

Practices Involving Public Speaking

To overcome a fear of speaking in front of others, it is helpful to take advantage of opportunities that come up during the course of your job or other activities in your day-to-day life. If public speaking opportunities don't normally arise in your life, there are many ways of creating these situations. Some of these include the following:

- **Speak up in meetings at work.** For example, share your opinions about issues being discussed. Ask and answer questions. If the opportunity to make a brief presentation arises, take advantage of it.

- **Offer to give a presentation at work or in another situation.** For example, if you belong to a book club or reading group, offer to present a summary of the book that your group is reading. If you have some special expertise, offer to share it with your coworkers, colleagues, or friends by giving a formal presentation.

- **Go to a public lecture and ask questions.** Public lectures are often advertised in the newspaper, on the Internet, on the radio, or on television (for example, on your local cable access channel). Also, check out advertisements on community bulletin boards and posters at the library, supermarket, local colleges, or other public places.

- **Take a course at a college, university, or any school that offers adult education courses.** Try to choose courses that provide the opportunity to give presentations. If these are not available, make a point of asking questions several times during each class. If you are unable to enroll in a course, another option is to simply audit or sit in on a large class at a local university. Professors will sometimes give guests permission to observe a class without formally enrolling. Often, undergraduate classes contain hundreds of students, so no one would notice an extra person in the room. Auditing a large class will save you from having to pay registration fees while still providing you with an opportunity to ask questions in public.

- **Make an impromptu speech or toast at a wedding, party, group dinner, or other social gathering.** If you are invited to a party or are planning to have a party of your own, offer to make a short speech in front of the other guests.

- **Take a public speaking course.** There are numerous companies that offer public speaking courses (especially for businesspeople). These classes are sometimes expensive, but it may be worth finding out more about the available options (perhaps your workplace would help to cover the costs). Check the Internet or your local Yellow Pages to learn about courses. There are many options available, including, for example, courses by Dale Carnegie Training (www.dalecarnegie.com) and The Leader's Institute (www.leadersinstitute.com).

- **Join Toastmasters International.** Toastmasters is an organization that holds meetings for individuals who are interested in learning to speak more effectively in front of others. They have more than 11,000 clubs located in ninety countries around the world. Typically, groups include about twenty individuals who meet for one to two hours each week. Annual membership is inexpensive. For more information, visit www.toastmasters.org.

- **Take a drama or music class.** Taking a theater, drama, or music class will provide you with opportunities to perform in front of others. Classes may be available at local high schools or colleges, professional theater or music schools, the YMCA, or through other agencies.

- **Give a lecture at a local elementary school, high school, or college about your work.** Sometimes schools will hold career days through which students have opportunities to learn about particular jobs or careers. Additionally, teachers sometimes invite guests to speak to their classes about particular types of careers or jobs. Call a local school principal to find out about opportunities in your neighborhood school. Or, if you have a child in school, you may have the opportunity to speak to his or her class about what you do at work.

- **Read a passage in front of others.** For some people, reading a newspaper article or a passage from a book in front of a few family members may be anxiety provoking. For others, it may be important to try something more challenging, such as reading an introduction for a guest speaker who is about to give a presentation at your workplace.

Now, can you think of other possible practices that involve public speaking? If so, record them in the space below:

Other Practices

[space left intentionally blank in the original book]

Practices Involving Making Small Talk, Casual Conversation, and Informal Socializing

Casual conversation and small talk can take place anywhere. The list below provides a few examples of situations where you might have the opportunity to practice these skills. In addition to planning several large practices per week, you should try to engage in several mini-practices throughout the day.

- **Have friends over for a get-together.** For example, invite several coworkers over for dinner or to watch a movie or sports event on TV. Or, have a birthday party for a friend or family member. Make sure that you interact with your guests! Don't come up with excuses to avoid them (like serving food and drinks to the exclusion of conversation, cleaning up, or washing the dishes).

- **Speak to strangers on elevators, while waiting in lines, at bus stops, or at other public locations.** With repeated practice, making small talk will become easier. Prolonged exposure works best, so try to talk to many different people over the course of an hour or two to get the most benefit. Smile, say hello, and use humor, if appropriate. Although you should be prepared for some people to react negatively (remember, other people may also be shy or they may be uninterested in making small talk), most people will probably react positively.

- **Ask for directions or for the time.** Walk up to a stranger in a mall or store and ask what time it is. Or, ask how to find a particular location. As mentioned earlier, prolonged exposure works best, so try to do this repeatedly over an hour or two or until your anxiety decreases.

- **Talk to coworkers or classmates.** Try arriving at school or work a bit early so that you will have the opportunity to chat with others. Make a point of saying hello to your coworkers or classmates during breaks. Simple questions such as, "How was your weekend?" are often a great way to get a conversation started.

- **Talk to dog owners who are walking their dogs.** Dog owners often love to talk about their dogs. If you have a dog, try going for walks in areas where other people walk their pets. Make comments or ask questions about other people's dogs (for example, "Nice dog" or "What kind of dog is that?"). If you return to the same routes frequently, you will likely see the same people over and over again. You may even make some new friends.

- **Talk to cashiers or other staff personnel in stores.** For example, comment on the weather, ask for advice or information ("Does this shirt go with these pants?"), or special order a book or CD.

- **Give or receive compliments.** Offer someone else a compliment. For example, tell a coworker that you like her sweater or new haircut, tell an artist that you like his work, or compliment a waiter on the quality of your food. If you are uncomfortable receiving compliments, just say "Thank you" when someone praises you. Don't discount the praise by telling the person all the reasons why you don't deserve it.

- **Express a controversial opinion.** If you have a controversial opinion about some issue, express it, particularly in situations where the consequences are likely to be minimal. For example, if you didn't like a movie that someone else is raving about, let them know what you didn't like about the film. If you disagree with someone else's political views, explain your perspective on the issue. Try not to put down the other person or to discount that person's views when you are expressing your own opinions. Differing views should be expressed in a friendly and supportive way, and you should make an effort to communicate understanding of the other person's perspective.

- **Join an ongoing conversation.** In some circumstances, it is perfectly appropriate to join an ongoing conversation. For example, at parties people often walk about, moving in and out of different conversations. See if you can join in with a group of people who are discussing some issue that interests you.

- **Talk to parents of other children.** Just as pet owners enjoy talking to other pet owners, parents usually enjoy talking about their children with other parents. If you have children, get involved in situations where you might have the opportunity to talk to other parents. For example, attend parents' night at your children's school or enroll your children in a class (such as swimming, hockey, crafts, music) with other children. Take advantage of any opportunities to talk to the other parents.

- **Meet two or three friends at a cafe.** Invite several coworkers or friends to meet you after work or school for a coffee, drink, or snack. Alternatively, invite others to join you for lunch.

Can you think of other possible practices that involve informal socializing, casual conversation, or making small talk? If so, record them in the space below:

Other Practices

[space left intentionally blank in the original book]

Practices Involving Meeting New Friends and Dating

Many of the situations listed in the previous section on practices involving small talk and casual conversation also provide opportunities to meet new people.

Similarly, several of the situations listed in this section also provide opportunities for casual conversation. Most new friendships and relationships start with a casual conversation, so it's no surprise that these sections might overlap. Also, developing new relationships often requires repeated encounters with new people you meet. In other words, two people will typically become acquaintances before they become friends. The list below provides examples of practices that involve a possibility of meeting new people, developing new friendships, developing new business relationships, or fostering opportunities for dating. Remember that the main goal of an exposure practice should be to become more comfortable in these situations. For now, developing new relationships should be a secondary goal. Focus on the process of reducing your fear rather than whether you develop new friends or relationships through these practices.

- **Go to a social event.** For example, attend your annual office holiday party, a class reunion, a community dance, a local art gallery opening, or a book signing. Situations such as these will provide you with opportunities to meet people, as well as to mingle and make small talk. Be sure to take social risks in these situations (for example, talking to other people).

- **Talk to your neighbors.** Go for walks in the neighborhood and say hello to your neighbors—particularly those you have not had a chance to meet. If you have a new neighbor, consider asking him or her over for a drink or dessert. Invite some of your other neighbors as well.

- **Join a club, take a class, or join an organization.** For example, join a bowling league, aerobics class, volleyball league, bingo group, self-help group, church group, art class, or other group. Ideally, the group should meet frequently (for instance, weekly) for you to get the most benefit from attending it.

- **Ask friends or colleagues to introduce you to new people.** Take advantage of opportunities to meet new people through friends, coworkers, or other people you know.

- **Invite people you know to socialize.** For example, invite several coworkers or acquaintances for lunch, dinner, a movie, or a concert. Or, invite several coworkers or acquaintances away on a vacation, ski weekend, or conference-related trip.

- **Meet people through online social networks or dating services.** Consider joining an online social networking site, such as Facebook (www.facebook.com) or MySpace (www.myspace.com). Join online chat rooms. Meet people through online dating services (for example, www.matc h.com). Two cautions: first, although the Internet can be a useful tool for meeting people, it's important that you not rely exclusively on online relationships *instead* of in-person relationships. Rather, consider using the Internet as a tool for meeting people who you might eventually meet in person. Second, if you are meeting people in person for the first time, use appropriate caution. For example, a first date should happen in a public place, and you should not give others your home address until you know them fairly well.

- **Arrange for dates through personal ads or dating services.** In addition to meeting people through the Internet, you can also find opportunities for dating through professional dating services and through personal ads in local newspapers.

Can you think of other possible practices that involve meeting new friends, dating, or related situations? If so, record them in the space below:

Other Practices

[space left intentionally blank in the original book]

Practices Involving Possible Conflict with Others

These practices should be planned carefully. Unlike the other practices recommended in this chapter, these are likely to cause another person to become a bit angry or impatient with your behavior. Choose practices in which the risks are minimal—if you are unsure of the risks, ask a friend or family member for a second opinion. You may also want to skip ahead to the sections on assertive communication in chapter 10 to prepare yourself for this kind of inter-action. It's important that potential conflict situations be dealt with assertively rather than with aggression, which is likely to escalate the other person's anger.

It may seem rude to do things purposefully that will inconvenience others. On the other hand, as you continue to read this section, you will see that most of these practices involve only minor inconvenience to other people, and many of these are situations that people often encounter anyway. The substantial gains that you may obtain from these practices are likely to outweigh any inconvenience that you create for others.

Listed below are some examples of practices that others have found useful for becoming more comfort-able with conflict situations:

- **Ask someone else to change his or her behavior.** For example, ask your roommate to wash his or her dishes rather than leaving dirty dishes lying around. Or, ask another person to stop talking in a movie theater.

- **Stay stopped in your car for a few seconds when the light turns green.** Pretend you are changing the radio station or that you didn't notice the light turn green. The drivers who are backed up behind you eventually may become frustrated and honk their horns. This should be your signal to drive away.

- **Say no when you don't want to do something.** If someone asks you to do something that you don't want to do (for example, donate money that you can't afford, purchase an item from a telemarketer, do more than your fair share of work, and so on), say no in an assertive (though polite) way. Again, we recommend that you read chapter 10 for suggestions regarding assertive communication.

- **Return an item to a store.** Return a book, an article of clothing, or some other item to a store. In most cases, the staff at the store will gladly take back the item. However, sometimes you may encounter a negative response, which will provide you with the opportunity to get used to this uncomfortable situation. To really test yourself, try to return an item without a receipt, without the original packaging, or after the allowed period for returns has passed. The store may not take back the item, but you will get an opportunity to practice dealing with possible conflict.

- **Send food back in a restaurant.** Ask your server to take your food back (for instance, to change the dressing on your salad, make your soup hotter, cook your food more thoroughly, or bring you a different drink).

- **Take an extra long time at a bank machine when there are people waiting behind you.** For example, make several deposits, transfer funds from one account to another, and withdraw cash from two or more different accounts. Make eye contact with others in line to see if they are looking impatient.

- **Forget your money when paying for an item in a store.** For example, when you reach the front of a supermarket line, tell the cashier that you have forgotten your wallet. Or, have more items in your cart than you can afford to purchase. This will help you to better tolerate the possibility of inconveniencing the cashier and the people in line behind you.

- **Ask a stranger to stop smoking.** If you are in a restaurant or bar, or even in a public place outdoors, try asking the person next to you to stop smoking. Use some discretion. For example, don't practice this if the other person seems aggressive, likely to get angry, or is much bigger than you are.

Now, can you think of other possible practices that involve some risk of mild conflict? If so, record them in the space below:

Other Practices

[space left intentionally blank in the original book]

Practices Involving Being the Center of Attention

Here are some suggestions for ways to draw attention to yourself. If you are afraid of looking foolish, standing out in a crowd, or simply being observed by others, try some of these exercises:

- **Say something incorrectly.** Purposefully answer a question incorrectly in class, provide someone with incorrect information, or mispronounce a word.

- **Speak loudly.** Speak loudly in a public place (for example, at a mall, in a bus, or on the subway), so that others around you can hear your conversation.

- **Have a mobile phone or pager go off in a public place.** Arrange for someone to page you or call you on your cell phone while you are at the dentist, eating at a restaurant, or walking through a public place. Use some discretion here. For example, don't try this practice during a college exam, a job interview, or while at a movie, unless your intention is to annoy the people around you.

- **Drop something.** Drop your keys, your books, or some other item in a public place. Or, spill water all over your shirt.

- **Talk about yourself.** When speaking with other people, talk about your family, your job, your hobbies, or some other aspect of your personal life. Offer your opinions about political issues, books that you have read recently, or movies that you have seen.

- **Participate in a party game.** For example, play Twister, Pictionary, Scattergories, Outburst, Trivial Pursuit, or some other game with friends, coworkers, or your family.

- **Wear your shirt or dress inside out or backward.** Walk around a public place while making a fashion faux pas. The more outrageous, the better. For example, wear shoes that don't match. Wear a plaid shirt with striped pants. Wear your dress or shirt inside out (this exercise is even better if your dress or shirt has shoulder pads), or wear a formal evening gown during the day. With practice, you will become much less concerned about looking conspicuous.

- **Knock over a display in a store.** For example, knock over a few rolls of paper towels or toilet paper in the supermarket. Again, it is important to use good judgment. For example, don't knock over glass jars of tomato sauce. That would be going too far!

Now, can you think of other possible practices that involve being the center of attention? If so, record them in the space below:

Other Practices

[space left intentionally blank in the original book]

Practices Involving Eating or Drinking with Others

People who fear drinking in front of others are often concerned about having shaky hands and spilling their drinks. Those who are fearful of eating in front of others may be nervous about making a mess, looking unattractive while eating, or feeling flushed from eating hot foods. You should choose to practice exposure in situations that will challenge your specific anxieties. For example, if you are more anxious when eating messy foods, you should order foods that are more likely to be messy. If you're nervous about blushing or sweating, order hot soup or a spicy meal. A list of situations offering an opportunity to eat or drink in front of others is provided here:

- **Eat a snack at your desk.** If your desk at work is in an open area, eat a snack at your desk. This may be easier than eating with your coworkers. When this exercise becomes easier, you can move to other practices, such as those in the rest of this list.

- **Hold a drink at a party or gathering.** If you tend to be anxious when holding a glass of wine or a soft drink in front of others, try doing just that the next time you're at a party or other social gathering. Try not to hide your hands if they begin to shake. If alcohol tends to decrease your anxiety, make sure you don't drink wine, beer, or spirits until after your anxiety has decreased on its own.

- **Have lunch with coworkers.** You probably eat lunch every day. You might as well eat with other people, if the opportunity arises. If your natural tendency is to eat at your desk or to eat lunch in restaurants alone, invite a coworker to join you for lunch once or twice every week.

- **Meet a friend at a restaurant for dinner.** If you tend to feel safer in dark restaurants, challenge yourself by choosing a more brightly lit location. Try to choose a seat where you are more likely to be observed by the other people in the restaurant.

- **Invite people over for a meal.** For example, invite two or three friends or neighbors over for dinner.

- **Dine at other people's homes.** If you tend to decline invitations to eat at other people's homes, accept the invitation next time. You may find it more difficult to do so if you are concerned about not being able to control the environment (such as the lighting), who the other guests are, and what types of food are served, but don't use these as reasons to avoid the situation.

- **Dine alone in a restaurant, food court, or another public place.** If eating alone in public makes you anxious, having lunch alone in a restaurant or food court is an appropriate practice. You might also want to consider eating in other public places, such as sitting on a bench in a park or in a shopping mall.

Can you think of other possible practices that involve eating or drinking in front of others? If so, record them in the space below:

Other Practices

[space left intentionally blank in the original book]

Practices Involving Writing in Front of Others

As a rule, people who are uncomfortable writing in front of others are concerned about having shaky hands while they are writing. They also may be fearful of others judging their handwriting or noticing personal information that they may be recording. Examples of situations that can provide an opportunity to write in front of others include the following:

- **Pay for items using a check.** Instead of paying with cash or a debit card, write a check when purchasing merchandise in a store. Be sure to complete the check in front of the cashier (don't write out the check before you get to the store: that's cheating). If you're concerned about having the cashier notice your shaky hands, try making your hands shake purposefully. In fact, to really challenge your fear, let your hands shake so much that you have to write a whole new check.

- **Write a letter while seated in a public place.** Write a letter to a friend while sitting in a cafe, riding on a bus, or relaxing on a public bench. Make sure that there are others around who can see you writing.

- **Fill out forms or applications in front of other people.** For example, complete an application for a new credit card or loan at a bank (with the bank officer watching), complete an application for a new video-store membership, fill out a contest ballot in front of a cashier, or sign documents in front of your coworkers.

Can you think of other possible practices that involve writing in front of other people? If so, record them in the space below:

Other Practices

[space left intentionally blank in the original book]

Practices Involving Job Interviews

To become more comfortable with job interviews, the best exposure practices are those that provide experiences similar to real job interviews. Some examples include:

- **Apply for a volunteer position.** Many volunteer opportunities (for example, in hospitals, schools, theater companies, charitable organizations, community agencies, and so on) begin with an interview process that is very similar to an interview for a paying job. You may feel less pressure if you know that you're applying for a nonpaying position. If so, this would be a good place to start. In addition to giving the employer the opportunity to meet you, another purpose of an interview is to give you a chance to evaluate the position. Applying for a volunteer position does not commit you to accepting it if it's offered. If you decide it isn't for you, you can always turn it down. If you apply for several volunteer jobs, you will become more comfortable with the entire interview process.

- **Practice interviews with family members or friends.** Practicing job interviews with friends or family members is another good way to begin the process of overcoming anxiety over job interviews. You will need to coach your friend or family member about the nature of the interview and the role that he or she should take. You may also want to work up to having some of these role-play interviews become particularly challenging (for example, have your helper play the role of a hostile interviewer), so you can learn to be more comfortable with difficult interviews in real life.

- **Apply for jobs that are not particularly interesting to you.** A great way of learning to overcome a fear of job interviews is to practice interviewing for jobs that are not high on your list. You might as well learn how to interview more effectively in situations in which you have little to lose. By practicing interviewing for jobs you don't particularly want, you will be better prepared when it comes time to interview for a job that interests you.

- **Apply for jobs that interest you.** If you are looking for a new job, eventually you must be able to interview for the job you want. The more jobs you apply for, the more interviews you will be offered. The more interviews that you get, the more opportunities you will have to practice your interviewing skills and to overcome your fear of being interviewed. Although it's reasonable to start the process by interviewing for jobs that are not particularly interesting to you, you should also be applying for jobs that you might really be interested in accepting.

Can you think of other possible practices that involve interviewing for a job? If so, record them in the space below:

Other Practices

[space left intentionally blank in the original book]

Practices Involving Being in Public

For some people, just being around other people is anxiety provoking, even if there is no interaction or direct social contact. If being in a public place is difficult for you, here are some examples of public places where you may be able to practice exposure. Remember to practice frequently and to stay long enough for your fear to decrease. If you must leave the situation, try to return to it as soon as possible.

- **Go to a mall or supermarket.** Shopping is a good way of exposing yourself to other people in a public place. Try shopping when the stores are more crowded to challenge your fearful thoughts even more.

- **Make eye contact in a public place.** If appropriate, make eye contact with other people while you walk down the street or while sitting on a bus or subway. Of course, for safety reasons, this may not be wise in some cities, particularly at night, or in dangerous parts of town.

- **Go to a concert or sporting event.** A guaranteed place to encounter lots of other people is at a large concert, sporting event, movie theater, or other entertainment venue. If you prefer to sit in an aisle seat or near the exit (for a quick escape), try sitting in the middle of the row and away from the exit.

- **Read in a public place.** Spend some time reading your favorite book, a newspaper, or a new novel at a coffee shop or library.

- **Join a gym or take an aerobics class.** Rather than exercising alone, practice exercising in front of others. For example, join an aerobics class and take a spot near the front of the room. Or, lift weights near other people who are more experienced and stronger than you are.

Can you think of other possible practices that involve being in public? If so, record them in the space below:

Other Practices

[space left intentionally blank in the original book]

Practices Involving Speaking to Authority Figures

Going out of your way to make contact with people in authority who make you feel uncomfortable is an effective way to learn how to be more comfortable with authority figures. Examples of relevant exposure practices are listed below. If any of these are situations in which you would like to feel more comfortable, they may be appropriate practices for you to try.

- **Have a meeting with your boss or teacher.** If you are a student, ask your teacher to meet with you to discuss a difficult homework assignment. If you are working, ask your boss for an appointment to discuss your performance or some other aspect of your job.

- **Ask a pharmacist questions about a medication.** If you are taking any medications, ask a pharmacist to answer particular questions about the medication (for example, side effects, interactions with other medications, how to get refills, and so on). If you're not taking any medications, you can still ask questions, perhaps on behalf of a friend or family member.

- **Ask your doctor to explain a particular medical issue.** Make an appointment with your family doctor to ask questions about symptoms that you may be experiencing. Be sure to have your questions answered.

- **Meet with your bank manager.** For example, arrange to meet with your bank's manager or loan officer to discuss the possibility of obtaining a loan or mortgage.

- **Meet with a lawyer.** For example, meet with a lawyer to discuss estate planning (writing a will) or some other legal issue that you are dealing with.

- **Meet with an accountant or financial advisor.** Hire an accountant with whom you feel intimidated to do your taxes, or meet with an intimidating financial advisor to get investment advice.

Can you think of other possible practices that involve interacting with people in authority? If so, record them in the space below:

Other Practices

[space left intentionally blank in the original book]

CHALLENGING YOUR WORST FEARS

By repeatedly exposing yourself to anxiety-provoking situations, you will continue to challenge most of your deeply held beliefs and predictions concerning your ability to cope with social and performance situations. Ideally, exposure practices should be designed to test the validity of your anxious assumptions. For example, if you are fearful of saying something foolish during a conversation at a party, it's not enough simply to attend parties, although just attending may be a reasonable first step. To more thoroughly challenge such an anxiety-provoking belief, you also would need to talk to other people at the party. By having numerous conversations with others, eventually you will learn that most of what you say is not foolish at all.

After reaching a certain level of comfort talking to other people at parties, the next step might be to practice saying something silly or foolish purposefully and to evaluate the consequences. This exercise would help to challenge your anxious beliefs at an even deeper level. Chances are that even if you did say something foolish at a party, the consequences would be minimal. With this type of exposure practice, you would learn not only that you can engage in effective conversations with others, but that even if you make a mistake from time to time, it doesn't really matter.

The strategies discussed in this section are useful for increasing the intensity of your exposure practices by testing out the validity of your "What if?" thoughts. Rather than dwelling on questions like "What if I make a mistake?" or "What if I draw attention to myself?"

we suggest that you try to answer these questions by purposefully making a mistake or purposefully drawing attention to your behavior. In all likelihood, you will discover that nothing terrible happens.

Purposefully Making Mistakes or Trying to Look Stupid

When you have begun feeling more comfortable in some of your feared situations, a reasonable next step is to make some small mistakes purposefully, or to do things that make you look foolish or stupid. Examples of this kind of purposeful behavior include pronouncing a word incorrectly while speaking to your boss, asking an obvious question in class, or bumping into a door. There is no need to make big mistakes (for example, purposefully failing an exam or crashing your car). Small mistakes will work just fine, and the consequences will be minimal.

Purposefully Drawing Attention to Yourself

If being the center of attention is difficult for you, your exposure practices should include attempts to draw the attention of others to your behavior. For example, rather than arriving early or on time for a movie or a class, try arriving a few minutes late, so that everyone is aware of you when you enter the room. You may feel embarrassed momentarily, but you will learn from the practice that the whole experience doesn't matter, even minutes later. Your embarrassment will be temporary. Also, people probably will forget about your late arrival almost instantly and soon will be thinking about other things.

Purposefully Increasing Your Anxiety Symptoms

In addition to entering the situations you fear, a more complete test of your anxiety-provoking beliefs is to deliberately arouse some of the symptoms that frighten you in social or performance situations. Chapter 9 discusses these strategies in some detail. Some examples of possible exposure exercises include the following: wetting your forehead (to simulate sweating) before giving a presentation, purposefully appearing to lose your train of thought during a meeting or presentation, and purposefully allowing your hands to shake while writing or holding a drink. By deliberately bringing on the symptoms you fear (in a predictable and controlled way), you will learn to be less frightened of having these symptoms show in front of others.

Expressing Personal Opinions

Finally, if you are afraid to express personal opinions during a conversation, just engaging in conversations, without expressing personal opinions, will not be enough to test the validity of your fearful beliefs. Conversation alone will not teach you that your fears are unfounded. Instead, you should make sure that you express your feelings or opinions during your exposure practices.

DEVELOPING A SITUATIONAL EXPOSURE HIERARCHY

Before beginning exposure therapy, it is helpful to generate a list of very specific situations that range in difficulty from mildly to extremely anxiety-producing. This list of situations, called a *situational exposure hierarchy,* will help to guide your exposure practices.

Usually, the situations on the hierarchy include details that take into account particular themes that contribute to how much fear you are likely to experience. These themes may include the size of the group or audience (for example, it may be easier to talk to one person than five people; five people may be easier to handle than fifty), the length of time involved (for instance, a five-minute conversation vs. a thirty-minute conversation), your relationship with the other person (for example, a family member vs. a stranger), and so on.

Two examples of situational exposure hierarchies follow. The first hierarchy is for a person with the fear of public speaking, and the second is for someone who experiences social anxiety in many different situations (in other words, generalized social anxiety). Note that the hierarchy items are very specific with respect to the duration of the practice, the types of people present, and other relevant variables. Developing specific items is important because it's difficult to develop practices based on overly vague hierarchy items. Fear and avoidance ratings are based on a scale ranging from 0 (no fear, no avoidance) to 100 (maximum fear, complete avoidance). (Table 8.1 and 8.2)

Sample Situational Exposure Hierarchy: Public Speaking Situation

Situation	Fear	Avoidance
1. Give a 1-hour, formal lecture to 200 strangers about a topic that I don't know well.	100	100
2. Give a 1-hour, formal lecture to 30 strangers about a topic that I don't know well.	99	100
3. Give a 1-hour, formal lecture to 200 strangers about a familiar topic.	90	100
4. Give a 1-hour, formal lecture to 30 strangers about a familiar topic.	85	100
5. Give a 1-hour, informal presentation to 20 coworkers about an unfamiliar topic.	85	90
6. Give a 1-hour, informal presentation to 20 coworkers about a familiar topic.	70	70
7. Give a 1-hour, informal presentation to 20 young children about my work.	65	65
8. Make comments or ask questions in a large meeting (more than 15 people).	50	60

Situation	Fear	Avoidance
9. Make comments or ask questions in a small meeting (5 or 6 people).	40	40
10. Offer to make a toast at a family dinner.	35	35

Table 8.1

Sample Situational Exposure Hierarchy: Generalized Social Anxiety

Situation	Fear	Avoidance
1. Give a 1-hour, formal lecture to 30 coworkers about a familiar topic.	100	100
2. Have a party at my home for my coworkers.	95	95
3. Ask Pat out for a dinner date.	90	100
4. Answer a personal ad in the newspaper.	85	100
5. Attend the annual holiday party at work without drinking alcohol.	85	85
6. Attend a tea for a coworker who is retiring.	70	70
7. Have a formal dinner with Rita (a friend).	70	75
8. Talk about personal feelings or opinions with my coworkers.	60	60
9. Have a fast-food lunch with Rita.	60	50
10. Have a conversation with the person sitting next to me on a bus.	50	50
11. Ask someone for directions or for the time.	45	45
12. Call Rita on the telephone.	40	40
13. Eat alone in a crowded food court at the mall.	40	40
14. Walk around at a crowded mall.	35	35
15. Answer the telephone without checking my caller ID.	30	30

Table 8.2

To generate your own hierarchy, refer back to the suggested exposure practices in this chapter as well as to the results of your self-assessment in chapter 3. Choose situations that range in difficulty from slightly anxiety-provoking to completely overwhelming.

Record these situations in order of difficulty (starting with the most anxiety-provoking at the top) in the spaces provided on the following blank Situational Exposure Hierarchy Form. Next, rate each situation to describe the level of fear you would feel if you were in that situation right now (use any number from 0 to 100, where 0= no fear; 25= mild fear; 50= moderate fear; 75= intense fear; and 100= very intense fear). Finally, using a 0- to 100-point scale, indicate how much you would tend to avoid each situation on your hierarchy (0= do not avoid the situation; 25= hesitate to enter situation, but rarely avoid it; 50= sometimes avoid the situation; 75= usually avoid the situation; 100= always avoid the situation). (Table 8.3)

Situational Exposure Hierarchy Form

Situation	Fear (0–100)	
1. _____	_____	_____
2. _____	_____	_____
3. _____	_____	_____
4. _____	_____	_____
5. _____	_____	_____
6. _____	_____	_____

Situation	Fear (0–100)	
7. _____	_____	_____
8. _____	_____	_____
9. _____	_____	_____
10. _____	_____	_____
11. _____	_____	_____
12. _____	_____	_____
13. _____	_____	_____
14. _____	_____	_____
15. _____	_____	_____

Table 8.3

IMAGINED EXPOSURE TO SOCIAL SITUATIONS

Whenever possible, in vivo exposure (actual exposure to feared situations) is preferable to exposure in the imagination. In fact, imagined exposure is rarely used for treating social anxiety. Still, exposure in the imagination may be useful either when the real situation is too overwhelming for you to enter or when you are unable to confront the actual situation for practical reasons (for instance, you have an upcoming college exam and no earlier opportunities to practice taking it).

Imagined exposure may be helpful to prepare you to enter the actual situation. When you are using imagined exposure, the guidelines are generally the same as for in vivo exposure. For example, practices should be frequent (if possible, daily) and should continue until your fear decreases (for example, thirty to sixty minutes). Whenever possible, imagined exposure should be followed by in vivo exposure in the actual situation.

When conducting imagined exposure practices, close your eyes and try to imagine the situation as vividly as possible. Some people find it helpful to make a tape recording describing the situation in detail and then listen to the tape during subsequent practices. Other people find it helpful simply to imagine being in the situation, without the help of a recorded description. Either way, it's important to imagine the experience vividly, so that it feels as real as possible. Your imagined exposure practices should produce many of the same feelings that are produced by real exposure, although the intensity of these feelings may be lower during imagined exposure. We recommend that you ask yourself the following questions to help bring the experience to life:

- What do I see around me? What do my surroundings look like? Who else is here?

- What is happening in this situation?

- What emotions am I feeling?

- What thoughts am I thinking?

- What physical sensations am I experiencing? How intense are they?

- What is my environment like? Is it hot? Humid?

- What am I doing while in this situation?

- What sounds am I hearing?

- What odors am I sensing?

SITUATIONAL ROLE-PLAY

A *situational role-play* is an exposure practice in which you rehearse being in a simulated social situation before actually entering the real situation. Role-play can provide you with exposure practice without creating the same social risks that are sometimes present in the actual situation. In other words, you have less to lose during simulated exposures, compared with real-life exposures. Below are some examples of how to use situational role-plays to improve your level of comfort, as well as to improve your skills for dealing with particular social situations:

- Before giving a formal presentation at work, practice giving your talk to several friends and relatives. Ask your simulated audience for feedback. If possible, repeat this role-play practice several times.

- If you're nervous about making small talk with strangers at parties, ask your partner (or any close friend or relative) to pretend to be an unfamiliar person. Imagine that you have both arrived early for a party and are waiting in the living room while the host prepares food in the kitchen. Practice engaging in small talk, as if you have just met for the first time.

- If you have an upcoming job interview, you can prepare by having friends or relatives simulate interviewing you for a job.

- In order to practice asking another individual out on a date, you could rehearse what you might say with a close friend or relative.

In the spaces below, record several more simulated exposure role-plays you could use to begin confronting the situations that you fear:

1. _____

[space left intentionally blank in the original book]

2. _____

[space left intentionally blank in the original book]

3. _____

[space left intentionally blank in the original book]

4. _____

[space left intentionally blank in the original book]

5. _____

[space left intentionally blank in the original book]

USING EXPOSURE RECORDS AND DIARIES

Keeping good records during exposure practices will help you to monitor your progress over time. The Exposure Monitoring Form at the end of this chapter is an example of a diary that can be used to record your experiences during exposure practices. In addition, this form is designed to help you challenge your anxious thoughts during exposure practices. Note that although the Exposure Monitoring Form may seem somewhat complex at first, with practice it will become easier to complete.

At the top of the form, you should describe the particular situation that you're practicing; the date, time, and duration of the practice; and your fear level before and after the practice (use a 0- to 100-point scale, where 0= no fear and 100= maximum fear). The middle part of the form is used for testing the validity of your fearful beliefs and predictions regarding the exposure practice. The first three columns are completed before the practice, and the last column is completed after the practice.

In the first column, record your emotional response to the upcoming practice (responses like fear or nervousness). The second and third columns are used for recording your fearful beliefs and predictions, as well as the evidence regarding the validity of these predictions. (Chapter 6 has many examples of possible fearful beliefs as well as instructions on how to evaluate the evidence concerning these thoughts.) After the practice is completed, record the outcome of the practice (what actually happened), any new evidence generated by the practice, and what you learned about the accuracy of your original anxiety-provoking thoughts and predictions.

In the lower part of the form, there is space to record your fear level periodically during the practice, using a scale ranging from 0 (no fear) to 100 (maximum fear). The frequency with which you record your fear ratings will depend on the duration of the practice. For example, ratings might be recorded every minute for a practice lasting ten minutes, or every thirty minutes for a practice lasting all day. There is space to provide up to twenty fear ratings during the practice, though you will probably not need that many. The last step is to plan for your next practice by answering the question, "Based on this experience, what exposure will I do next?"

A STEP-BY-STEP GUIDE TO CONDUCTING EXPOSURE TO SOCIAL SITUATIONS

A comprehensive exposure-based treatment should include the following steps:

- **Develop a situational exposure hierarchy.** Although the hierarchy should be used to guide your exposure practices, you can be flexible. For example, feel free to work on situations that are not on your hierarchy. In addition, you may decide to revise your hierarchy as particular situations become less anxiety-provoking.

- **Plan your exposure practices on a week-by-week basis.** At the start of each week, you should have a good idea of the types of practices that you will conduct over the coming week, as well as the dates and times you'll conduct these practices.

- **Develop a long-term exposure plan.** You should have an idea of the types of situations in which you are likely to conduct exposure practices over the coming months. Of course, this plan probably will change frequently, depending on the results of your practices each week.

- **Start with exposure to situations that are near the bottom or middle of your hierarchy.** If a situation is too difficult, try something easier. If a practice doesn't create anxiety, try something more difficult.

- **Gradually increase the difficulty level of practices.** As exposures to particular situations become easier, begin practicing exposure in situations that are more anxiety-provoking.

INTEGRATING SITUATIONAL EXPOSURE STRATEGIES INTO YOUR TREATMENT PLAN

Although exposure to feared situations is perhaps the most important technique for overcoming your fear, the exposure methods described in this chapter (and in chapter 7) are often most effective when they are used as part of a comprehensive treatment plan. In addition to situational exposure, your treatment should include the cognitive strategies described in chapter 6, which will help you to reinterpret your experiences during exposure to feared situations. As we reviewed earlier in this book, we recommend that you first practice the cognitive techniques for several weeks before formally beginning exposure practices.

Also, your treatment program may include medication (chapter 5), exposure to feared sensations (chapter 9), and social-skills practices (chapter 10), depending on your own personal needs and preferences. As you will see, these strategies are typically used in the context of your own situational exposure practices. Exposure is the foundation around which the other treatment strategies are introduced. (Table 8.4)

338

Table 8.4

Exposure Monitoring Form

Exposure Situation _____ Date and Time _____

Initial Fear Level (0–100) _____ Fear Level at End (0–100) _____ Duration of Exposure _____

COMPLETE BEFORE THE EXPOSURE PRACTICE		COMPLETE AFTER THE EXPOSURE PRACTICE
What emotions (e.g., fear, anger) do you have as you think about doing this exposure?	What anxiety-provoking thoughts, predictions, and assumptions do you have about the exposure? What do you expect will happen during the exposure practice?	What evidence do you have that your fearful thoughts are true?	1. What was the **outcome** of this practice? What actually happened? 2. What **evidence** did you gain from this practice? How accurate were your original thoughts and predictions?
			1. Outcome of Practice 2. Evidence Gained

Fear Ratings (0–100)

Provide occasional **fear ratings** (0–100) over the course of the exposure practice. For example, for a 20-minute exposure practice, record ratings every 5 minutes or so. For a 2-hour exposure practice, record ratings every 15 minutes or so. Space is provided for a total of 20 ratings over the course of the practice.

1. ____ 2. ____ 3. ____ 4. ____ 5. ____ 6. ____ 7. ____ 8. ____ 9. ____ 10. ____
11. ____ 12. ____ 13. ____ 14. ____ 15. ____ 16. ____ 17. ____ 18. ____ 19. ____ 20. ____

Based on this experience, what exposure practice will you complete next? _____

© 2000 Peter J. Bieling, Ph.D., and Martin M. Antony, Ph.D. Reprinted with permission.

CHAPTER 9

Exposure to Uncomfortable Sensations

Symptom exposure (also called *interoceptive exposure*), involves intentional exposure to internal physical sensations, such as dizziness, racing heart, sweating, shaking, and blushing. This technique was originally developed as a treatment for an anxiety-based condition known as *panic disorder.* Panic disorder is a problem in which people experience sudden rushes of fear without any obvious trigger or cause. People with panic disorder tend to be very fearful of the physical sensations they experience during their panic attacks, and they often interpret these symptoms as a sign of imminent danger or threat (like an impending heart attack or a complete loss of control). Symptom exposure was developed to teach those with panic disorder to stop fearing the physical feelings associated with physical arousal and anxiety. With repeated exposure to these induced physical symptoms, people learn that these feelings are not dangerous, and they eventually become less frightened of their own internal feelings and sensations.

Anxiety over experiencing physical arousal symptoms is not unique to panic disorder. A number of studies

(Chambless and Gracely 1989; Taylor, Koch, and McNally 1992) have found that people with other anxiety-based problems are also often anxious about experiencing certain physical sensations. This includes people with social anxiety, where the fear may be strongest for sensations that might be visible to others, including blushing, sweating, shaking, and losing one's train of thought. Just as symptom exposure leads to reduced fear of sensations in people with panic disorder, it makes sense that deliberately exposing oneself to feared symptoms while in social situations might lead to decreased fear of sensations for people with high levels of social anxiety. By combining symptom exposure and situational expo-sure, you will learn that you can not only tolerate being in feared situations with your usual levels of physical arousal, but that you can tolerate the situation even when your feared physical sensations are particularly intense. By bringing on these sensations in a controlled and predicable way, you will learn to be less anxious about experiencing them in social situations.

Although there hasn't been much research on the use of symptom exposure in social anxiety, we have found that this technique is often helpful for those who suffer from excessive social and performance fears (Antony and Swinson 2000; Antony and Rowa 2008). The techniques described in this chapter are not meant to be used instead of the strategies described in earlier chapters. In fact, to overcome your social anxiety, the most important strategies are the cognitive techniques described in chapter 6 and the situational exposure strategies described in chapters 7 and 8. You should not attempt to use symptom exposure until you have practiced the strategies described in chapters 6 through 8 and are thoroughly familiar with them.

Furthermore, before attempting the symptom exposure techniques, you should be very familiar with the basic rules of exposure. As reviewed in chapter 7, exposure works best if it is practiced frequently, if each practice lasts long enough to show that your feared consequences don't come true, and if practices are predictable and under your control. In addition, the cognitive strategies described in chapter 6 should be used to combat anxious thinking before, during, and after your exposure practices. Finally, during your exposure practices, you should not use subtle avoidance techniques such as distraction, drug or alcohol use, or other safety behaviors (for example, wearing makeup to hide blushing).

INTRODUCTION TO SYMPTOM EXPOSURE

Symptom exposure involves using specific exercises to bring on physical sensations that make you uncomfortable or anxious. Initially, the exercises are practiced in "safe" situations, like your home. After you get used to the exercises, the next step is to try them in anxiety-provoking situations, such as immediately before entering a social or performance situation. Examples of symptom exposure exercises are listed here, along with the sensations they typically trigger (Antony et al. 2006; Antony and Swinson 2000). In addition to this list, there are many other possible exercises that can be used. For example, if you are afraid of a choking or gagging feeling in your throat, wearing a necktie or scarf may be a good way of creating this feeling for the purpose of exposure therapy. It's best to consider these exercises only as a partial list. At the end of the list, there is space for you to record additional exercises that might be useful for triggering symptoms that you fear. (Table 9.1 and 9.2)

Examples of Symptom Exposure Exercises and Typical Sensations Experienced

Symptom Exposure Exercise	Typical Sensations
Shake head from side to side (30 sec.)	Dizziness, faintness, lightheadedness
Spin around in a swivel chair (60 sec.)	Dizziness, faintness, lightheadedness
Hyperventilate (shallow breathing at a rate of about 100–120 breaths per min.; 60 sec.)	Breathlessness or smothering feelings, dizziness or lightheadedness, racing or pounding heart, feeling unreal, trembling or shaking, numbness or tingling sensations

Symptom Exposure Exercise	Typical Sensations
Breathe through a small, narrow straw (plug your nose if necessary; 2 min.)	Breathlessness or smothering feelings, racing or pounding heart, choking feelings, dizziness or lightheadedness, chest tightness, trembling or shaking
Tense all the muscles in the body (60 sec. or as long as possible)	Trembling or shaking, breathlessness or smothering feelings, racing or pounding heart, dizziness or lightheadedness, blushing
Carry heavy weights or bags (60 sec. or as long as possible)	Trembling or shaking, breathlessness or smothering feelings, racing or pounding heart, dizziness or lightheadedness, hot flushes
Run on the spot or run up and down stairs (60 sec.)	Racing or pounding heart, breathlessness or smothering feelings, chest tightness, sweating, trembling or shaking, blushing
Sit in a hot, stuffy space (for example, a sauna, hot car, or small room with a space heater; 5 to 10 min.) or wear overly warm clothing	Sweating, breathlessness or smothering feelings, hot flushes, blushing
Have a hot drink or hot soup	Sweating, blushing, hot flushes

Table 9.1

Other Exercises to Trigger Sensations I Fear

Exercise   Symptoms

_____   _____

_____   _____

_____   _____

_____   _____

_____   _____

Table 9.2

IS SYMPTOM EXPOSURE FOR YOU?

Although symptom exposure is likely to be helpful for many who suffer from social anxiety, it's usually possible to reduce social anxiety without this particular strategy. In fact, for some people, there may be little reason to use these exercises at all. Symptom exposure is likely to be helpful to you if either of the following statements is true:

- You are generally afraid of experiencing anxiety symptoms such as a rapidly beating heart, dizziness, shaking, blushing, or sweating.

- You are afraid of experiencing anxiety symptoms in front of other people.

If you're fearful of experiencing physical arousal feelings in general or when in social or performance situations, we recommend trying the exercises described in this chapter. However, if you are not fearful of the sensations that you experience when anxious, and you are not concerned about others noticing your anxiety symptoms, then there is no need to practice these exercises. In fact, you can skip ahead to chapter 10.

HOW DOES SYMPTOM EXPOSURE WORK?

Like situational exposure, symptom exposure is believed to decrease fear by disproving a person's fearful beliefs, assumptions, and predictions. By deliberately bringing on uncomfortable feelings in a controlled and predictable way, you will learn that (1) you can control the sensations that normally appear to be uncontrollable and (2) even if you do experience noticeable physical feelings in front of other people, the consequences are likely to be minimal.

By learning to allow yourself to be anxious in front of other people, and to allow others to observe your anxiety symptoms, eventually you will become less concerned about your anxiety reactions and about what people think when they notice your shaking, sweating, blushing, or other signs of anxiety. By becoming less concerned about experiencing these feelings, you will probably become less anxious when exposed to social and performance situations.

A WARNING ABOUT SYMPTOM EXPOSURE

If you are healthy, the exercises described in this chapter are safe. However, if you have certain health problems, some of the exercises could worsen your condition. For example, if you have asthma or a bad cold, you should probably not practice hyperventilation or breathing through a straw. If you experience neck or back pain, we recommend against shaking your head from side to side or engaging in any exercises that could aggravate your condition. To be safe, we recommend checking with your doctor to see if any of these exercises are likely to be dangerous or problematic for you.

A STEP-BY-STEP GUIDE TO SYMPTOM EXPOSURE

This section describes the four main steps involved in using symptom exposure to overcome the fear of experiencing physical arousal sensations. These include (1) discovering which exercises are most effective for bringing on feared symptoms, (2) developing a symptom exposure hierarchy, (3) practicing the exercises in nonsocial situations, and (4) combining the symptom exposure exercises with exposure practices in social situations.

Step 1: Symptom Induction Testing

Before beginning to practice symptom exposure exercises on a regular basis, you should first determine which exercises are most likely to be effective for you. This can be achieved by attempting each exercise at home and paying attention to the types of symptoms that you experience, the effect of the exercises on your fear level, and how similar the experience is to the fear that you normally experience in social situations. The following Symptom Induction Testing Form can be used to record your responses to each exercise. We have included space for additional exercises that you may have identified earlier in the chapter.

Symptom Induction Testing Form
Instructions: After trying each symptom exposure exercise, (1) record the physical sensations that were experienced and (2) rate the intensity of fear experienced using a scale of 0 (no fear) to 100 (maximum fear). (Table 9.3)

Exercise	Sensations Experienced	Fear (0–100)
Shake head from side to side (30 sec.)		
Spin around in a swivel chair (60 sec.)		
Hyperventilate (shallow breathing at a rate of about 100–120 breaths per min.; 60 sec.)		
Breathe through a small, narrow straw (plug your nose if necessary; 2 min.)		

348

Exercise	Sensations Experienced	Fear (0–100)
Tense all the muscles in the body (60 sec. or as long as possible)		
Carry heavy weights or bags (60 sec. or as long as possible)		
Run on the spot or run up and down stairs (60 sec.)		
Sit in a hot, stuffy space (for example, a sauna, hot car, or small room with a space heater; 5 to 10 min.) or wear overly warm clothing		
Have a hot drink or hot soup		
Other Exercise		
Other Exercise		

Table 9.3

Step 2: Developing Symptom Exposure Hierarchies

Just as the situational exposure hierarchy described in chapter 8 is used to guide your situational exposure practices, *symptom exposure hierarchies* are useful for choosing appropriate symptom exposure exercises. In most cases, we recommend that you develop two symptom exposure hierarchies: one for practicing the exercises outside of social situations (see step 3) and a second hierarchy for practicing symptom exposure while in (or immediately before entering) social or performance situations (see step 4). If you are not at all fearful of experiencing anxiety sensations outside of social situations, then developing a hierarchy for practicing symptom exposure in nonsocial situations is less important. Instead, you should focus on exercises to practice while exposed to social and performance situations.

To develop a hierarchy for symptom exposure, first eliminate any exercises that you know will not make you anxious (based on the results of your symptom induction testing, completed in step 1). For example, if the sensations created by physical exercise (something like jogging) are not frightening to you at all, eliminate this exercise from your list. Next, take the remaining exercises and put them in order of difficulty, with the least anxiety-provoking exercise at the bottom and the most anxiety-provoking item at the top. Record your level of expected fear for each exercise, using a scale ranging from 0 (no fear) to 100 (maximum fear). Examples of symptom exposure hierarchies reflecting practices outside of social situations and practices in social situations follow. We have also included space to record your own hierarchies. (Table 9.4, 9.5, 9.6 and 9.7)

Sample Symptom Exposure Hierarchy for Practices in Nonsocial Situations

Exercise	Fear Rating (0–100)
1. Hyperventilate at home alone (1 minute).	60
2. Breathe through a straw at home alone (2 minutes).	45
3. Spin in a chair at home alone (1 minute).	35

Exercise	Fear Rating (0–100)
4. Shake head from side to side at home alone (30 seconds).	30

Table 9.4

My Symptom Exposure Hierarchy for Practices in Nonsocial Situations Exercise

Exercise	Fear Rating (0–100)
1. _____	_____
2. _____	_____
3. _____	_____
4. _____	_____
5. _____	_____
6. _____	_____
7. _____	_____
8. _____	_____
9. _____	_____
10. _____	_____

Table 9.5

Sample Symptom Exposure Hierarchy for Practices in Social Situations Exercise

Exercise	Fear Rating (0–100)
1. Hold a heavy bag for 60 seconds immediately before holding a filled glass in front of others (to induce shaky hands).	100
2. Breathe through a straw for 2 minutes immediately before entering a cocktail party and making small talk.	80
3. Wear a warm sweater while giving a presentation.	80

Exercise	Fear Rating (0–100)
4. Eat hot soup to induce flushing and sweating at a dinner party.	60
5. Run around the block before entering a party.	40
6. Hyperventilate just before calling someone on the telephone.	35

Table 9.6

My Symptom Exposure Hierarchy for Practices in Social Situations

Exercise	Fear Rating (0–100)
1. _____	_____
2. _____	_____
3. _____	_____
4. _____	_____
5. _____	_____
6. _____	_____
7. _____	_____
8. _____	_____
9. _____	_____
10. _____	_____

Table 9.7

Step 3: Practicing Symptom Exposure in Nonsocial Situations

If you are not fearful of practicing the symptom exposure exercises in nonsocial situations, it is not necessary to spend a lot of time on step 3. However, if there are exercises that you intend to practice in social situations (step 4), we recommend that you first try them a few times in nonsocial situations to make sure that you are familiar with the exercise.

If there are exercises that are anxiety-provoking for you in nonsocial situations, we recommend that you practice them repeatedly at home or in another comfortable location place before practicing in social situations. Use your symptom exposure hierarchy for nonsocial situations to help you choose which exercises to practice. Begin with exercises that are challenging but unlikely to be so overwhelming that you cannot complete them. After you have chosen an exercise, set aside about fifteen minutes twice a day to practice the exercise repeatedly. After each repetition of the exercise, take a short break (from thirty seconds to a few minutes) until the symptoms decrease. Continue to practice the exercise another five or six times or until your fear has decreased. Later in this chapter, you will find a diary you can use to record the results of each practice and to challenge any anxiety-provoking thoughts that arise during the practice.

Each time you complete an exercise, you will experience the physical symptoms associated with it. However, your fear of the symptoms should decrease across individual practices and across days. For example, if you are practicing hyperventilation, you will likely continue to become hot and lightheaded each time you do the exercise. However, over time, these feelings should become less frightening.

Step 4: Practicing Symptom Exposure in Social Situations

After you have practiced situational exposure (chapter 8) and symptom exposure in nonsocial situations, the next step is to combine these two approaches. Combining symptom and situational exposure is one of the most challenging types of exposure that you can practice. However, this type of exposure can also provide you with the strongest possible evidence that your anxious predictions are exaggerated or untrue. By entering the social and performance situations that you fear and purposefully inducing arousal sensations to enhance your fear, you will learn that these situations are manageable even when you feel extremely uncomfortable. To select possible exercises for combining symptom and situational exposure, refer back to your symptom exposure hierarchy for practices in social situations (step 2).

INTEGRATING SYMPTOM EXPOSURE INTO YOUR TREATMENT PLAN

As discussed earlier, we recommend that your psychological treatment program (cognitive behavioral ther-

354

apy) begin with the cognitive strategies discussed in chapter 6. After practicing the cognitive techniques for several weeks, you should practice situational exposure for several more weeks or months until you feel more comfortable in social situations (chapters 7 and 8). Only then should you consider adding symptom exposure if you are still fearful of experiencing anxiety symptoms in front of others. As your fear continues to decrease through exposure and cognitive therapy, you may also consider working on your social and communication skills (chapter 10).

USING SYMPTOM EXPOSURE RECORDS AND DIARIES

Keeping good records during symptom exposure practices will help you to monitor your progress over time. The Symptom Exposure Diary at the end of this chapter will help you to measure changes in your fear across symptom exposure practices. Furthermore, this diary is designed to help you challenge your anxious thoughts during exposure practices. The first column indicates the trial number (1, 2, 3, and so on). In the second column, you should record the specific sensations that you experience. In the third column, record your fear level during each exercise trial. Finally, the fourth and fifth columns are for recording your anxious thoughts during the exercise and for countering your thoughts with more realistic beliefs.

TROUBLESHOOTING

Problem: The symptom exposure exercises don't frighten me.

Solution: If the exercises don't cause anxiety when you practice them in nonsocial situations, try practicing them immediately before entering social situations. If they still don't increase your fear, then discontinue the symptom exposure exercises. However, you should continue to use the cognitive strategies (chapter 6) and the situational exposure exercises (chapters 7 and 8).

Problem: The symptom exposure exercises are too overwhelming for me to complete.

Solution: If a symptom exposure exercise is too overwhelming, even when conducted in a nonsocial situation, try an easier exercise from your hierarchy and don't move on to the more difficult exercises until the easier ones become manageable. If you find that a symptom exposure exercise is overwhelming only when practiced in the context of a social or performance situation, you can practice an easier exercise from your symptom exposure hierarchy and work your way up to the more difficult exercises. Or, you can continue to practice situational exposure without the symptom exposure exercises. Hold off on introducing symptom exposure practices in social situations until you are able to manage the situation on its own (without symptom exposure).

Symptom Exposure Diary

Instructions: This form should be completed each time you practice symptom exposure. For each symptom exposure trial: (1) list the physical symptoms that you experienced; (2) rate the intensity of your fear using a scale of 0 (no fear) to 100 (maximum fear); (3) list your specific anxious predictions regarding the exercise (What might happen during the exercise?); and (4) list alternative nonanxious predictions and evidence supporting these nonanxious predictions (countering).

Exposure Exercise _____

Date and Time _____ (Table 9.8)

Symptom Exposure Diary

Instructions: This form should be completed each time you practice symptom exposure. For each symptom exposure trial: (1) list the physical symptoms that you experienced; (2) rate the intensity of your fear using a scale of 0 (no fear) to 100 (maximum fear); (3) list your specific anxious predictions regarding the exercise (What might happen during the exercise?); and (4) list alternative nonanxious predictions and evidence supporting these nonanxious predictions (countering).

Exposure Exercise _____

Date and Time _____

Trial #	Sensations Experienced	Fear	Anxiety-Provoking Thoughts and Predictions	Countering
1				
2				
3				
4				
5				
6				
7				

Table 9.8

Adapted from Antony, M.M., and R. P. Swinson. 2000. *Phobic Disorders and Panic in Adults: A Guide to Assessment and Treatment.* Washington, DC: American Psychological Association. Used with permission.

CHAPTER 10

Communicating More Effectively

Are there times when your behavior communicates to others a message that's different from what you are trying to communicate? Do you freeze up in interviews? Do you tend to avoid eye contact when talking to other people? Does your body language tell others to *stay away?* Do you read your presentations verbatim so you don't make any mistakes? Do others often feel as though you aren't listening to them? Do people misinterpret your shyness as a sign of aloofness or a snobby attitude? This chapter is all about how to communicate effectively and to get your message across in the way you intend.

GETTING YOUR MESSAGE ACROSS

For some people, a consequence of avoiding social situations is never having the opportunity to master the communication skills that would help them deal effectively with others. For example, if your fear has stopped you from applying for jobs or asking people out on dates, you may not always know how to best deal with these situations (what to say, what to wear, how to behave, and so on). The ability to interact effectively with other people must be learned and it takes practice, just like learning to play the piano or training to run a marathon. As you get more experience being in the situations you avoid, and learning what works and what doesn't, your performance is likely to improve. This chapter provides ideas for enhancing the quality of your interactions with other people. Most of these strategies can be used during the course of your situational exposure practices (chapters 7 and 8).

As you read this chapter, there are a few important points to keep in mind. First, our purpose in writing this chapter is not to suggest that you lack social skills. In fact, most people we have worked with who have problems with social anxiety have fine social skills overall. If anything, your social and communication skills are probably already much better than you think they are. Rather, our aim is to help you increase your awareness of the different ways in which your behavior may impact others and to change specific behaviors where appropriate.

You should also bear in mind that there is no such thing as perfect social skills. What works best in one situation or with one group of people may not work well in another situation or with another group. For example, the best way to ask one person out on a date may cause a rejection from someone else. Although a particular style may help you get one job, it may work against you for another job or with another interviewer. In other words, no matter how well-developed your social skills are, they can never be perfect. Like everyone, you will continue to stumble from time to time and occasionally you will make a bad impression on other people.

Finally, the strategies described in this chapter should not be thought of as rules to be followed by everyone. Rather, they are suggestions and guidelines that you may find helpful in some situations. For example, we suggest that certain types of body language (for example, standing too far away from another person during a conversation) may be interpreted as a sign of aloofness or that you are uninterested in talking. However, standing too close also may cause other people to feel uncomfortable. Unfortunately, it's very difficult to determine the ideal amount of "personal space." What works well with one person may not work as well with another. Personal space preferences also vary across ethnic groups and subcultures. That is, among some groups, standing quite close to the person with whom you're speaking is the norm. But in another group that norm might cause great discomfort. Given that it is often difficult to know how to behave in a particular situation, it's best not to get too caught up in whether you are using these strategies perfectly or whether you're making a perfect impression on others.

Examples of communication skills discussed in this chapter are provided here. As you read through the list, pay attention to the specific skills you are interested in improving. (Table 10.1)

Skill	Examples
Listening skills	• Listening carefully to others when they are speaking, instead of comparing yourself to the other person, ruminating about what you will say next, and so on
Nonverbal communication skills	• Making appropriate eye contact when talking to other people
	• Attending to body language
	• Standing at an appropriately close distance to other people during conversations
	• Smiling appropriately
	• Speaking with a confident tone and a volume level that others can hear
Conversation skills	• Starting and stopping conversations
	• Keeping conversations flowing
	• Not putting yourself down in front of others
	• Not apologizing unnecessarily
	• Disclosing information about yourself when appropriate
Interview skills	• Preparing for interviews
	• Deciding what to wear
	• Anticipating the interviewer's questions
	• Preparing questions to ask
	• What to do after the interview is over
Assertiveness skills	• Communicating assertively rather than in a way that is either too passive or too aggressive; asking for what you want

Skill	Examples
	• Dealing with conflict, particularly with people with whom you disagree or who might be angry or hostile toward you
	• Learning the difference between imposing on others' time and privacy vs. making a reasonable request for help or social contact
Skills for meeting new people and dating	•Basic manners
	• Finding people to date
	• Asking someone to lunch or dinner
	• Generating conversation topics
	• Ending a date gracefully
	• Dealing with rejection
Public speaking and presentation skills	• Engaging the audience
	• Designing slides and other audiovisual aids
	• Organizing your talk
	• Handling questions from the audience

Table 10.1

Of course, it is impossible to thoroughly cover all of these topics in a single chapter. Indeed, numerous books have been written on each of these particular domains (presentations, interviews, dating, assertiveness, listening, and so on). For more detailed suggestions, consult some of the recommended readings cited throughout this chapter and in the list of additional recommended readings at the back of the book. In addition, there are a number of good books that cover a wide range of topics related to social and communication skills. Some examples include *Messages: The Communication Skills Book* (McKay, Davis, and Fanning 1995), *The Messages Workbook: Powerful Strategies for Effective Communication at Work & Home* (Davis, Paleg, and Fanning 2004), and Robert Bolton's classic book, *People Skills* (1979).

Finally, you may want to check out a website that uses video to demonstrate how to do a wide range of things—everything from sewing to cooking to magic tricks. The site is www.videojug.com. In addition to being a great place to learn all sorts of interesting skills, the site includes video demonstrations of various social behaviors, including making a good first impression, dating, hugging, kissing, complaining appropriately, looking approachable, and even how to give a great handshake! Just search for the behavior you want to see.

LEARNING TO LISTEN

Communication is a two-way street. Listening effectively when you are in a conversation, being interviewed, or participating in a meeting is as important as what you say. When you feel anxious, your attention tends to shift from the situation itself to your own experiences in the situation. In other words, you become aware of how you're feeling, and you begin to wonder whether your anxiety symptoms are noticeable to the other people in the room and whether those people are judging you negatively. At the same time, you become less aware of other aspects of the situation, including what other people are saying. This lack of concentration on what others are saying may reinforce your uncertainty about whether your responses are appropriate. Often, even when you think you are listening, you may be only partially aware of what is being said.

There are several costs to not listening. First, you may miss important information that the other person is trying to communicate. You may hear only the parts of the message that are consistent with your anxious beliefs, thereby increasing your anxiety. For example, if you hear only your boss' negative comments and miss his or her praise during a performance evaluation, you will undoubtedly feel worse than if you had heard the entire evaluation. Not hearing the entire message also may lead you to respond inappropriately, sometimes to something completely different than what was actually said. Furthermore, the other person may sense that you are not listening to what is being said. As a result, you may be perceived by that person as aloof, distracted, or bored by the conversation.

Blocks to Effective Listening

In *Messages: The Communication Skills Book,* authors McKay, Davis, and Fanning list a number of different factors that frequently interfere with our ability to listen to others during conversations, meetings, arguments, and other types of social interactions. Of these, five are especially common when people feel anxious in a social situation. These listening blocks include the following:

- **Comparing yourself to the other person.** We all compare ourselves to others as a way to evaluate our own behavior and accomplishments. However, excessive social anxiety may be associated with the tendency to do this more often, to make unfavorable comparisons (for instance, comparisons with those who are more successful on a particular dimension), and to feel bad after making such comparisons. This tendency to make negative comparisons while conversing (for example, criticizing yourself with unspoken comments such as, "I'm not as smart as he is" or "She is more attractive than I am") interferes with your ability to listen to and hear what is being said.

- **Filtering what the other person says.** Filtering involves listening only to certain parts of what the other person is saying. In social anxiety, this can involve paying attention only to those parts of the conversation that seem to indicate that the other person is being critical or judgmental.

- **Rehearsing what to say next.** When people are overly concerned about saying the right thing during conversations or meetings, they often rehearse mentally how they will respond to other people's comments rather than truly listening to what is being said. Although you may engage in rehearsal to make sure you say the right thing, this practice, if used too often, may have the opposite effect.

- **Derailing the conversation.** Derailing involves switching the topic of conversation when it becomes either boring or uncomfortable. In social anxiety, derailing may take place when the conversation moves into anxiety-provoking areas. For example, if a coworker asks you about your weekend and you are embarrassed to admit that you stayed home alone all weekend, you might shift the conversation back to a work-related topic, rather than disclose what you perceive to be overly personal information. Derailing can make the other person feel as though you are not listening or are not interested in the conversation.

- **Placating the other person.** Placating involves agreeing with the other person regardless of what he or she says in an effort to avoid potential conflict. Because social anxiety is associated with a fear of being disliked or negatively judged, people who are socially anxious often go out of their way to agree with others. However, most people don't expect to have others agree with them all the time. If you always agree with whatever is said, it may raise the other person's suspicions about whether you're really listening.

Improving Your Listening Skills

The authors of *Messages* provide a number of suggestions for improving listening skills. First, they suggest that effective listening should involve active participation rather than just sitting quietly and absorbing the information. Active listening involves maintaining appropriate eye contact, paraphrasing what the person has said ("So, in other words, what you are saying is..."), asking for clarification (asking questions to help you understand what was said), and providing the other person with feedback (or your reactions to what he or she said). Whenever possible, feedback should be immediate (as soon as you understand the communication), honest (reflecting your true feelings), and supportive (in other words, gentle and unlikely to be hurtful to the other person).

In addition, it's important to listen with *empathy.* Being empathic means conveying the idea that you genuinely understand the other person's message as well as the feelings he or she is experiencing. As discussed in chapter 6, there are many different ways of interpreting a given situation. By trying to understand another person's perspective, you will be better able to listen and to communicate that fact. Note that it is not necessary for you to agree with the other person's perspective—just to understand it. However, even when someone says something that you believe to be completely incorrect, you probably can identify at least a small part of the message that is true. Letting the person know that you understand his or her perspective conveys empathy, even if you don't agree with the overall content of what was said.

Finally, effective listening requires listening with openness and awareness. *Openness* involves listening without trying to find fault. *Awareness* involves (1) being aware of how a communication fits in with your own knowledge and experiences, and (2) being aware of any inconsistencies in the verbal message itself and the nonverbal aspects of the communication, such as tone, posture, and facial expressions.

Exercise: Effective Listening

The next time you're in a conversation, try some of the effective listening skills described above:

1. Make eye contact during the conversation.

2. Paraphrase what the other person says, and ask for clarification if you're unsure about any aspect of the communication.

3. Give feedback when appropriate, making sure that your feedback is immediate, honest, and supportive.

4. Finally, make sure that you are listening with empathy, openness, and awareness.

After trying this exercise in a real-life situation, come back to this chapter and list on the lines below any ways in which the experience was different from your usual conversations. Did the conversation last longer? Was it more gratifying? Did the other person respond differently to you? Did you experience less anxiety than usual?

[space left intentionally blank in the original book]

NONVERBAL COMMUNICATION

When you feel anxious in a social situation, you probably engage in behaviors designed to subtly avoid communicating with others. These may include avoiding eye contact, speaking very quietly, or even avoiding the situation completely. Despite your efforts to avoid communication, however, it's virtually impossible *not* to communicate. In fact, what you actually say in words during a conversation makes up a very small component of the messages you communicate to others. Nonverbal aspects of communication, including your physical distance from others, eye contact, posture, tone of voice, and vocal volume communicate at least as much information as your verbal messages. In fact, even when you completely stay away from a feared social situation, you communicate a message to others. For example, if you repeatedly avoid meetings at work, others may assume that you are shy, uninterested, or even unfriendly.

Despite wanting others to respond positively, people who are shy or socially anxious often exhibit nonverbal behaviors that communicate to others, "Stay away from me." Examples of these closed nonverbal behaviors include leaning back or standing far away from other people, avoiding eye contact, speaking quietly, crossing your arms over your chest, clenching your fists, and maintaining a serious facial expression. Although you may believe that these behaviors serve as a form of protection in anxiety-provoking situations, they tend to have the opposite effect.

Instead of protecting you from potential threat or from being judged by others, these behaviors probably increase the likelihood that others will react negatively. For example, at a party, people are most likely to approach someone who is smiling, making eye contact, and talking at a reasonable volume. When someone stands far away, speaks quietly, and avoids eye contact, it is natural to assume that the individual is either uninterested in speaking or difficult to get to know.

Of course, moderation is the key here. Too much eye contact can make others uncomfortable. In addition, someone who stands too close or smiles at inappropriate times may make others feel uneasy. Unfortunately, it is impossible to specify the appropriate intensity for each of these behaviors because so many variables play a role. What is appropriate in one situation is not necessarily appropriate in another. For example, although it's okay to stand several inches away from a romantic partner during an intimate conversation, you probably would want to stand farther back when talking to a coworker. With respect to nonverbal communication, there are differences across gender and across cultures. Therefore, we suggest that you experiment with using different nonverbal behaviors to find out what works best for you in the particular situations that you encounter from day to day.

Closed nonverbal behaviors are behaviors that close the channels of communication by sending the message that the opportunity for contact or communication with you is unavailable. Below is a list of closed nonverbal behaviors often associated with social anxiety:

- Leaning back while sitting (vs. leaning forward)

- Standing far away from another person (vs. standing closer)

- Avoiding eye contact (vs. making appropriate eye contact)

- Speaking quietly (vs. speaking at a volume that is easily heard)

- Crossing arms (vs. keeping arms uncrossed or making hand gestures)

- Clenching fists (vs. keeping hands open)

- Maintaining a serious facial expression (vs. smiling warmly)

- Speaking with a timid tone (vs. speaking with a confident tone)

- Sitting hunched over (vs. sitting up straight)

Exercise: Open Behaviors

Do you tend to overuse any of these behaviors? If so, try to replace some of your closed behaviors with open behaviors during the course of your exposure practices over the next week. Record your experiences in the provided space. For example, record whether people react differently to you when you smile more, make eye contact, or speak more loudly.

[space left intentionally blank in the original book]

CONVERSATIONAL SKILLS

Do you often struggle to find things to say when making casual conversation or small talk? Do you keep quiet at parties or meetings because you find it difficult to contribute to conversations? When you do get involved in a conversation, perhaps you find that the discussion fizzles quickly, as you and the other person run out of things to say. In this section, we discuss ways of starting and ending conversations, as well as methods of improving the quality of your conversations. These suggestions may be adapted for different types of conversations, including talking to a coworker or classmate, conversing on a date, or speaking with a stranger while waiting in line.

Keep in mind that the suggestions in this section are not always going to work smoothly. For example, if you start talking to someone in an elevator, the person may respond positively or may frown and ignore you. If an individual responds negatively when you try to make contact, remember that it's not necessarily because you did something wrong. The other person may be shy or may be concerned about his or her safety (having been raised never to talk to strangers). Also, it's possible that your communication will be misunderstood. If things don't work out during a particular practice, try to understand why and to figure out what you can do differently next time. Learning from your experiences will help you to plan future practices that are more likely to work out satisfactorily.

Finally, if you want to learn more about making conversation, we recommend that you read the third edition of Alan Garner's book, *Conversationally Speaking: Testing New Ways to Increase Your Personal and Social Effectiveness* (1997). Another excellent book on improving conversation skills is *Talk to Me: Conversation Tips for the Small-Talk Challenged* (Honeychurch and Watrous 2003).

Starting a Conversation

Although getting a conversation started is sometimes difficult, it often becomes easier with practice. Opportunities to start conversations are everywhere. For example, people often speak to strangers in grocery store lines and elevators, or on buses, subways, airplanes, and in other public places. People talk to others at parties, weddings, funerals, and work functions. If you are at a party, it is perfectly appropriate to walk up to a group of people who are already talking. After a minute or two of standing around with the group, you can join in the conversation. If you are a college student, you can increase your opportunities for casual conversation by always sitting in the same area of the classroom so you'll have repeated exposure to some of the same students each time. Also, arrive to class early so you can chat with others before class starts.

The topic of conversation should usually begin with something friendly and not too personal, particularly if you don't know the other individual very well. You may begin with a question (something like, "How was your weekend?"), a compliment ("I like your new haircut"), an observation (perhaps, "I notice that you're not driving your usual car"), or an introduction ("I don't believe we've met. My name is..."). Other appropriate topics include: hobbies, your job, a movie or TV show you recently saw, the weather, something you recently read, your vacation, a recent shopping trip or outing, and sports. After you've been talking for a while, it may be appropriate to discuss more controversial topics, such as politics, relationships, personal feelings, difficult family situations, and topics related to sexuality. However, you should introduce topics such as these slowly, and gauge the other person's reactions before deciding how far to take the conversation. Try to avoid getting too personal, unless you know the other person well or the other person is disclosing similar types of personal information. At a party or on a first date, it's fine to talk about your work or what your parents do for a living, but it is usually best to stay clear of weighty topics (like a past sexual assault, a recent history of depression, and so on).

Improving the Quality of Your Conversations

Here are a few tips for improving your conversations:

- **Conversations are a two-way street.** It's not enough to just listen to another person. Nor is it appropriate to talk only about yourself without giving the other person a chance to speak. Of course, there are exceptions. There are some people who are very happy to have you do all the talking or allow them to do all the talking. However, for most of us, a conversation is far more interesting if we have the opportunity to express our own thoughts, feelings, and experiences and also the chance to listen to another person's views and experiences.

- **Use active listening skills.** The active listening skills described earlier in the chapter will enhance the quality of your conversations. In particular, be sure to reflect back that you are understanding what the other person is saying.

- **Disclose some (but not too much) information about yourself.** As mentioned earlier, the information you disclose should not be overly personal at first. Instead, you can start by talking about your weekend's activities, your favorite sports team, a movie you recently saw, or a class that you're taking, for example.

- **Show interest in the other person.** For instance, follow up what the other person says by asking for clarification or requesting more details.

- **Try a light touch.** In some situations, it may be appropriate to touch the other individual (for example, a light touch on the arm). However, only use touch if it can be done naturally, in a way that doesn't seem overly forced. Note that the appropriate use of touch varies between men and women and across cultures. It may also be frowned on in professional settings.

- **Pay attention to detail.** When telling stories, take your cues from others when trying to decide how much detail to include. See how detailed others are in their conversations, and model your own conversations after them. If you notice that others are starting to look bored or look at their watches while you tell a story, take that as a sign that it's time to wrap it up. On the other hand, make sure your conversation is not completely devoid of details. Either too much detail or not enough detail can make a conversation less engaging.

- **Give and receive compliments.** When complimenting others, make sure you are honest (don't say you like something if you don't), and don't overdo it. Although it's nice to receive a compliment from time to time, it can be uncomfortable to receive too many compliments or to receive compliments that are felt to be undeserved. If you receive a compliment from someone else, simply say thank you. Don't discount the compliment or make the other person feel bad for giving it.

- **Pay attention to your nonverbal behaviors.** For example, make eye contact and speak so the other person can hear you.

Asking Questions

Asking the other person questions will communicate that you are interested in what he or she has to say. You can ask about your conversation partner's experiences (for example, "How was that restaurant you went to last night?") or you can ask for the other person's reaction to something you've said. If possible, try to use open-ended questions rather than closed-ended questions. A *closed-ended question* is one that elicits a response of only one or two words. For example, the closed-ended question "Did you like the movie?" could easily lead to responses like "Yes" or "No," at which point you would be back at square one, trying to find another topic of conversation. Closed-ended questions usually begin with words like "are," "do," "who," "when," "where," and "which."

In contrast, *open-ended questions* usually can elicit more detailed answers. Open-ended questions are more likely than closed-ended questions to generate longer and more interesting conversations. These types of question usually begin with words or phrases like "how," "why," and "in what way." For example, the question "What did you think about the movie?" draws out a more thorough response than "Did you like the movie?"

Here are some examples of closed-ended and open-ended questions: (Table 10.2)

Closed-Ended Questions	Open-Ended Questions
Did you have a good weekend?	What did you do this weekend?
Who is your favorite candidate?	What do you like about the different candidates?
What do you do for a living?	How did you get into your current line of work?

Closed-Ended Questions	Open-Ended Questions
Do you like your psychology professor?	Why do you like your psychology professor?

Table 10.2

Note that a question can be too open-ended, so that it is responded to as if it were a closed-ended question. For example, questions like "How are you?" or "How was your day?" typically lead to a one-word response such as "Fine."

Ending Conversations

All conversations eventually come to an end. Furthermore, in informal social situations (at a party, on a date, on the phone), conversations almost always end because one or both people lose interest in what is being talked about or they reach a point at which they would rather be doing something else or talking to someone else.

If you are especially sensitive to rejection, you may become more anxious as a conversation nears its end. Or you may be hurt if you think that the other person seems less interested in continuing to converse. Nevertheless, if you begin to pay attention to other people's conversations, you will notice that all discussions reach a point at which there is little more to be said. Sometimes this point is reached in a few seconds. Other times, it may take a few minutes or even an hour for a particularly interesting conversation to end.

Running out of things to talk about is not a failure and does not mean that you are boring. It is a normal feature of all conversations.

Typically, people try to find graceful ways to get out of conversations that have run their course. At a party, you might excuse yourself to refill your drink or visit the bathroom. Or, it may be appropriate to mention politely that you need to catch up with another person at the party. In a work setting, people often end the conversation with a reference to work (for instance, "Well, I need to get back to work") or a pledge to continue the conversation later ("Perhaps we can have lunch together some time soon"). Often, simply saying something like, "It's been nice talking to you, but I need to run" is sufficient. If you have enjoyed the conversation, be sure to let your conversation partner know that ("I've really enjoyed talking to you. I hope we get a chance to talk again").

Exercise: Conversations

Try using some of these conversational strategies the next time you're having a conversation. If you rarely encounter situations that allow for conversation, you may need to go out of your way to seek out such situations. During the practice, pay special attention to using the strategies for starting the conversation, improving the quality of the conversation, and ending the conversation. In the spaces below, record your experiences after using the relevant strategies for each phase of the conversation.

Starting the conversation:

[space left intentionally blank in the original book]

Improving the quality of the conversation:

[space left intentionally blank in the original book]

Ending the conversation:

[space left intentionally blank in the original book]

JOB INTERVIEWS

Most people feel somewhat nervous when being interviewed for a job. In fact, showing no signs of anxiety could work against you in some interview situations. Not showing any signs of anxiety during an interview might be interpreted by the interviewer as a sign that you are overconfident or disinterested. But if you're particularly anxious in social situations, interviews may be even more anxiety-provoking for you than they are for the average person. Chapter 6 reviewed strategies for changing the beliefs that contribute to your anxiety in situations such as interviews. Chapters

7 and 8 recommended practicing exposure to interviews (using both real interview practices and role-play simulations) as a strategy for learning to become less anxious. In this section, we provide additional suggestions for improving interview skills. These suggestions are meant to be used along with the cognitive and exposure-based techniques discussed in earlier chapters.

Essentially, being prepared for an interview involves knowing what to do before the interview, how to behave during the interview, and what to do when the interview is over. We provide suggestions for each of these interview phases. For a more detailed discussion of this topic, we suggest reading *Messages: The Communication Skills Book.* There are several other excellent resources on interviewing for jobs listed in the recommended readings section at the end of this book.

Preparing for the Interview

Here are some suggestions for preparing for an interview. These are all things to do before you get there:

- Before the interview, practice interviewing with friends and family members. Also, practice interviewing for other jobs that are of less interest to you. As we discussed in chapters 7 and 8, practicing being interviewed will help to decrease your anxiety when you are in the actual situation.

- Keep the situation in perspective. Remember that it's only an interview. If it doesn't work out, there will be other opportunities. Think of the interview as a learning experience or an opportunity to improve your interviewing skills.

- Take time to understand the purpose of the interview, learn who will be interviewing you, what the structure of the interview will be, and how long the interview will run. If possible, find out the interviewer's name and make sure you remember it. If that's not possible, when the interviewer introduces himself or herself to you, pay attention and try to use the name when you say good-bye.

- Learn as much as possible about the organization or company and about the person who is interviewing you. If the organization has a website, make sure you study it carefully. You may even be able to learn about your interviewer beforehand. Being knowledgeable about the organization during the interview will show that you really are interested in the position.

- Take some time to identify your strengths and have a good idea of what you can contribute to the organization, in case you're asked. You may want to take some notes with you to prevent forgetting something that you want to mention.

- Plan a response in case you are asked about your weaknesses or limitations. There is no need to list every flaw that comes into your mind. Instead, you can mention one or two limitations, phrasing them in such a way that they are unlikely to be viewed as a problem that cannot be solved. For example, you can choose to focus on a minor limitation in your experience or training that is unlikely to be viewed as serious. Or, you can deflect the question by talking about a limitation that you had in the past that is no longer a problem (something like, "When I first started my previous job, I didn't have much experience working with computers. However, over the past few years, I got a lot of computer experience, so that's not an issue anymore"). However, don't emphasize limitations that could be viewed as weaknesses in your character or a reflection of your work habits (for example, "I get angry easily" or "I'm very unorganized"), since a potential employers may view these as harder to change. Also, avoid answering a question about your weaknesses with a response about how you work too hard (for instance, "I tend to work too hard, so I need to remind myself to take breaks"). This is a very cliché response that employers will see through (no employer would see that as a weakness). For more ideas on how to answer difficult interview questions, check out Ron Fry's book, *101 Great Answers to the Toughest Interview Questions* (2007).

- Prepare at least ten questions you can ask during the interview. Write them down so you won't forget. For example, you should consider asking questions about the types of responsibilities that you are likely to have, the hours you will be expected to work, who you will be working with, and the structure of a typical day. Questions about salary, vacations, and benefits generally should be asked after you have received an offer, although for certain positions it may be appropriate to ask these questions during the interview, particularly if the interviewer brings these topics up.

- Bring extra copies of your resume and other supporting documents, in case the interviewer does not have easy access to these materials or wishes to share your resume with someone else in the organization.

During the Interview

So, your interview day has arrived. Here are some suggestions for how to make the most of it:

- Under no circumstances should you be late. Give yourself enough time to get to the interview and arrive a bit early. If you are unfamiliar with where the interview is being held, make sure to visit the site the previous day so you know how to get there.

- Your appearance is important. Make sure that you are dressed attractively and that your hair is neat. Note that appropriate attire for one job interview may be quite inappropriate for another type of job. If you're not sure what to wear, err on the side of dressing in a more conservative and professional manner.

- Remember to use some of the strategies discussed earlier in this chapter. For example, really listen to what the interviewer asks or tells you. Pay attention to your nonverbal communication and try to maintain eye contact.

- Be courteous, polite, and tactful. Remember to say please and thank-you. Don't disparage the organization, the interview process, or the person interviewing you. In fact, avoid appearing overly negative about previous jobs and employers, even if you were unhappy in a previous position.

- Appear flexible and willing to compromise. For example, if the hours aren't perfect, let the interviewer know that you will do what you can to accommodate the schedule. After you get the offer, you can renegotiate the hours. If it doesn't work out to your satisfaction, you can always turn down the position.

- Ask questions. A job interview has two purposes: (1) to allow the interviewer to decide about you and (2) to give you an opportunity to decide whether you want to work for that particular organization. Make sure you ask questions during the interview. Not only will asking questions help you to find out more about the position, but it will also convey to the interviewer that you are serious about the job.

- In general, be yourself during the interview and answer questions honestly. However, don't offer too much unnecessary personal information. For example, if the interviewer asks whether you are nervous, it's okay to say that you are feeling a bit anxious. On the other hand, there is no need to provide details about any personal difficulties or stresses that you may be experiencing, including frequent panic attacks, depression, or marital problems.

- At the end of your interview, ask the interviewer what the next steps are. For example, if the organization will be interviewing other candidates, when can you expect to hear their decision? Is there likely to be a second or third interview for the finalists?

After the Interview

Your work isn't quite over once the interview ends. Here are a couple of suggestions for things to do after the interview has ended:

- After the interview, send a letter thanking the interviewer for his or her time.

- Take some time to think about what went well during the interview and what you might have preferred to do or say differently. This information will be helpful for planning your next set of interviews if you don't get the job.

ASSERTIVE COMMUNICATION

This section describes three ways of communicating: passive communication, aggressive communication, and assertive communication. Passive and aggressive styles of communication rarely have the desired effect; assertive communication is more likely to get positive results. This section will help you to understand the differences among these three types of communication and will provide you with an introduction to methods for ensuring that you communicate assertively.

Passive Communication

Generally, shyness and social anxiety are associated with a tendency to communicate passively. Passive communication involves expressing one's needs indirectly, often in a quiet voice, and perhaps with frequent pauses and hesitations. Passive communication places the other person's wants, needs, and desires ahead of your own. This style of communicating is often associated with a strong desire to avoid any possibility of offending or inconveniencing the other individual. However, because your message is not communicated directly, the other person may never receive the message that you intended to communicate. Therefore, passive communication closes the channels of communication and may cause you to feel hurt and resentful. In fact, this resentment eventually may put you at risk for communicating in an aggressive manner later on. For example, a passive way of inviting someone to socialize is the vague statement, "We should get together sometime."

Aggressive Communication

Aggressive communication involves expressing your feelings, needs, or wants at the expense of another's feelings, needs, and wants. Aggressive communication tends to be judgmental, critical, and accusatory in content and tone. Like passive communication, this style of responding closes the channels of communication and can result in hurt feelings, grudges, anger, and alienation from the other person. An example of an aggressive way of asking someone to socialize is the statement, "If you cared about me and weren't so selfish, you would invite me to get together with you more often."

Assertive Communication

Often, people assume that passive and aggressive styles of communicating are their only two options. However, there is a third option. In contrast to aggressive and passive styles of communicating, assertive communication takes into account one's own feelings, needs, and wants, as well as those of the other person. Assertive communication has many of the features of good communication, including a tendency to be direct, clear, and immediate. An example of an assertive way to invite someone to socialize is the question, "Would you like to see a movie with me this weekend?"

In addition, assertive communication should include actively listening to the other person's perspective (including trying to hear and understand the other person's point of view, validating the other person's feelings, asking for clarification, and so on). Although assertive communication does not guarantee that you will get your way, compared with aggressive and passive styles of communication, assertive statements are more likely to keep the channels of communication open and to maximize the chances of reaching a mutually satisfactory resolution.

Dealing Assertively with Conflict Situations

If your goal is to convince someone else to change his or her behavior, an appropriate way of doing that is to make sure that your message is neither passive nor aggressive. Instead, you should try to communicate your message in a way that is factual, direct, and empathic.

Begin by describing your observations regarding the situation. Observations reflect your perspective regarding the facts, rather than your interpretations of those facts. Observations should be based on reality and therefore are usually very difficult to argue with. For example, "You arrived home too late" is not an observation because whether the person's arrival is "too" late is open to interpretation. However, the statement "You arrived home an hour later than you said you would" is an observation (assuming it's true) and is therefore less likely to lead to a defensive response from the other person.

After describing your observations, the next step is to describe your feelings about the situation. Feelings are emotions such as anger, anxiety, worry, and sadness. Feelings are not thoughts. For example, the statement "I feel that you should not be late" is not really a feeling statement. In contrast, "I feel hurt and worried when you arrive home later than you say you will" is a feeling statement. As is the case with communicating your observations, it's difficult to argue with a feeling statement. Only you know how you really feel.

Finally, it is important to communicate the ways in which you would like things to change. To follow the earlier example through, you might say, "I would like you to phone me if you are going to be more than thirty minutes late."

After you communicate your message in terms of these three components, you need to make sure that you give the other person a chance to express his or her perspective on the situation. Make sure you take advantage of the active listening skills that were discussed earlier in this chapter.

In addition to these basic assertiveness skills, there are a number of other strategies that may help you to deal with conflict situations:

- Make sure that you choose an appropriate time to talk about the situation. Don't put it off indefinitely. On the other hand, don't talk about the issue during the height of your anger. Also, don't insist that the issue be discussed right away if the other person is busy or unwilling to talk. Sometimes it's best to schedule a meeting at a mutually convenient time and to discuss the matter then.

- Make sure that you challenge the beliefs that contribute to your anxiety, anger, or hurt feelings. As discussed in chapter 6, our feelings are influenced by our beliefs, and our beliefs may be exaggerated or unrealistic at times. In other words, the situation may not matter as much as you think it does. When discussing the situation with the other person, try to maintain your cool by thinking about the situation realistically.

- Before confronting a situation, decide whether it is worth it. Is it a situation that matters? Will it take care of itself, even if you don't say anything? For example, if your difficult neighbor is moving away next week, perhaps it's not important to complain about the way he or she maintains the lawn.

- Try bouncing your thoughts off a neutral third party. Hearing another person's views regarding the issue may help you to see things in a different way. This can be particularly useful to determine whether your expectations about the situation are distorted.

- Try to understand the other person's perspective. Like you, the other individual is just trying to survive the best way that he or she can. Hostility and anger often are triggered by feelings of threat or hurt. If you develop an empathic understanding of the other person's perspective and beliefs, you will have a greater chance of finding a compromise and resolving the conflict, particularly if the other person can see that you are genuinely trying to understand.

- Consider writing a letter to the other person. Sometimes it's easier to communicate your thoughts and feelings in writing. However, even in a letter, you should use an assertive communication style rather than a passive or aggressive one. It is usually best not to use e-mail in these situations.

MEETING NEW PEOPLE, MAKING FRIENDS, AND DATING

This section describes ways of improving the skills that are important for meeting new people and developing new relationships. The topics covered include suggestions for where to meet new people and ways to deal with certain stresses associated with developing relationships, such as the possibility of being rejected.

Places to Meet New People

In a survey of more than 3,000 Americans, Laumann, Gagnon, Michael, and Michaels (1994) studied the ways and places in which people meet. Among married people, the ways that individuals met their spouses are shown by percentages as follows: (Table 10.3)

Way of Meeting	Percent*
Introduction by a friend	35%
Introduction by self	32%
Introduction by a family member	15%
Introduction by a coworker	6%
Introduction by a classmate	6%
Introduction by someone else	2%
Introduction by a neighbor	1%

Table 10.3: *Note: The numbers do not add up to 100 percent because a small number of people gave multiple answers.

In the same survey, the places where married individuals met their spouses were broken down into percentages as follows: (Table 10.4)

Location of Meeting	Percent
School	23%
Work	15%
Party	10%
Place of worship (e.g., church)	8%
Bar	8%

Location of Meeting	Percent
Gym or social club	4%
Personal ad	1%
Vacation	1%
Elsewhere	30%

Table 10.4

The statistics were similar for people in unmarried partnerships (couples cohabiting, couples in long-term partnerships, and couples in short-term partnerships), although some of the numbers were different in these other groups. For example, compared with married people, unmarried people in short-term relationships were more likely to have met their partners at a bar (17 percent) or a party (25 percent) and less likely to have met them at a place of worship (1 percent). Note that this survey was conducted before the Internet boom, so it doesn't include information about online dating. We will return to this topic shortly.

There are many other locations where it can be relatively easy to develop new friendships or to meet a potential partner. Some examples include the following: through a hobby (for example, joining a photography club or a theater group), getting involved in a sport (joining a bowling league, a running club, or a hiking group), getting in shape (for instance, lifting weights in a gym, joining an aerobics class, taking swimming lessons), taking dance classes, volunteering for an organization, forming a book club or reading group, attending public lectures, taking a part-time job, enrolling in an adult education course, or traveling (perhaps with a group).

The best way to meet new people is to do the things that you enjoy doing. That way, you are likely to meet people who enjoy the same things you do. For example, if you don't enjoy drinking alcohol or spending time in bars, you should think twice about trying to meet people there. At a bar, you are likely to meet people who enjoy going to bars. You should also keep in mind the types of people you are likely to meet by getting involved in a particular activity. For example, if you want to meet people close to your own age, try to get involved in activities that attract people in your age group.

It's not enough just to be around other people. To meet them, it will be necessary to take social risks in the situation. For openers, you should maintain eye contact, make a point of saying hello, and be sure to smile from time to time. Casual contact is more likely to develop into a friendship or relationship if you purposely engage in conversation. As you get to know someone, you will need to take bigger risks such as asking that person to meet you for coffee, go to a movie, or join you for a day's outing to a park or a museum.

Meeting People Online

Internet dating is a very popular way to meet people. *The Internet Dating Guide* (www.theinternetdatinggu ide.com) reports that about 30 percent of American singles have used matchmaking sites. According to *Online Dating Magazine* (www.onlinedatingmagazine. com), twenty million Americans visit an online dating service each month, 120,000 marriages per year occur as a result of an online dating service, and about a third of Americans know someone who has used an online dating service. The Internet is also a great source of information about ways for singles to meet. Simply enter the name of your city and the word "singles" into a search engine (for example, Google), and you will likely come up with all sorts of ideas, ranging from "speed dating" groups to singles travel opportunities, personal ad listings, and social events.

In addition to online dating, the Internet is a popular way to meet new friends. An anonymous survey of 191 college students (Knox et al. 2001) found that friendship (as opposed to dating) was the most important reason for using the Internet among this group. In this survey, 60 percent of respondents reported that they had successfully established an online friendship, and about half reported being more comfortable meeting people online than in person. However, note that 40 percent of people reported having lied online! More recently, online social networking sites like Facebook.com and MySpace .com have become popular ways to meet friends.

It is important for you not to use online relation- ships as a replacement for in-person relationships. Rather, you should view online relationships as a stepping stone toward meeting people in person. The recommended readings section at the end of the book provides additional resources on online dating.

Dating Skills

Regardless of how it may seem, there are lots of potential partners out there, regardless of whether you are old or young, male or female. Further- more, the idea that there is only one person out there who is your soul mate is a myth. There are many different people who are potentially excellent partners, each having very different qualities to bring to a relationship. Although it may sound like a cliché, it is often true that someone comes along when you least expect it, and often it occurs when you're not even looking. So relax. Rushing the process can lead to feelings of disappointment or failure when a hoped-for relationship doesn't work out. There are several excellent published guides to dating, a number of which are listed in the recommended readings at the end of the book.

PREPARATION

The first step in dating is preparation. What does preparation in this context mean? It means you figure out what you're looking for. What is the purpose of your search? Are you looking for a serious relationship, marriage, and children? Or are you looking for a sexual partner? Companionship? A way to alleviate boredom? The purpose of the relationship will influence what kind of person you will seek and attract. For example, if you are looking for excitement, meeting someone who is aloof, mysterious, and gorgeous may be your aim. On the other hand, if you want a more serious relationship, you should choose to emphasize qualities that will continue to be important to you after the thrill of a new relationship wears off, like a sense of humor, shared values, kindness, honesty, stability, responsibility, and respect.

Despite the saying "opposites attract," the cliché "birds of a feather flock together" is probably closer to the truth. Generally, research in social psychology has found that people are most attracted to those who are similar to them with respect to values, appearance, interests, and other attributes. Being aware of your own interests and attributes will help you to know what you are looking for in another person. In addition, *being* the type of person who you would like to meet will help you to attract that person. To meet the right person, you need to make a point of being in places where that person is likely to be. For example, if you're interested in meeting someone who loves reading, then make a point of spending time in the library, visiting bookstores, or attending book signings.

NETWORKING

One very helpful activity for meeting new people is called networking. *Networking* can be defined as an exchange of information or services among individuals or groups. As we mentioned earlier, more than two thirds of married people are introduced to their spouses by a third person (Laumann et al. 1994). Therefore, let your friends and family know that you are interested in meeting someone. If nothing romantic develops, you may add to your circle of friends. By adding new friends (without actually giving up on old friendships), you will increase your chances of finding a partner.

FIRST DATES

When you do meet someone who interests you, the initial date can be quite informal. For example, you might go for a walk during a break at work, run an errand together between classes, or offer the person a ride home. After you've had more contact with the person, you could suggest a more formal outing, like going out for lunch or dinner, seeing a concert or movie, or visiting a gallery or museum. If you are a student, you might suggest taking a class with the other person to increase your chances of having repeated contact.

On your date, pay attention to small details, especially your physical appearance and hygiene. Dress appropriately for the situation. Wear clothes you like, but err on the side of conservative or classic fashions if you are unsure about the other person's taste. In other words, don't wear your most outrageous outfit on a first date.

REJECTION

Be prepared for rejection. Much more often than not, a particular dating situation does not lead to a long-term relationship. It's normal for one person to be more interested in pursuing a relationship than the other person is. If the other individual ends up not wanting to continue the relationship, make sure that you keep the rejection in perspective (see chapter 6 for suggestions). A rejection does not mean that there is something wrong with you or that going out on dates will never lead to a long-term relationship. Rather, rejection speaks more to the fit between you and the specific person with whom things didn't work out. Experiencing some form of rejection is a necessary part of dating. The more dating experiences you seek out, the more rejection you will experience. However, increasing the frequency of your dates will also provide opportunities to improve your dating skills and increase the likelihood of developing a positive relationship in the future.

PRESENTATIONS AND PUBLIC SPEAKING SKILLS

This section provides a basic primer on public speaking and giving presentations. In particular, it includes suggestions for preparing for presentations or talks and describes ways to improve the quality of your presentations.

For a more detailed treatment of this topic, we suggest that you check out the recommended readings on public speaking at the end of this book. Although the emphasis in most of these books is on business presentations, many of the skills suggested apply to other types of presentations as well, such as giving a speech at a wedding or party. In addition to providing suggestions for how to organize and deliver presentations, most of these recommended books also provide ideas for managing anxiety during presentations. One that provides an excellent mix of information on presentation skills and managing anxiety is *The Confident Speaker: Beat Your Nerves and Communicate at Your Best in Any Situation* (Monarth and Kase 2007).

Preparing for Presentations

Preparing for presentations involves seven important steps: (1) identifying the purpose of the presentation, (2) determining the nature of the audience, (3) deciding upon the subject matter, (4) organizing the presentation, (5) making your talk interesting and compiling supporting materials, (6) rehearsing the presentation, and (7) managing your anxiety.

STEP 1: DETERMINING THE PURPOSE OF THE PRESENTATION

Before preparing a lecture or speech, you must first be clear about the purpose of the presentation. Essentially, presentations can have one or more of the following functions:

- **To persuade.** For example, a presentation may be designed to sell a particular product or to convince a group of coworkers to change a procedure in the workplace.

- **To explain.** Examples include a half-day orientation meeting to explain company procedures to new employees, a lecture designed to teach a complex topic to college students, or a seminar to provide in-depth information to colleagues about a particular subject.

- **To instruct.** These may include presentations regarding how to perform a task (like how to use a new computer program) or how to develop a new skill (for example, learning to dance).

- **To brief.** Some presentations are designed to brief an audience regarding some matter. For example, this may include a four-minute presentation to update management about the status of union negotiations or to brief your customers about changes in the price of a product.

- **To entertain.** Examples of presentations designed to entertain include theatrical presentations (for instance, stand-up comedy) and sometimes speeches at weddings, anniversaries, or parties.

STEP 2: DETERMINING THE NATURE OF THE AUDIENCE

Before planning a presentation in detail, it is helpful to know something about the nature of your audience. In some cases, you may even need to ask the audience questions about their background at the start of the presentation and adapt your style or content to meet their needs. Some questions that are helpful to consider include the following:

- How big is the audience?

- What is the likely composition of the audience (factors such as age, gender, professional background)?

- What is the audience expecting?

- How much does the audience already know? What do they still need to learn?

- Why is the audience attending the presentation—because they have to or because they want to?

STEP 3: DECIDING UPON THE SUBJECT MATTER

Before giving your presentation, you should have an idea of the main message that you want to convey. In most cases, the main point of the presentation should be simple and clear. The audience should be aware of the key points that you plan to make so that the content of the presentation can be understood in the proper context. In most cases, it's helpful to pique the group's interest (perhaps with a joke, anecdote, or illustration) early in the talk. If the purpose of your presentation is to persuade the audience about some issue, you should ensure that you have gained their confidence (for example, by making the members of the audience aware of your expertise and credentials). Also, persuasive presentation should include specific instructions on how to implement the suggestions you provide (for example, where to obtain the product you are selling).

STEP 4: ORGANIZING THE PRESENTATION

One of the most common suggestions made to people who prepare presentations is to pay close attention to the three phases of the talk: the introduction, the main body of the talk, and the conclusion. The *introduction* should include an overview of the presentation so audience members know what to expect. The *main body* of the presentation is where you discuss the main content of the talk, with all of the important details. At the *conclusion,* you should provide a brief summary, as well as some interpretations and inferences about the content (for instance, why the presentation was important).

If possible, your presentation should be organized so it tells a story. For example, before describing a new method of performing some task, you might provide the audience with a history of how that particular task has been performed in the past so they have a context in which to understand the new information. Or, the presentation can be laid out so that a series of problems are described, each followed by one or more solutions.

STEP 5: MAKING THE PRESENTATION INTERESTING

In addition to making sure your main points are conveyed to the audience, it is important that they are conveyed in a way that is interesting. To help you do this, consider strategies like humor, analogies, personal stories, examples, illustrations, and relevant statistics. Be careful not to use humor that could offend audience members. You never know who is in your audience and whether their backgrounds, beliefs, or experiences might cause them to take a joke the wrong way. Another strategy is to involve the audience members in some way. For example, you might ask them questions or encourage them to ask you questions during your presentation. Or you could have them do something (demonstrate the skill you are trying to teach, complete a survey or take a test, and so on). Supporting materials can be another useful way to bring your presentation to life.

Supporting materials. Supporting materials often take the form of visuals (for example, PowerPoint slides and other projected images, videos, white boards, flip charts, CD ROMs, and so on). These visuals can include text, photos, illustrations, cartoons, graphics, and maps. Here are a few suggestions to keep in mind regarding supporting materials:

- If you are going to use cartoons, make sure they are funny. Ask some friends, family members, or coworkers for their opinions about the cartoons you intend to use.

- In some cases, it may be helpful to have props. For example, if you mention particular books in your presentation, have copies with you for audience members to look at. If you are describing a product, bring it with you and display it during the presentation.

- If possible, provide handouts containing copies of your slides and overheads so that audience members can listen to you instead of having to take notes. Audience members generally appreciate getting handouts.

- Make sure that your slides and overheads are attractive and that the type is large enough to be seen from the back of the room.

- Avoid the temptation to have too much information on your slides and overheads.

STEP 6: REHEARSING THE PRESENTATION

If at all possible, rehearse your presentation beforehand. There are several ways of rehearsing. Ideally, you can rehearse in front of an audience of friends, family, or coworkers, preferably in a location similar to where the actual talk will be held. Ask your rehearsal audience for feedback, and make changes to the presentation accordingly. If you cannot rehearse in front of a live audience, try rehearsing in front of a video camera or camcorder and watch the recording afterward. If that's not possible, practice out loud in front of a mirror. As you become more experienced in giving presentations, practicing beforehand will become less important.

STEP 7: MANAGING YOUR ANXIETY

Preparing for a presentation should also include strategies for managing your anxiety. Before the presentation, make sure that you have used the cognitive strategies (chapter 6) to challenge your anxious thoughts. In addition, use the exposure-based strategies (chapters 7 through 9) to confront your fears whenever possible. When you're actually in the situation, make sure that your breathing is slow and regular. Overbreathing or holding your breath will increase your anxiety symptoms. Don't fight your fear. Just let the symptoms happen. Fighting your fear is likely to cause anxiety symptoms to intensify. It's okay to be nervous during a presentation. In fact, audience members often expect it. Depending on the nature of the presentation, it may even be helpful to tell the audience you are feeling nervous. Saying so may help you to calm down, and it very likely will help to win the audience over to your side.

Delivering the Presentation

Here is a list of suggestions to keep in mind when you are giving a presentation.

- Pay attention to the way you deliver your speech. Before the talk, check any pronunciations you're not sure about. Make sure that your voice does not drop off at the end of your sentences. Be sure you are projecting at a reasonable volume (imagine you are delivering your speech to the back wall of the room). Speak crisply and pronounce your words clearly. Avoid saying "uh" and "um." Finally, avoid speaking too quickly. Going too fast is one of the most common mistakes people make during presentations, particularly when they are feeling anxious.

- Make eye contact with the audience members during the talk.

- Try to move around when you are speaking. Walk around the front of the room rather than staying planted at a podium. Don't put your hands in your pockets. Instead, gesture with your hands to emphasize key points. However, keep your hands away from your face and hair.

- Presentations are often less interesting when they are read verbatim. If you read a presentation word for word, you also run the risk of panicking if you lose your place. Instead, we recommend speaking from a detailed outline with lots of headings, bullets, and so on. An outline will make sure that all the information you need is available and easy to access, even if you lose your place. It will also force you to be somewhat spontaneous during the presentation. If the thought of not reading your speech is too scary, another option is to bring both an outline version and a fully written version. If necessary, you can switch to reading your presentation if using the outline alone doesn't work.

- Don't talk down to your audience. They probably know more than you think they do. Even if the material is new to them, they will not appreciate being talked to like children—unless, of course, they are children! Make sure your tone of voice and the things you say are not condescending.

- Repeat the main points of the presentation frequently. Audience members will not hear everything you say, and if they miss an important point you may lose them for the rest of the presentation unless the important points are repeated.

- Keep it simple. Don't try to discuss more than your time allows.

- Make sure you are prepared to handle questions. Consider bringing additional information (a reference book, notes, and so on) that may be needed to answer certain types of questions. No matter how silly a question is, try to answer it tactfully and show respect for the person who asked the question (for example, "That's an interesting question..."). Finally, repeat all audience questions before you answer them. Chances are good that people in the back of the room will not be able to hear some of the questions the first time they are asked.

- Be yourself during the talk. Audiences prefer a speaker who is down to earth and genuine rather than someone who looks as if he or she is trying too hard to be entertaining or to impress the audience.

After the Presentation

Following your presentation, it is helpful to evaluate the quality of your performance, basing your evaluation on whether you followed the suggestions provided in this chapter. Don't base your self-evaluation on whether you were anxious during the presentation or whether your anxiety symptoms showed. The presenter's anxiety or lack thereof is only one small aspect of what makes an effective presentation.

Social anxiety is associated with the tendency to be an overly harsh critic of one's own performance. Therefore, we suggest that you obtain objective feedback from your audience members as well. This can be done informally by asking people what they thought of the talk. Or, if appropriate, it can be done more formally by handing out an anonymous evaluation form that requires audience members to rate their impressions of certain aspects of the presentation, such as the format of the presentation, the content (for example, interest level, relevance, difficulty, and so on), the speaker (for example, presentation skills, organization, expertise, clarity), use of audiovisual resources, and the location (for instance, lighting, temperature, seating comfort). In addition, make sure to include space on the form for audience members to write their impressions (strengths of the presentation, areas for improvement) in their own words.

CHAPTER 11

Maintaining Your Improvements and Planning for the Future

The purpose of this final chapter is to discuss strategies for ensuring that the gains you have made so far are maintained over the coming months and years. Perhaps the most important suggestion we can offer is that you should continue to use the strategies described in the first ten chapters. Continuing to use approaches that were helpful in getting you to where you are now will ensure that you maintain your gains and that your anxiety continues to decrease over time.

THE END OF TREATMENT

In some ways, treatment is never finished. Although most people experience improvements using the strategies described in this book, it's common for people to continue to suffer from anxiety in some social situations from time to time. Like back pain, depression, and high blood pressure, anxiety is often a chronic problem that comes and goes, but it can also be controlled. It will be helpful for you to continue to use the methods described in this book to make sure that your anxiety doesn't worsen. In fact, an important goal of cognitive behavioral therapy is to teach people to be their own therapists. If this book has been effective, chances are that your anxiety is much better than it was and you have learned some strategies that you can continue to use as you move forward.

If treatment has been less effective than you would have liked, this is a time to figure out why. Here are some possible reasons to consider:

- **Inadequate dosage.** Typically, we think of dosage in the context of medication treatments, and certainly an inadequate dosage of medication (taking too little medication or taking medication for too short a time) can lead to a lack of improvement. However, the term "dosage" can also be applied to cognitive behavioral strategies. There is evidence that improvement is directly related to the amount of homework a person completes. So, if your exposure practices are too short or too infrequent or you don't practice challenging your anxiety-provoking thoughts, your anxiety may not have improved as much as you had hoped.

- **Stress.** If you were under a lot of stress while working on the strategies in this book, you may have found only limited benefit. For example, if you were working very long hours, dealing with family stresses, or coping with serious health problems, you may not have been able to devote as much time to this treatment as you might have liked. Our recommendation is to try again once the stress in your life has subsided. Stress can also lead to a return of fear, an issue to which we will return shortly.

- **Other psychological problems.** In some cases, shyness and social anxiety are part of another problem. For example, someone with an eating disorder may have high levels of social anxiety for fear of looking fat in front of others. Although the strategies in this book may help in such a case, it would also be important to directly address the eating issues.

- **Other life issues.** For some people, years of social anxiety can lead to various long-term problems, including chronic unemployment, extreme loneliness, severe depression, or substance-use problems. Without addressing these larger issues, the strategies described in this book may not have much impact on improving your overall quality of life. It will be important to find some help and support for these larger issues as well. Chapter 4 includes some recommendations for finding a therapist. Professional help may be able to steer you in a direction toward solving these other problems in addition to your anxiety.

WHY FEAR RETURNS AND WHAT YOU CAN DO ABOUT IT

Most people who receive treatment for social anxiety experience long-lasting improvements in their anxiety, particularly following cognitive and behavioral treatment. Nevertheless, there are a number of different reasons why fear may return for some individuals. If your fear returns, the best thing to do is to resume using the strategies that were most helpful to you the first time you overcame your fear. Social anxiety that comes back sometime after a period of improvement may even be easier to overcome the second time around.

Discontinuing the Treatment Strategies Too Early or Too Quickly

Discontinuing your cognitive therapy and exposure practices may increase the likelihood of experiencing a return of fear, particularly if you stop using these techniques before you have completely overcome your anxiety. We recommend that you continue to challenge your anxiety-provoking thoughts from time to time for as long as you continue to feel anxious. When your fear has decreased significantly, you can stop using the cognitive diaries. However, you should continue to use the cognitive techniques informally, by silently asking yourself appropriate questions (for example, "Is there some other, nonanxious way of interpreting this situation?").

In addition, you should take advantage of opportunities to expose yourself to previously feared situations even after your fear has been reduced. Sometimes life circumstances (such as being busy at work or school, or recovering from the flu) make it hard to practice exposure on a regular basis. Whenever possible, continue to confront your feared situations from time to time. Occasional exposures should help to prevent your fear from returning.

Stopping medication too early may also increase the risk of your anxiety returning. As discussed in chapter 5, relapse following discontinuation from treatment with antidepressants is believed to be less likely when treatment has continued for at least a year. So, it's best not to stop medication treatment the moment you start to feel better.

Coming off medication suddenly may also increase the risk of your fear returning. Discontinuation from some antidepressants and from almost all anti-anxiety medications is associated with symptoms of withdrawal, which often mimic the symptoms of anxiety. These withdrawal symptoms may prompt some people to resume their old habits of avoidance and fearful thinking. The best way of preventing withdrawal symptoms following discontinuation from medication is to reduce the dosage very slowly over time. We strongly recommend that you not reduce or stop your medication without first consulting with your doctor.

Life Stresses

Sometimes, an increase in the stress in your life can lead to a return of anxiety and fear. For example, if you experience a stressful life event (increased hours at work, relationship problems, financial difficulties, health problems, family tensions, death of a close friend, and the like), you may find that your anxiety in social situations gets worse. Sometimes, this worsening of anxiety occurs while the stress is ongoing; other times it may occur shortly after the stress has ended.

The relationship between stress and increased social anxiety is not surprising. Most people respond to stress in characteristic ways. Some tend to respond physically by experiencing more colds, headaches, increased blood pressure, and other physical ailments. Others may fall into bad habits, such as smoking more, increasing alcohol or caffeine consumption, eating unhealthy foods, or exercising less. Still others may respond emotionally by becoming more anxious, depressed, or irritable. If your natural pattern has been to experience anxiety in social situations, stress may cause some of your old responses to resurface.

Stress tends to increase a person's arousal level, so breathing becomes heavier, heart rate increases, and other symptoms of arousal become more intense. When you're under stress, it doesn't take much change in your anxiety level for the feeling to become more noticeable than usual. Situations that are normally okay may seem overwhelming when you are experiencing other stresses in your life.

Most of the time, the increase in social anxiety following stress is temporary; when the stress level improves, the anxiety decreases again. However, if you respond to your increased anxiety by falling back into your old habits of anxious thinking and avoidance behaviors, you may find that the increased social anxiety continues even after the stress has passed. If your anxiety returns following a stressful life event, the best thing to do is to reread the relevant sections of this book and resume using some of the strategies that you found helpful the first time around.

Encountering a New and Unexpectedly Difficult Situation

Although you may think you have overcome a particular fear, it is possible that some fear remains but that you just haven't had a chance to encounter a sufficiently challenging situation until now. One of our clients was recently surprised to experience intense fear while unexpectedly having to give a toast at his father's birthday party. He had worked very hard to overcome his fear of public speaking at work. After a few months of practice, he found he could speak comfortably in meetings, and he even gave long presentations to groups of 200 or more with almost no fear. One day, he was asked on the spur of the moment to make a toast at his father's birthday party to about thirty friends and relatives whom he had known his whole life. This made him very nervous. Although he had successfully overcome his fear of speaking in formal work situations, he had never had the opportunity to speak in an informal and personal situation like a family party. For him, giving a toast in front of friends and relatives was actually a new situation that he hadn't had the chance to practice previously.

Experiencing a Trauma in the Feared Situation

Sometimes, experiencing a trauma in a social situation can lead to a return of fear. For example, if your audience during a presentation is particularly cold and unfriendly, if you are rejected by someone whom you care about, or if your boss is extremely critical of your performance in a meeting, you may find that you're more anxious the next time you return to the situation. The fact that you had a particular anxiety in the past makes it more likely that it will return if you experience a negative event in a situation that mirrors this old fear.

If you experience a negative event in a situation that you previously feared, the best thing to do is to return to the situation as soon as possible. If you begin to avoid the situation, your anxiety will be more likely to return. In addition to exposure, try challenging your anxious beliefs by considering alternative, nonanxious interpretations of the negative event you experienced.

PREVENTING YOUR FEAR FROM RETURNING

Although your anxiety is unlikely to return after you have learned to be more comfortable in social and performance situations, there are no guarantees. Nevertheless, there are a number of things that you can do to improve your chances of maintaining your gains.

Continue to Use the Cognitive Therapy and Exposure Strategies

As we've discussed, continuing to challenge your anxious thoughts informally and to practice exposure from time to time will help you to maintain the improvements that you have made so far. We also recommend that you reread relevant sections from this book occasionally to reinforce what you have learned and to make sure that you haven't forgotten any important principles.

Practice Exposure in a Range of Situations and Contexts

Your gains are likely to last longer if you practice exposure in a wide variety of situations and contexts. For example, if you're fearful of starting conversations, rather than practicing starting conversations only at work, we recommend that you practice making conversation in other situations as well (for example, at home, at parties, at the bus stop, in the elevator, and so on).

Take Advantage of Opportunities to Overlearn

Overlearning involves (1) practicing exposure so many times that it becomes boring and second nature, and (2) practicing exposure in situations more difficult than those you encounter in your everyday life. For example, if you are fearful of having your hands shake while having a drink, you can practice having them shake so much that you actually spill some of your drink. (Make sure your glass is filled with water and not grape juice!) Repeat this practice until it no longer causes anxiety. Or, if you're fearful of making a minor mistake when talking to a stranger, you can practice purposely making obvious mistakes while speaking to people you don't know.

Overlearning is thought to offer protection from experiencing a return of fear. There are several advantages of practicing exposure to more difficult situations than those you normally encounter. First, practicing in more challenging situations will automatically make the less challenging situations seem easier. Second, practices in difficult situations will further challenge your anxious beliefs. For example, if you learn that nothing bad happens even if you purposely make a big mistake during a presentation, you may become less fearful of accidentally making a small mistake when speaking in public. Finally, overlearning provides room for some of your fear to return without causing significant impairment in your life.

WHERE TO GO FOR MORE INFORMATION

For those who want additional information on social anxiety and related topics, we have included more useful information at the back of this book. Our list of recommended readings includes books on social anxiety, other anxiety problems, cognitive behavioral therapy, and related topics. This list also includes information on two videos on the treatment of social anxiety. Readings are included both for consumers and professionals. We have also included a resource list of national and international organizations that provide information (including referrals to experienced therapists) to people who suffer from social anxiety and for professionals who have an interest in this topic. Finally, we have included a list of websites that provide information on social anxiety and effective treatments.

We hope that you have found the strategies described in this book helpful. Chances are that you will need to continue to use these tools for some time before experiencing a reduction in social anxiety that has a noticeable impact on your day-to-day life. We recommend that you reread the sections that were particularly useful or inspiring to you. Most of all, we wish you good luck as you learn to deal with stressful social situations with a new, well-earned sense of confidence.

Recommended Readings

SHYNESS AND SOCIAL ANXIETY: SELF-HELP BOOKS

Antony, M.M. 2004. *10 Simple Solutions to Shyness: How to Overcome Shyness, Social Anxiety, and Fear of Public Speaking.* Oakland, CA: New Harbinger.

Hope, D.A., R.G. Heimberg, H.R. Juster, and C.L. Turk. 2000. *Managing Social Anxiety.* New York: Oxford.

Rapee, R.M. 1998. *Overcoming Shyness and Social Phobia: A Step-by-Step Guide.* Lanham, MD: Jason Aronson.

Stein, M.B., and J.R. Walker. 2002. *Triumph Over Shyness: Conquering Shyness and Social Anxiety.* New York: McGraw-Hill.

SOCIAL AND COMMUNICATION SKILLS: SELF-HELP BOOKS

Dating and Meeting New People

Berry, D.M. 2005. *Romancing the Web: A Therapist's Guide to the Finer Points of Online Dating.* Manitowoc, WI: Blue Water Publications.

Burns, D.D. 1985. *Intimate Connections.* New York: Signet (Penguin Books).

Jacobson, B., and S.J. Gordon. 2004. *The Shy Single: A Bold Guide to Dating for the Less-than-Bold Dater.* Emmaus, PA: Rodale.

Katz, E.M. 2003. *I Can't Believe I'm Buying this Book: A Commonsense Guide to Successful Internet Dating.* Berkeley, CA: 10 Speed Press.

Tessina, T. 1998. *The Unofficial Guide to Dating Again.* New York: Macmillan.

Interviews

Fry, R. 2007. *101 Great Answers to the Toughest Interview Questions,* 5th ed. Clifton Park, NY: Thomson Delmar Learning.

McKay, D.R. 2004. *The Everything Practice Interview Book: Be Prepared for Any Question.* Avon, MA: Adams Media Corporation.

Stein, M. 2003. *Fearless Interviewing: How to Win the Job by Communicating with Confidence.* New York: McGraw-Hill.

Public Speaking and Presentations

Kosslyn, S.M. 2007. *Clear and to the Point: 8 Psychological Principles for Compelling PowerPoint Presentations.* New York: Oxford.

MacInnis, J.L. 2006. *The Elements of Great Public Speaking: How To Be Calm, Confident, and Compelling.* Berkeley, CA: 10 Speed Press.

McClain, G.R. 2007. *Presentations: Proven Techniques for Creating Presentations that Get Results,* 2nd ed. Avon, MA: Adams Media Corporation.

Monarth, H., and L. Kase. 2007. *The Confident Speaker Beat Your Nerves and Communicate at Your Best in Any Situation.* New York: McGraw-Hill.

Morrisey, G.L., T.L. Sechrest, and W.B. Warman. 1997. *Loud and Clear How to Prepare and Deliver Effective Business and Technical Presentations,* 4th ed. Reading, MA: Addison-Wesley.

Other Communication Skills

Bolton, R. 1979. *People Skills.* New York: Simon & Schuster.

Davis, M., K. Paleg, and P. Fanning. 2004. *The Messages Workbook: Powerful Strategies for Effective*

432

Communication at Work & Home. Oakland, CA: New Harbinger.

Fleming, J. 1997. *Become Assertive!* Kent, United Kingdom: David Grant Publishing.

Garner, A. 1997. *Conversationally Speaking: Testing New Ways to Increase Your Personal and Social Effectiveness,* 3rd ed. Los Angeles: Lowell House.

Honeychurch, C., and A. Watrous. 2003. *Talk to Me: Conversation Tips for the Small-Talk Challenged.* Oakland, CA: New Harbinger.

McKay, M., M. Davis, and P. Fanning. 1995. *Messages: The Communication Skills Book,* 2nd ed. Oakland, CA: New Harbinger.

Patterson, R.J. 2000. *The Assertiveness Workbook: How to Express Your Ideas and Stand Up for Yourself at Work and in Relationships.* Oakland, CA: New Harbinger.

ANXIETY DISORDERS AND COGNITIVE BEHAVIOR THERAPY: SELF-HELP BOOKS

Antony, M.M., and R.E. McCabe. 2004. *10 Simple Solutions to Panic: How to Overcome Panic Attacks,*

Calm Physical Symptoms, and Reclaim Your Life. Oakland, CA: New Harbinger.

Antony, M.M., and R.P. Swinson. 2008. *When Perfect Isn't Good Enough Strategies for Coping with Perfectionism,* 2nd ed. Oakland, CA: New Harbinger.

Bieling, P.J., and M.M. Antony. 2003. *Ending the Depression Cycle: A Step-by-Step Guide for Preventing Relapse.* Oakland, CA: New Harbinger.

Bourne, E.J. 2005. *The Anxiety and Phobia Workbook,* 4th ed. Oakland, CA: New Harbinger.

_____. 2003. *Coping with Anxiety: 10 Simple Ways to Relieve Anxiety, Fear & Worry.* Oakland, CA: New Harbinger.

Burns, D.D. 1999. *The Feeling Good Handbook, Revised Edition.* New York: Plume.

Butler, G., and T. Hope. 2007. *Managing Your Mind: The Mental Fitness Guide,* 2nd ed. New York: Oxford.

Davis, M., E.R. Eshelman, and M. McKay. 2008. *The Relaxation and Stress Reduction Workbook,* 6th ed. Oakland, CA: New Harbinger.

Greenberger, D., and C.A. Padesky. 1995. *Mind Over Mood: Change How You Feel by Changing the Way You Think.* New York: Guilford.

Gyoerkoe, K.L., and P.S. Wiegartz. 2006. *10 Simple Solutions to Worry How to Calm Your Mind, Relax Your Body, & Reclaim Your Life.* Oakland, CA: New Harbinger.

Hyman, B.M., and C. Pedrick. 2005. *The OCD Workbook: Your Guide to Breaking Free from Obsessive-Compulsive Disorder,* 2nd ed. Oakland, CA: New Harbinger.

McKay, M., M. Davis, and P. Fanning. 2007. *Thoughts and Feelings: Taking Control of Your Moods and Your Life,* 3rd ed. Oakland, CA: New Harbinger.

Zuercher-White, E. 1997. *An End to Panic: Breakthrough Techniques for Overcoming Panic Disorder,* 2nd ed. Oakland, CA: New Harbinger.

SOCIAL ANXIETY: BOOKS FOR PROFESSIONALS

Antony, M.M., and K. Rowa. 2008. *Social Anxiety Disorder: Psychological Approaches to Assessment and Treatment.* Göttingen, Germany: Hogrefe.

Beidel, D.C., and S.M. Turner. 2007. *Shy Children, Phobic Adults: Nature and Treatment of Social Anxiety Disorder,* 2nd ed. Washington, DC: American Psychological Association.

Crozier, W.R., and L.E. Alden, eds. 2005. *The Essential Handbook of Social Anxiety for Clinicians.* Hoboken, NJ: Wiley.

Heimberg, R.G., and R.E. Becker. 2002. *Cognitive-Behavioral Group Therapy for Social Phobia: Basic Mechanisms and Clinical Strategies.* New York: Guilford.

Hofmann, S.G. 2008. *Cognitive-Behavior Therapy of Social Phobia: Evidence-Based and Disorder Specific Treatment Techniques.* New York: Routledge.

Hofmann, S.G., and P.M. DiBartolo. 2001. *From Social Anxiety to Social Phobia: Multiple Perspectives.* Needham Heights, MA: Allyn and Bacon.

Hope, D.A., R.G. Heimberg, and C.L. Turk. 2006. *Managing Social Anxiety: A Cognitive Behavioral Therapy Approach (Therapist Guide).* New York: Oxford.

Kearney, C.A. 2005. *Social Anxiety and Social Phobia in Youth: Characteristics, Assessment, and Psychological Treatment.* New York: Springer.

Stravynski, A. 2007. *Fearing Others: The Nature and Treatment of Social Phobia.* New York: Cambridge.

ANXIETY DISORDERS AND COGNITIVE BEHAVIOR THERAPY: BOOKS FOR PROFESSIONALS

Andrews, G., R. Crino, M. Creamer, C. Hunt, L. Lampe, and A. Page. 2002. *The Treatment of Anxiety Disorders: Clinician's Guide and Patient Manuals,* 2nd ed. New York: Cambridge.

Antony, M.M., and D.H. Barlow, eds. 2002. *Handbook of Assessment, Treatment Planning, and Outcome Evaluation: Empirically Supported Strategies for Psychological Disorders.* New York: Guilford.

Antony, M.M., and M.B. Stein. 2008. *Oxford Handbook of Anxiety and Related Disorders.* New York: Oxford University Press.

Antony, M.M., and R.P. Swinson. 2000. *Phobic Disorders and Panic in Adults: A Guide to Assessment and Treatment.* Washington, DC: American Psychological Association.

Antony, M.M., D.R. Ledley, and R.G. Heimberg, eds. 2005. *Improving Outcomes and Preventing Relapse in Cognitive Behavioral Therapy.* New York: Guilford.

Antony, M.M., S.M. Orsillo, and L. Roemer, eds. 2001. *Practitioner's Guide to Empirically-Based Measures of Anxiety.* New York: Springer.

Barlow, D.H. 2002. *Anxiety and Its Disorders: The Nature and Treatment of Anxiety and Panic,* 2nd ed. New York: Guilford.

_____ed. 2008. *Clinical Handbook of Psychological Disorders,* 4th ed. New York: Guilford.

Beck, A.T., and G. Emery. 1985. *Anxiety Disorders and Phobias: A Cognitive Perspective.* New York: Basic Books.

Beck, J.S. 1995. *Cognitive Therapy: Basics and Beyond.* New York: Guilford.

_____. 2005. *Cognitive Therapy for Challenging Problems: What To Do When the Basics Don't Work.* New York: Guilford.

Bernstein, D.A., T.D. Borkovec, and H. Hazlett-Stevens. 2000. *New Directions in Progressive Relaxation Training: A Guidebook for Helping Professionals.* Westport, CT: Praeger.

Bieling, P.J., R.E. McCabe, and M.M. Antony. 2006. *Cognitive Behavioral Therapy in Groups.* New York: Guilford.

Eifert, G.H., and J.P. Forsyth. 2005. *Acceptance and Commitment Therapy for Anxiety Disorders: A Practitioner's Treatment Guide to Using Mindfulness, Acceptance, and Values-Based Behavior Change Strategies.* Oakland, CA: New Harbinger.

Kase, L., and D. Ledley. 2007. *Anxiety Disorders.* Hoboken, NJ: Wiley.

Miller, W.R., and S. Rollnick. 2002. *Motivational Interviewing: Preparing People for Change,* 2nd ed. New York: Guilford.

Orsillo, S.M., and L. Roemer, eds. 2005. *Acceptance- and Mindfulness-Based Approaches to Anxiety: Conceptualization and Treatment.* New York: Springer.

Richard, D.C.S., and D. Lauterbach. 2007. *Handbook of Exposure Therapies.* New York: Academic Press.

Wright, J.H., M.R. Basco, and M.E. Thase. 2006. *Learning Cognitive-Behavior Therapy: An Illustrated Guide.* Washington, DC: American Psychiatric Press.

VIDEO RESOURCES

Albano, A.M. 2006. *Shyness and Social Phobia.* DVD. Washington, DC: American Psychological Association.

Rapee, R.M. 1999. *I Think They Think ... Overcoming Social Phobia.* DVD or VHS. New York: Guilford.

National and International Associations Providing Referrals

NATIONAL ASSOCIATIONS (UNITED STATES)

Note that most of these associations offer information for finding therapists and other resources in the United States and Canada, and several offer information on resources in other countries.

Anxiety Disorders Association of America

8730 Georgia Ave., Suite 600
Silver Spring, MD 20910
USA
Tel: 1-240-485-1001
Fax: 1-240-485-1035
Web: www.adaa.org

- Annual conference (for professionals and consumers)

- Consumer memberships and professional memberships

- Information on support groups in the United States, Canada, South Africa, Mexico, and Australia

- Names of professionals who treat anxiety disorders in the United States, Canada, and elsewhere

Association for Behavioral and Cognitive Therapies

305 Seventh Ave., 16th Floor
New York, NY 10001-6008
USA
Tel: 1-212-647-1890
Fax: 1-212-647-1865
Web: www.abct.org

- Professional memberships only, but offers referrals to consumers

- Find a therapist: http://abct.org/members/directory/flnd_a_therapist.cfm

Academy of Cognitive Therapy

One Belmont Ave., Suite 700
Bala Cynwyd, PA 19004-1610
USA
Tel: 1-610-664-1273
Fax: 1-610-664-5137

E-mail: info@academyofct.org
Web: www.academyofct.org

- Professional memberships only, but offers referrals for consumers to certified cognitive therapists

American Academy of Cognitive and Behavioral Psychology

Attn: E. Thomas Dowd, Ph.D., ABPP
Department of Psychology
Kent State University
Kent, OH 44242
USA
Tel: 1-330-672-7664
Fax: 1-330-672-3786
E-mail: edowd@kent.edu
Web: www.americanacademyofbehavioralpsychology.
 org

- Professional memberships only, but offers referrals for consumers to board-certified psychologists in cognitive behavioral psychology www.americanaca demyofbehavioralpsychology.org/AABP/FellowDire ctory.htm

Freedom From Fear

308 Seaview Ave.
Staten Island, NY 10305

USA
Tel: 1-718-351-1717, ext.24
Web: www.freedomfromfear.org
E-mail: help@freedomfromfear.org

- National nonprofit advocacy organization for people with anxiety disorders and depression

- Newsletter, blogs, bookstore

- Information on support groups and other resources

American Psychological Association

750 First St., N.E.
Washington, DC 20002-4242
USA
Tel: 1-800-374-2721
Web: www.apa.org

- Professional memberships only, but offers referrals to consumers

- Referral line: 1-800-964-2000

- Find a psychologist: http://locator.apa.org/

American Psychiatric Association

APA Answer Center

1000 Wilson Blvd., Suite 1825
Arlington, VA 22209
USA
Tel: 1-888-35-PSYCH or 1-703-907-7300
E-mail: apa@psych.org
Web: www.psych.org

- Professional memberships only, but offers referrals to consumers

INTERNATIONAL ASSOCIATIONS

Anxiety Disorders Association of Canada

ADAC/ACTA
P.O. Box 117
Station Cote St-Luc
Montreal, QC H4V 2Y3
Canada
Tel: 1-514-484-0504 or 1-888-223-2252
Fax: 1-514-484-7892
E-mail: contactus@anxietycanada.ca
Web: www.anxietycanada.ca

- Consumer memberships and professional memberships

- Website provides links to other sites with referral options in Canada

International Association for Cognitive Psychotherapy

Web: www.cognitivetherapyassociation.org

- Professional memberships only, but offers referrals for consumers to cognitive therapists: http://www.cognitivetherapyassociation.org/refhome.aspx

British Association for Behavioural and Cognitive Psychotherapies

Victoria Buildings
9-13 Silver Street
Bury BL9 0EU
United Kingdom
Tel: 0161-797-4484
Fax: 0161-797-2670
E-mail: babcp@babcp.com
Web: www.babcp.com

- Professional memberships only, but website includes a "find a therapist" feature for consumers.

Australian Association for Cognitive and Behaviour Therapy

Web: www.aacbt.org

- Professional memberships only, but website includes a list of CBT practitioners for consumers (click on the "state branches" link at the top, and then click the link near the bottom of the list).

Internet Resources

Although the information in this section was up to date when this book went to press, Web pages come and go, and addresses for Internet resources change frequently. For additional information on Internet resources, we suggest doing a search using keywords such as social phobia, social anxiety, and shyness. Note that although we have screened each of these sites, we have not reviewed them in detail and cannot take responsibility for the accuracy of the information they contain.

Anxieties.com

www.anxieties.com

- A very informative anxiety self-help site run by the Anxiety Disorders Treatment Center (and Dr. R. Reid Wilson) in Durham, NC

Anxiety-Panic.com

www.anxiety-panic.com

- A search engine for anxiety-related links

Anxiety Disorders Association of America

www.adaa.org

- National association for professionals and consumers with an interest in anxiety disorders

CPA Clinical Practice Guidelines for the Management of Anxiety Disorders

http://ww1.cpa-apc.org:8080/Publications/CJP/supplements/july2006/anxiety_guidelines_2006.pdf

- Downloadable treatment guidelines published in 2006 by the Canadian Psychiatric Association

Internet Mental Health

www.mentalhealth.com

- Comprehensive website with information on mental health issues

NIMH Anxiety Disorders Brochure

http://www.nimh.nih.gov/health/publications/anxiety-disorders/summary.shtml

- Downloadable brochure on anxiety disorders published in 2007 by the National Institute of Mental Health

Shyness Home Page

www.shyness.com

- Provides links to information about shyness

Resources for Shy People

www.gordoni.com/shy

- A list of resources compiled by self-identified shy person, Gordon Irlam (Gordoni)

Social Anxiety Support

www.socialphobia.org.nz

- A New Zealand-based site on social anxiety and related topics

Social Phobia/Social Anxiety Association

www.socialphobia.org

- Site for a nonprofit organization focused on social phobia and social anxiety

Social Phobia World

www.socialphobiaworld.com

- A place for online forums and chats about social phobia

References

American Psychiatric Association. 2000. *Diagnostic and Statistical Manual of Mental Disorders* (4th ed., Text Revision). Washington, DC: Author.

Antony, M.M., D.R. Ledley, A. Liss, and R.P. Swinson. 2006. Responses to symptom induction exercises in panic disorder. *Behaviour Research and Therapy* 44:85-98.

Antony, M.M., and K. Rowa. 2008. *Social Anxiety Disorder: Psychological Approaches to Assessment and Treatment.* Göttingen, Germany: Hogrefe.

_____. 2005. Evidence-based assessment of anxiety disorders. *Psychological Assessment* 17: 256-266.

Antony, M.M., and R.P. Swinson. 2000. *Phobic Disorders and Panic in Adults: A Guide to Assessment and Treatment.* Washington, DC: American Psychological Association.

Antony, M.M., C.L. Purdon, V. Huta, and R.P. Swinson. 1998. Dimensions of perfectionism across the anxiety disorders. *Behaviour Research and Therapy* 36:1143-1154.

452

Antony, M.M., K. Rowa, A. Liss, S.R. Swallow, and R.P. Swinson. 2005. Social comparison processes in social phobia. *Behavior Therapy* 36:65-75.

Barlow, D.H. 2002. *Anxiety and Its Disorders: The Nature and Treatment of Anxiety and Panic,* 2nd ed. New York: Guilford.

Beck, A.T. 1963. Thinking and depression: 1. Idiosyncratic content and cognitive distortions. *Archives of General Psychiatry* 9:324-333.

_____. 1964. Thinking and depression: 2. Theory and therapy. *Archives of General Psychiatry* 10:561-571.

_____. 1967. *Depression: Causes and Treatment.* Philadelphia: University of Pennsylvania Press.

_____. 1976. *Cognitive Therapy of the Emotional Disorders.* New York: New American Library.

Beck, A.T., G. Emery, and R.L. Greenberg. 1985. *Anxiety Disorders and Phobias: A Cognitive Perspective.* New York: Basic Books.

Bezchlibnyk-Butler, K.Z., J.J. Jeffries, and A.S. Virani. 2007. *Clinical Handbook of Psychotropic Drugs,* 17th ed. Göttingen, Germany: Hogrefe.

Bieling, P.J., R.E. McCabe, and M.M. Antony. 2006. *Cognitive Behavioral Therapy in Groups.* New York: Guilford.

Bögels, S.M., G.F.V.M. Sijbers, and M. Voncken. 2006. Mindfulness and task concentration training for social phobia: A pilot study. *Journal of Cognitive Psychotherapy* 20: 33-44.

Bolton, R. 1979. *People Skills.* New York: Simon and Schuster.

Briggs, S.R. 1988. Shyness: Introversion or neuroticism? *Journal of Research in Personality* 22: 290-307.

Britton, J.C., and S.L. Rauch. Forthcoming. Neuroanatomy and neuroimaging of anxiety disorders. In *Oxford Handbook of Anxiety and Related Disorders,* ed. M.M. Antony and M.B. Stein. New York: Oxford University Press.

Burns, D.D. 1999. *The Feeling Good Handbook, Revised Edition.* New York: Plume.

Carducci, B.J. and P.G. Zimbardo. 1995. Are you shy? *Psychology Today,* November/December: 34-41, 64, 66, 68, 70, 78, 82.

454

Chambless, D.L., and E.J. Gracely. 1989. Fear of fear and the anxiety disorders. *Cognitive Therapy and Research* 13:9-20.

Cheek, J.M., and A.K. Watson. 1989. The definition of shyness: Psychological imperialism or construct validity? *Journal of Social Behavior and Personality* 4:85-95.

Clark, D.M., and A. Wells. 1995. A cognitive model of social phobia. In *Social Phobia: Diagnosis, Assessment, and Treatment,* ed. R.G. Heimberg, M.R. Liebowitz, D.A. Hope, and F.R. Schneier, 69-93. New York: Guilford.

Connor, K.M., and S. Vaishnavi. Forthcoming. Complementary and alternative approaches to treating anxiety disorders. In *Oxford Handbook of Anxiety and Related Disorders,* ed. M.M. Antony and M.B. Stein. New York: Oxford University Press.

Crippa, J.A., A.S. Filho, M.C. Freitas, and A.W. Zuardi. 2007. Duloxetine in the treatment of social anxiety disorder. *Journal of Clinical Psychopharmacology* 27:310.

Davidson, J.R., E.B. Foa, J.D. Huppert, F.J. Keefe, M.E. Franklin, J.S. Compton, N. Zhao, K.M. Connor, T.R. Lynch, and K.M. Gadde. 2004. Fluoxetine, comprehensive cognitive behavioral therapy, and placebo in generalized social phobia. *Archives of General Psychiatry* 61:1005-1013.

Davis, M., K. Paleg, and P. Fanning. 2004. *The Messages Workbook: Powerful Strategies for Effective Communication at Work and Home.* Oakland, CA: New Harbinger.

Eifert, G.H., and J.P. Forsyth. 2005. *Acceptance and Commitment Therapy for Anxiety Disorders: A Practitioner's Treatment Guide to Using Mindfulness, Acceptance, and Values-Based Behavior Change Strategies.* Oakland, CA: New Harbinger.

Ellis, A. 1962. *Reason and Emotion in Psychotherapy.* Secaucus, NJ: Lyle Stuart.

_____. 1989. The history of cognition in psychotherapy. In *Comprehensive Handbook of Cognitive Therapy,* ed. A. Freeman, K.M. Simon, L.E. Beutler, and H. Arkowitz, 5-19. New York: Plenum Press.

_____. 1993. Changing the name of rational emotive therapy (RET) to rational emotive behavior therapy (REBT). *The Behavior Therapist* 16:257-258.

Emmelkamp, P.M.G., and H. Wessels. 1975. Flooding in imagination vs. flooding in vivo: A comparison with agoraphobics. *Behaviour Research and Therapy* 13:7-15.

456

Fry, R. 2007. *101 Great Answers to the Toughest Interview Questions,* 5th ed. Clifton Park, NY: Thomson Delmar Learning.

Furmark, T., M. Tillfors, I. Marteinsdottir, H. Fischer, A. Pissiota, B. Langstrom, and M. Fredrikson. 2002. Common changes in cerebral blood flow in patients with social phobia treated with citalopram or cognitive-behavioral therapy. *Archives of General Psychiatry* 59:425-433.

Garner, A. 1997. *Conversationally Speaking: Testing New Ways to Increase Your Personal and Social Effectiveness,* 3rd ed. Los Angeles: Lowell House.

Greenberger, D., and C.A. Padesky. 1995. *Mind over Mood: A Cognitive Therapy Treatment Manual for Clients.* New York: Guilford.

Hartley, L.R., S. Ungapen, I. Dovie, and D.J. Spencer. 1983. The effect of beta-adrenergic blocking drugs on speakers' performance and memory. *British Journal of Psychiatry* 142:512-517.

Hayes, S.C., and S. Smith. 2005. *Get Out of Your Mind and into Your Life: The New Acceptance and Commitment Therapy.* Oakland, CA: New Harbinger.

Hedges, D.W., B.L. Brown, D.A. Shwalb, K. Godfrey, and A.M. Larcher. 2007. The efficacy of selective serotonin reuptake inhibitors in adult social anxiety disorder: A meta-analysis of double-blind, placebo-controlled trials. *Journal of Psychopharmacology* 21: 102-111.

Heimberg, R.G., and R.E. Becker. 2002. *Cognitive-Behavioral Group Therapy for Social Phobia: Basic Mechanisms and Clinical Strategies.* New York: Guilford.

Henderson, L., and P. Zimbardo. 1999. Shyness. In *Encyclopedia of Mental Health,* ed. H.S. Friedman. San Diego: Academic Press.

Hirsch, C.R., and D.M. Clark. 2004. Information processing bias in social phobia. *Clinical Psychology Review* 24:799-825.

Honeychurch, C., and A.Watrous. 2003. *Talk to Me: Conversation Tips for the Small-Talk Challenged.* Oakland, CA: New Harbinger.

James, I.M., W. Burgoyne, and I.T. Savage. 1983. Effect of pindolol on stress-related disturbances of musical performance: Preliminary communication. *Journal of the Royal Society of Medicine* 76:194-196.

Jerremalm, A., J. Johansson, and L.G. Öst. 1980. Applied relaxation as a self-control technique for social phobia. *Scandinavian Journal of Behavioral Therapy* 9:35-43.

Kendler, K., L. Karkowski, and C. Prescott. 1999. Fears and phobias: Reliability and heritability. *Psychological Medicine* 29:539-553.

Kendler, K., J. Myers, C. Prescott, and M.C. Neale. 2001. The genetic epidemiology of irrational fears and phobias in men. *Archives of General Psychiatry* 58:257-265.

Kessler, R.C., P. Berglund, O. Demler, R. Jin, and E.E. Walters. 2005. Lifetime prevalence and age-of-onset distributions of DSM-IV disorders in the National Comorbidity Survey Replication. *Archives of General Psychiatry* 62:593-602.

Kessler, R.C., A.M. Ruscio, K. Shear, and H.U. Wittchen. Forthcoming. Epidemiology of anxiety disorders. In *Oxford Handbook of Anxiety and Related Disorders,* ed. M.M. Antony and M.B. Stein. New York: Oxford University Press.

Knox, D., V. Daniels, L. Sturdivant, and M.E. Zusman. 2001. College student use of the internet for mate selection. *College Student Journal* 35:158-161.

Kobak, K.A., L.V. Taylor, G. Warner, and R. Futterer. 2005. St. John's wort versus placebo in social phobia:

Results from a placebo-controlled pilot study. *Journal of Clinical Psychopharmacology* 25:51-58.

Laumann, E.O., J.H. Gagnon, R.T. Michael, and S. Michaels. 1994. *The Social Organization of Sexuality: Sexual Practices in the United States.* Chicago: University of Chicago Press.

Liebowitz, M.R., R.G. Heimberg, F.R. Schneier, D.A. Hope, S. Davies, C.S. Holt, D. Goetz, H.R. Juster, S.H. Lin, M.A. Bruch, R.D. Marshall, and D.F. Klein. 1999. Cognitive-behavioral group therapy versus phenelzine in social phobia: Long term outcome. *Depression and Anxiety* 10:89-98.

Lipsitz, J.D., A.J. Fyer, J.C. Markowitz, and S. Cherry. 1999. An open trial of interpersonal psychotherapy for social phobia. *American Journal of Psychiatry* 156:1814-1816.

Lochner, C., S. Hemmings, S. Seedat, C. Kinnear, R. Schoeman, K. Annerbrink, M. Olsson, E. Eriksson, J. Moolman-Smook, C. Allgulander, and D.J. Stein. 2007. Genetics and personality traits in patients with social anxiety disorder: A case-control study in South Africa. *European Neuropsychopharmacology* 17:321-327.

Mathew, S.J., and S. Ho. 2006. Etiology and neurobiology of social anxiety disorder. *Journal of Clinical Psychiatry* 67(suppl. 12):9-13.

McCabe, R.E., and M.M. Antony. Forthcoming. Anxiety disorders: Social and specific phobias. In *Psychiatry,* 3rd ed, ed. A. Tasman, J. Kay, J.A. Lieberman, M.B. First, and M. Maj. Chichester, UK: John Wiley and Sons.

McCabe, R.E., M.M. Antony, L.J. Summerfeldt, A. Liss, and R.P. Swinson. 2003. A preliminary examination of the relationship between anxiety disorders in adults and self-reported history of teasing or bullying experiences. *Cognitive Behaviour Therapy* 32: 187-193.

McKay, M., M. Davis, and P. Fanning. 1995. *Messages: The Communication Skills Book,* 2nd ed. Oakland, CA: New Harbinger.

Meichenbaum, D.H. 1977. *Cognitive Behavior Modification: An Integrative Approach.* New York: Plenum Press.

Miller, W.R., and S. Rollnick. 2002. *Motivational Interviewing: Preparing People to Change,* 2nd ed. New York: Guilford.

Moalem, S., and P. Prince. 2007. *Survival of the Sickest: A Medical Maverick Discovers Why We Need Disease.* New York: Harper Collins.

Monarth, H., and L. Kase. 2007. *The Confident Speaker Beat Your Nerves and Communicate at Your Best in Any Situation.* New York: McGraw-Hill.

Moore, E., A.E. Braddock, and J.S. Abramowitz. 2007. Efficacy of bibliotherapy for social anxiety disorder. Paper presented at the meeting of the Anxiety Disorders Association of America, St. Louis, MO.

Muehlbacher, M., M.K. Nickel, C. Nickel, C. Kettler, C. Lahmann, F. Pedrosa Gil, P.K. Leibereich, N. Rother, E. Bachler, R. Fartacek, P. Kaplan, K. Tritt, F. Mitterlehner, J. Anvar, M.K. Rother, T.H. Loew, and C. Egger. 2005. Mirtazepine treatment of social phobia in women: A randomized, double-blind, placebo-controlled study. *Journal of Clinical Psychopharmacology* 25:580-583.

Mulkens, S., P.J. de Jong, A. Dobbelaar, and S.M. Bögels. 1999. Fear of blushing: Fearful preoccupation irrespective of facial coloration. *Behaviour Research and Therapy* 37: 1119-1128.

Nesse, R.M., and G.C. Williams. 1994. *Why We Get Sick: The New Science of Darwinian Medicine.* New York: Vintage Books.

Orsillo, S.M., and L. Roemer, eds. 2005. *Acceptance- and Mindfulness-Based Approaches to Anxiety: Conceptualization and Treatment.* New York: Springer.

Osberg, J.W. 1981. The effectiveness of applied relaxation in the treatment of speech anxiety. *Behavior Therapy* 12:723-729.

Ossman, W.A., K.G. Wilson, R.D. Storaasli, and J.W. McNeill. 2006. A preliminary investigation of the use of acceptance and commitment therapy in a group treatment for social phobia. *International Journal of Psychology and Psychological Therapy* 6:397-416.

Phan, K.L., D.A. Fitzgerald, P.J. Nathan, and M.E. Tancer. 2006. Association between amygdala hyperactivity to harsh faces and severity of social anxiety in generalized social phobia. *Biological Psychiatry* 59:424-429.

Pierce, K.A., and D.R. Kirkpatrick. 1992. Do men lie on fear surveys? *Behaviour Research and Therapy* 30:415-418.

Plomin, R. 1989. Environment and genes: Determinants of behavior. *American Psychologist* 44:105-111.

Pollack, M.H., N.M. Simon, J.J. Worthington, A.L. Doyle, P. Peters, F. Toshkov, and M.W. Otto. 2003. Combined paroxetine and clonazepam treatment strategies compared to paroxetine monotherapy for panic disorder. *Journal of Psychopharmacology* 17: 276-282.

Prochaska, J.O., C.C. DiClemente, and J. Norcross. 1992. In search of how people change. *American Psychologist* 47:1102-1114.

Rachman, S.J. 1976. The passing of the two-stage theory of fear and avoidance: Fresh possibilities. *Behaviour Research and Therapy* 14:125-131.

Rapee, R.M., M.J. Abbott, A.J. Baillie, and J.E. Gaston. 2007. Treatment of social phobia through pure self-help and therapist-augmented self-help. *British Journal of Psychiatry* 191:246-252.

Rodebaugh, T.L., R.M. Holaway, and R.G. Heimberg. 2004. The treatment of social anxiety disorder. *Clinical Psychology Review* 24:883-908.

Roemer, L., and S.M. Orsillo. 2007. An open trial of an acceptance-based behavior therapy for generalized anxiety disorder. *Behavior Therapy* 38:72-85.

Safren, S.A., R.G. Heimberg, and H.R. Juster. 1997. Clients' expectancies and their relationship to pretreatment symptomatology and outcome of cognitive-behavioral group treatment for social phobia. *Journal of Consulting and Clinical Psychology* 65:694-698.

Seedat, S., and M.B. Stein. 2004. Double-blind, placebo-controlled assessment of combined clonazepam with paroxetine compared with paroxetine monotherapy for generalized social anxiety disorder. *Journal of Clinical Psychiatry* 65:244-248.

Somers, J.M., E.M. Goldner, P. Waraich, and L. Hsu. 2006. Prevalence and incidence studies of the anxiety disorders: A systematic review of the literature. *Canadian Journal of Psychiatry* 51:100-113.

Stein, M.B., P.R. Goldin, J. Sareen, L.T. Zorrilla, and G.G. Brown. 2002. Increased amygdala activation to angry and contemptuous faces in generalized social phobia. *Archives of General Psychiatry* 59:1027-1034.

Stein, M.B., M.J. Chartier, A.L. Hazen, M.V. Kozak, M.E. Tancer, S. Lander, P. Furer, D. Chubaty, and J.R. Walker. 1998. A direct-interview family study of generalized social phobia. *American Journal of Psychiatry* 155:90-97.

Stein, M.B., K.L. Jang, and W.J. Livesley. 2002. Heritability of social anxiety-related concerns and personality characteristics: A twin study. *Journal of Nervous and Mental Disease* 190:219-224.

Stein, M.B., N.J. Schork, and J.A Gelernter. 2004. Polymorphism of the beta1-adrenergic receptor is associated with low extraversion. *Biological Psychiatry* 56:217-224.

Straube, T., I.T. Kolassa, M. Glauer, H.J. Mentzel, and W.H. Miltner. 2004. Effect of task conditions on brain responses to threatening faces in social phobics: An event-related functional magnetic resonance imaging study. *Biological Psychiatry* 56:921-930.

Suárez, L., S. Bennett, C. Goldstein, and D.H. Barlow. Forthcoming. Understanding anxiety disorders from a "triple vulnerability" framework. In *Oxford Handbook of Anxiety and Related Disorders,* ed. M.M. Antony and M.B. Stein. New York: Oxford University Press.

Sue, D.W. 1990. Culture-specific strategies in counseling: A conceptual framework. *Professional Psychology: Research and Practice* 21:424-433.

Swinson, R.P., M.M. Antony, P. Bleau, P. Chokka, M. Craven, A. Fallu, K. Kjernisted, R. Lanius, K. Manassis, D. McIntosh, J. Plamondon, K. Rabheru, M. Van Ameringen, and J.R. Walker. 2006. Clinical practice guidelines: Management of anxiety disorders. *Canadian Journal of Psychiatry* 51(suppl. 2):1S-92S.

Taylor, S., W.J. Koch, and R.J. McNally. 1992. How does anxiety sensitivity vary across the anxiety disorders? *Journal of Anxiety Disorders* 6:249-259.

466

Tessina, T. 1998. *The Unofficial Guide to Dating Again.* New York: Macmillan.

Turk, C.L., R.G. Heimberg, S.M. Orsillo, C.S. Holt, A. Gitow, L.L. Street, F.R. Schneier, and M.R. Liebowitz. 1998. An investigation of gender differences in social phobia. *Journal of Anxiety Disorders* 12:209-223.

Van Ameringen, M., C. Mancini, and B. Patterson. Forthcoming. Pharmacotherapy for social anxiety disorder and specific phobia. In *Oxford Handbook of Anxiety and Related Disorders,* ed. M.M. Antony and M.B. Stein. New York: Oxford University Press.

Van Veen, J.F., I.M. Van Vliet, and H.G. Westenberg. 2002. Mirtazapine in social anxiety disorder: A pilot study. *International Clinical Psychopharmacology* 17:315-317.

Weissman, M.M., J.C. Markowitz, and G.L. Klerman. 2007. *Clinician's Quick Guide to Interpersonal Psychotherapy.* New York: Oxford University Press.

Williams, M., J. Teasdale, Z. Segal, and J. Kabat-Zinn. 2007. *The Mindful Way Through Depression: Freeing Yourself from Chronic Unhappiness.* New York: Guilford.

Zimbardo, P.G., P.A. Pilkonis, and R.M. Norwood. 1975. The social disease of shyness. *Psychology Today* 8:68-72.

Martin M. Antony, Ph.D., is professor of psychology at Ryerson University in Toronto, ON, and director of research at the Anxiety Treatment and Research Centre at St. Joseph's Healthcare in Hamilton, ON. He is also president-elect of the Canadian Psychological Association. He has published twenty-four books and more than 100 scientific papers and book chapters in the areas of cognitive behavior therapy and anxiety disorders. He has received early career awards from the Society of Clinical Psychology (American Psychological Association), the Canadian Psychological Association, and the Anxiety Disorders Association of America, and is a fellow of the American and Canadian Psychological Associations. He is past president of the Anxiety Disorders Special Interest Group of the Association for Behavioral and Cognitive Therapies (ABCT) and has been program chair for the ABCT annual convention. He is actively involved in clinical research in the area of anxiety disorders, teaching, and education, and maintains a clinical practice. Visit him online at www.martinantony.com.

Richard P. Swinson, MD, is professor emeritus and past chair of the Department of Psychiatry and Behavioural Neurosciences at McMaster University in Hamilton, ON, Canada. He is also medical director of the Anxiety Treatment and Research Centre and past psychiatrist-in-chief at Joseph's Healthcare, also in Hamilton. He is a fellow of the Royal College of Physicians and Surgeons of Canada, the American

Psychiatric Association, and the Royal College of Psychiatrists UK. He was awarded an inaugural fellowship of the Canadian Psychiatric Association in 2006. His research interests lie in the theory, assessment and treatment of anxiety disorders, particularly obsessive-compulsive disorder and social anxiety disorder. He has published more than 180 peer-reviewed papers, thirty book chapters, and eight books. Dr. Swinson has held numerous research grants since 1966 and has been an invited speaker at many conferences around the world on anxiety disorders and substance use disorders. He also chaired the steering committee for the Canadian Anxiety Treatment Guidelines Initiative, leading to the publication of Canadian Clinical Practice Guidelines for the Management of Anxiety Disorders in 2006.

Books For ALL Kinds of Readers

At ReadHowYouWant we understand that one size does not fit all types of readers. Our innovative, patent pending technology allows us to design new formats to make reading easier and more enjoyable for you. This helps improve your speed of reading and your comprehension. Our EasyRead printed books have been optimized to improve word recognition, ease eye tracking by adjusting word and line spacing as well as minimizing hyphenation. Our EasyRead SuperLarge editions have been developed to make reading easier and more accessible for vision-impaired readers. We offer Braille and DAISY formats of our books and all popular E-Book formats.

We are continually introducing new formats based upon research and reader preferences. Visit our web-site to see all of our formats and learn how you can Personalize our books for yourself or as gifts. Sign up to Become A ⓇHYW Registered Reader.

www.readhowyouwant.com

Printed in Great Britain
by Amazon

17490998R00278